LSE MONOGRAPHS IN
INTERNATIONAL STUDIES

Turkish foreign policy during the Second World War

The strategic importance of Turkey at the outset of the Second World
War made it inevitable that the newly-born republic should be the
target of covetous glances from every great power. This book provides
the first comprehensive and systematic analysis of Turkish diplomacy
during the conflict, as the Turks successively fended off pressure from
both the Axis and Allied powers to enter the war. The Turkish
position of 'active neutrality' was criticised both at the time and
subsequently for its 'immorality', but Professor Deringil shows that
Turkey's own military and political weakness made any other course
of action impractical. Preservation of the nascent Turkish state had to
be the guiding principle behind her foreign policy, and this was
pursued with considerable tactical acumen by diplomats and strat-
egists still, to some extent, versed in the Ottoman tradition.

Based on a wide range of sources in Turkey and elsewhere, Selim
Deringil's lucid survey is likely to become the standard work on this
important but neglected theme.

Selim Deringil is an Associate Professor in the History Department,
Boğaziçi University, İstanbul.

LSE MONOGRAPHS IN INTERNATIONAL STUDIES

PUBLISHED FOR THE CENTRE FOR
INTERNATIONAL STUDIES, LONDON SCHOOL OF
ECONOMICS AND POLITICAL SCIENCE

The Centre for International Studies at the London School of Economics and Political Science was established in 1967 with the aid of a grant from the Ford Foundation. Its aim is to promote research and advanced training on a multi-disciplinary basis in the general field of international studies.

To this end the Centre sponsors research projects and seminars and endeavours to secure the publication of manuscripts arising out of them.

Whilst the Editorial Board accepts responsibility for recommending the inclusion of a volume in the series, the author is alone responsible for views and opinions expressed.

ALSO IN THIS SERIES

China's Policy in Africa, 1958–1971 – Alaba Ogunsanwo
Hitler's Strategy 1940–1941: The Balkan Clue – Martin van Creveld
The Totalitarian Party: Party and People in Nazi Germany and Soviet Russia – Aryeh L. Unger
Britian and East Asia, 1933–1937 – Ann Trotter
Britain and the Origins of the New Europe, 1914–1918 – Kenneth J. Calder
The Middle East in China's Foreign Policy, 1949–1977 – Yitzhak Shichor
The Politics of Soviet Cinema, 1917–1929 – Richard Taylor
The End of the Post-War Era: Documents on Great-Power Relations, 1968–75 – edited by James Mayall and Cornelia Navari
Anglo-Japanese Alienation 1919–1952: Papers of the Anglo-Japanese Conference on the History of the Second World War – edited by Ian Nish
Occupation Diplomacy: Britain, the United States and Japan 1945–1952 – Roger Buckley
The Defence of Malaysia and Singapore: The Transformation of a Security System 1957–1971 – Chin Kin Wah
The Politics of Nuclear Consultation in NATO 1965–1980 – Paul Buteux
British Policy towards Greece during the Second World War 1941–1944 – Procopis Papastratis
Détente and the Nixon Doctrine: American Foreign Policy and the Pursuit of Stability 1969–1976 – Robert S. Litwak
The Second Baldwin Government and the United States, 1924–1929: Attitudes and Diplomacy – B. J. C. McKercher
America's Commitment to South Korea: The First Decade of the Nixon Doctrine – Joo Hong Nam
The Politics of Oil in Indonesia – Foreign Company – Host Government Relations (Khong Cho Oon)
The Law of War – Ingrid Detter De Lupis

Turkish foreign policy during the Second World War: an 'active' neutrality

SELİM DERİNGİL

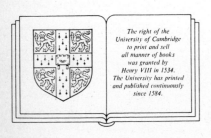

The right of the
University of Cambridge
to print and sell
all manner of books
was granted by
Henry VIII in 1534.
The University has printed
and published continuously
since 1584.

CAMBRIDGE UNIVERSITY PRESS
Cambridge
New York   New Rochelle   Melbourne   Sydney

Published by the Press Syndicate of the University of Cambridge
The Pitt Building, Trumpington Street, Cambridge CB2 1RP
32 East 57th Street, New York, NY 10022, USA
10 Stamford Road, Oakleigh, Melbourne 3166, Australia

© Cambridge University Press 1989

First published 1989

Printed in Great Britain by
Redwood Burn Limited, Trowbridge, Wiltshire

British Library cataloguing in publication data

Deringil, Selim
Turkish foreign policy during the Second
World War : an 'active' neutrality.
(LSE monographs in international studies)
1. Turkey. Foreign relations, 1939–1945
I. Title   II. Series
327.56

Library of Congress cataloguing in publication data

Deringil, Selim, 1951–
Turkish foreign policy during the Second World War : an active
neutrality / Selim Deringil.
    p.   cm. – (LSE monographs in international studies)
Bibliography: p.
Includes index.
ISBN 0 521 34466 2
1. Turkey – Foreign relations – 1918–1960.   2. Turkey – Nonalignment.
3. World War, 1939–1945 – Turkey.   I. Title.   II. Series.
DR477.D44   1988
327.561 – dc19   88–11989   CIP

ISBN 0 521 34466 2

To Selçuk

Bir, iki, üçler, yaşasın Türkler.
Dört, beş, altı, Polonya battı.
Yedi, sekiz, dokuz, Alman domuz.
On, onbir, oniki, İtalya tilki.
Onüç, ondört, onbeş, İngiltere Kardeş.

One, two, three, the Turks for me.
Four, five, six, Poland's in a fix.
Seven, eight, nine, Germany's a swine.
Ten, eleven, twelve, Italy, a fox herself.
Thirteen, fourteen, fifteen, England is a Queen.

Turkish children's hopscotch rhyme during the Second World War

CONTENTS

ACKNOWLEDGEMENTS

I would like to thank David Barras for his supervision of my work and his constant readiness to guide me. I would also like to thank Oral Sander of the Political Sciences Faculty of Ankara University for his help, and Mrs Nermin Streater for her kind permission to consult Numan Menemencioğlu's unpublished memoirs.

My thanks go also to Professor Donald Cameron Watt and Dr Michael Leifer of the London School of Economics for their help and for inviting me to the LSE as a Visiting Fellow in the summer of 1984.

I owe thanks also to Dr Binnaz Toprak, Mr Fahri Aral, Dr Şahin Alpay, and Miss Jülide Ergüder. All errors, omissions, and opinions are entirely my own.

INTRODUCTION

Turkish foreign policy during the period under review remains one of the major feats of diplomatic tightrope walking in the annals of recent international relations. Turkey managed to manoeuvre herself into a position where she had a formal and explicit Treaty of Mutual Assistance with Great Britain as well as a Friendship and Non-Aggression Pact with Germany. The country seen on the map of 1941 forms, 'a great oblong pad of poorly developed territory', jutting out into Nazi-dominated Europe, entirely surrounded by Axis or pro-Axis forces.[1] Encircled and enticed as she was, Turkey was able to achieve her primary aim of staying out of the universe of devastation which surrounded her.

She owed this entirely to the consistency of her foreign policy. This policy consisted of a set of realistically understood possibilities, limitations, advantages and handicaps which constantly guided the Turkish decision makers. This small and homogeneous body of men formed the ruling elite in Turkey and held the monopoly of real power. To a large extent Turkish foreign policy stemmed from their common experiences and beliefs. These men acknowledged the fact that Turkey was no longer the world power which the Ottoman Empire had once been, and that she had to order her policy accordingly. They knew also that the emerging forces in Europe had been for some time approaching a head-on collision.

As early as 1931, Mustafa Kemal had said: 'The Treaty of Versailles has not removed any of the causes that led to the First World War. Quite to the contrary it has deepened the rift between the former rivals . . .'[2] As the leader of the new Turkey lay on his death-bed in 1938 he advised his followers: 'A World War is near. In the course of this war international equilibrium will be entirely destroyed. If during this period we act unwisely and make the smallest mistake, we

1

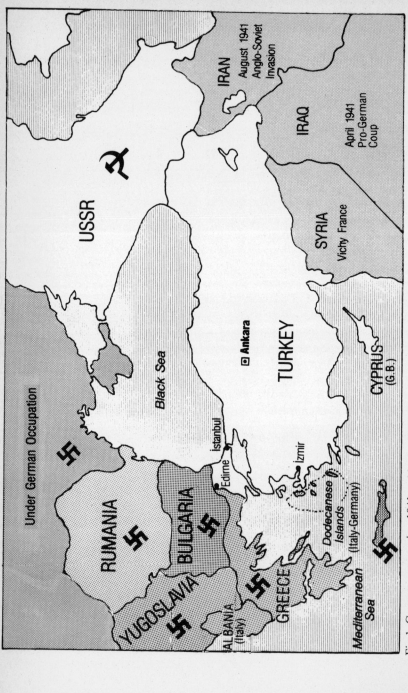

Fig.1 German occupation 1941.   *Map by: Hakan Derman*

will be faced with an even graver catastrophe than in the Armistice years.'[3]

Mustafa Kemal and his followers fully recognised the fact that the Turkey which emerged from the War of Liberation (1919–22) was a poor and tired country. They realised that a prolonged period of peace was necessary for Turkey to heal her wounds. Therefore they based their policy on the principle of 'Peace at Home, Peace Abroad.' The Turkish leaders were, however, undeniably of Ottoman upbringing and they adapted much of Ottoman diplomatic thinking to their new polity. The British Ambassador to Turkey, Sir Percy Loraine, reported on 9 April 1938: 'The Sick Man is dead, but he has left behind him a number of lusty children.'[4] Thus Loraine acknowledged the heritage of Turkey's leaders. But he also recognised that their aims were very different from those of a crumbling Empire: 'Turkey has not a second Empire to lose, nor has she today any wish to create one . . . in developing her still extensive territory . . . She has enough to keep her busy for a century.' The Ambassador pointed out that the Turks had wearied of war and stated, 'In their settled policy there is no room for adventure.'[5]

Loraine's astute assessment correctly defined the constant and ultimate goal of the Turkish leaders: the survival and continuity of Turkey as a sovereign independent state. This precluded any form of adventurism and demanded a very cautious approach to foreign policy. Thus the Turkish foreign policy formulators based their decision-making on the following premises:

(a) Turkey has an exceptional geopolitical location. This is both an advantage and a disadvantage. It is an advantage because she therefore assumes an importance greater than a non-strategically based small power. This enables her to have an influential voice in the foreign affairs arena, it also enables her to attract strong friends.[6]

(b) But this is also a disadvantage, being placed where she is makes it more difficult for Turkey to avoid confrontation with major powers. The strategic location draws covetous glances. The advantage which enables her to attract powerful friends can likewise lead to the unwelcome attentions of a 'protector'.

(c) Turkey is a 'small country at the crossroads', therefore she has to seek to maintain a maximum freedom of movement. This means she has to avoid the formation of power blocks, or if they exist already she has to avoid joining them. She must strive to dilute power into as many different nations as possible.[7]

(d) A small power ultimately stands or falls only according to the efficiency of its own resources. Formulas such as 'Traditional friendship', 'hereditary enemy', or 'long lasting history of cooperation' are devoid of any real meaning. Practical politics will inevitably triumph over idealism, promises and sentiment. In Tamkoç's words, 'The international system, despite the general lip service to the concept of community relationship based on friendship is basically anarchic . . . power is still the overriding consideration of nations'.[8]

(e) Because this is so Turkey should always be prepared to fight for the defence of her rights and territory. These should be clearly defined and the intention to defend them by force of arms if necessary should be clearly stated. But alongside this it must be emphasised that Turkey will go to war only in defence.

(f) Practical politics in the case of a small power inevitably involve bargaining. Bargaining is one of the key tools for the survival of a small state. 'Tough bargaining was considered by the Turks as the highest patriotism.'[9]

In view of the above, Turkish foreign policy was a synthesis of the experiences and convictions of the governing elite.

Leaders such as President İnönü and Foreign Ministers such as Saraçoğlu and Menemencioğlu employed a distinctly pragmatic approach in their foreign policy decision making. Their experience had taught them to be wary of European powers and this manifested itself in their dealings with them. Medlicott assesses the British–French–Turkish Treaty of 1939 in these terms: 'This intense nationalism, built on a suspicion of European powers with whom it was nevertheless desired to cooperate, meant that the alliance with Britain and France was a matter of the purest expediency for Turkey and had no basis of sentiment and habit.'[10] İnönü himself stated the position:

There was the possibility of an alliance with Britain, France and the Soviet Union. As a consequence it was possible that we would fight on the same side. I considered this from the very outset to be the least harmful to our interests . . . When events progressed beyond the limit of our predictions, precautions had to be suited to the time and the needs.[11]

Therefore, İnönü considered the alliance with the west as something of a necessary evil. And when events 'progressed beyond the limit of predictions', i.e. when the Soviet Union was not brought into the alliance, when France collapsed and Britain seemed on the brink of disaster, policy had to be adjusted accordingly. The British could not appreciate that their goal should not be exactly the goal of every honest man. The Turks, although largely sympathetic towards the British during their fight for survival, saw things differently. The alliance with Britain had been entirely a defensive measure, by making their alliance with Britain and France the Turkish leaders felt they were taking out an insurance policy for their own benefit. To the British, the treaty with Turkey was an instrument for securing Turkey's effective collaboration in the war effort.

This situation led to what I have called the Anglo-Turkish contradiction. The British felt they had the legitimate right to ask Turkey to muster all her strength and join in the fight for what they considered to be a common cause. The Turks, on the other hand, saw no reason to risk their very existence which had cost them so dear in what was primarily a war of the European powers' own making. They sought no territorial gain and desired no substantial revision of their international position. All Turkey would achieve by entering the war, Menemencioğlu believed, would be to serve as a battleground for the Great Powers.[12] On one occasion Menemencioğlu told the German Ambassador von Papen: 'The objective of our foreign policy is to protect our self-determination to the end. I am certain that if we entered the war, our self-determination will be destroyed, and there would not be the slightest gain for my country . . .'[13] The Turkish attitude was perhaps best expressed by Menemencioğlu's telling von Papen: 'We are egoists and fight exclusively for ourselves.'[14]

There is little doubt that in terms of foreign policy leadership Turkey was fortunate to have men of such a high level of competence as İnönü and Menemencioğlu. Morgenthau has named 'The quality of diplomacy' as, 'the most important of all the factors that make for the power of a nation.'[15] 'By using the power potentialities of a nation to best advantage, a competent diplomacy can increase the power of a nation beyond what one would expect it to be in view of all the other factors combined.'[16] In other words, quality of leadership in this crucial sphere is essential if a nation is to be successful in its policy.

But Morgenthau and Tamkoç make the mistake of generalising on the concept of 'National Character.'[17] In his section on 'Turkish Political Culture' Tamkoç states that the 'fundamental characteristics of political beliefs' held by Turks are as follows: 'The individual regards himself first and foremost as a Turk, endowed with special qualities, powers and obligations to protect and preserve the motherland of the Turkish polity . . . Almost equal in importance, however, is his belief in himself as a Moslem, which in his way of thinking is nearly synonymous with the word Turk.'[18] Tamkoç then points out that every Turk is 'suspicious of "strangers" (*yabancılar*) and

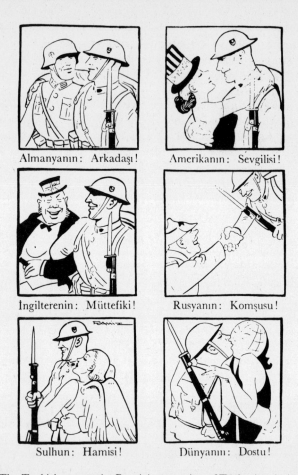

Fig. 2 The Turkish cartoonist Ramiz' perception of Turkey's relations with the major powers during the Second World War. Translation of captions from left to right reads: The Comrade of Germany; The Sweetheart of America; The Ally of Britain; The Neighbor of Russia; The Protector of Peace; The Friend of the World.   *(Source: Metin Tamkoç, 'The Warrior Diplomats'.)*

foreigners, usually identified as *gâvurlar* (e.g. *Moskof gâvuru*) bent upon exploiting the human and natural resources of his motherland'.[19]

Instead of vague and fragile generalisations about the 'national character' of a whole people this book will deal with the experiences and actions of a specific elite, those involved in the making of foreign policy during this period.

In the mid thirties, this elite perceived the major threat to Turkish security to be Italy, with its heavily fortified islands just off the Turkish coast, and Mussolini's trumpetings of 'Mare Nostrum'. The significance of Italy in Turkish thinking is often overlooked by writers who use the benefit of hindsight and take into account Italy's poor performance in the actual hostilities. Weisband focuses exclusively on the Soviets as the primary threat to Turkey and makes no mention of Italy,[20] yet Italy loomed large on the world scene in the twenties and thirties. Elizabeth Monroe comments in a book written in 1938: 'The Turkish dislike of Italy dates back to the war of 1911–12 and the capture of the Dodecanese and Libya. It simmered during the World War and grew vehement after the Armistice when Italy's aims were discovered to include a province in Asia Minor.'[21] After Italy was denied her prize in the Antalya region she, 'mourned aloud for the lost province'.[22] Contemporary apologists of Fascist foreign policy also mourned aloud the passing of, 'the good natured easy going Oriental race of the past with whom it was always possible to come to a friendly understanding'.[23] Fear and suspicion of Italy were the primary factors leading to Turkey's *rapprochement* with Britain.

A study of Turkish foreign policy should ideally be based on Turkish archives. But unfortunately this is not possible as the main Turkish archival material dealing with the foreign policy of this period is closed to private research.[24] The Soviet archives for this period are also unavailable. For instance one episode I have been unable to deal with as a result of this is the Turkish–Soviet agreement of non-aggression concluded in March 1941, as an increasingly more anxious Soviet Union cast about for contingency plans to guard against German aggression. Therefore I have had to use the British Foreign Office archives as my main unpublished source. I have attempted to balance this by using available Turkish material. As such I have made use of published and unpublished memoirs and the press. In particular Numan Menemencioğlu's unpublished memoirs, 'Les Détroits vus de la Mediterranée: aperçus, études, souvenirs,' constitutes a very useful source by a man who was a central figure at this time.[25] I have given special prominence to the press, therefore we need to consider what it can tell us. Given the fact that the press was controlled, it forms an invaluable source of information on government thinking. The media was strictly controlled by the government through a number of laws and press regulations. The most important of these was press regulation No. 1,881 which could be applied to impose fines and prison sentences on columnists as well as close down their papers if they published articles 'undermining public confidence in the State, or in the officials of the State'.[26] In addition to this first tier of control there was also the fact that martial law had been declared in six provinces including İstanbul. This meant that papers could also be closed by order of the martial law authorities. A recent article by Koçak gives an excellent summary of the government's relations with the press.[27]

The official organ by which the government regulated the press was the General Directorate of the Press (Matbuat Umum Müdürlüğü). This body supervised the papers down to the most minute details. It often issued general directives determining how much coverage was to be given to what item, even specifying the number of columns, the use or non-use of photographs, emphasising that official war bulletins of both sides should get exactly equal column space.[28]

Because of the low literacy rate the public which could read and follow the news constituted only a small minority. Much of Turkey's press comment during the war years seems therefore to be directed towards the outside world. The Allies as well as the Axis closely followed the editorial comments of Turkey's leading columnists. The British *Review of the Foreign Press* regularly gave translations of excerpts from Turkey's leading newspapers.[29] The most important of these was the *Ulus*. It was the official organ of the Republican Peoples' Party and under the direction of Falih Rıfkı Atay, a trusted figure in government circles.[30] The distinguished journalist Ahmet Şükrü Esmer was the foreign editor of the *Ulus* and was considered generally as one of the leading authorities on foreign affairs. The *Cumhuriyet* was generally regarded as favouring Germany.[31] But owner-editor Nadir Nadi has emphasised in his memoirs that he, along with his father Yunus Nadi, were merely trying to urge a more neutral policy.[32] Both *Cumhuriyet* and *Tasvir-i Efkâr* had men on their staffs who were billed as pro-German.

The most consistently anti-German paper was on the left of the political spectrum, the *Tan*. Owned and managed by Zekeriya Sertel and his wife Sabiha Sertel, it was destroyed by rioting right-wingers in 1945.[33] *Akşam* was regarded as being one of the more moderate papers, under the direction of Necmettin Sadak. One of Turkey's most eminent journalists was Hüseyin Cahit Yalçın. Known primarily for his outspoken criticism of Hitler and his equally anti-Russian attitude he directed *Yeni Sabah* and *Tanin*.[34] Although various papers came to be regarded as pro-Allied or pro-German it must be realised that such classification runs the risk of being arbitrary. Even *Cumhuriyet* was

Table 1. *List of closures in Turkish press (1939–45)*

Name of newspaper or magazine	Total period of closure	Number of closures	Deciding authority
Cumhuriyet	5 months and 9 days	5	3 times by government twice by martial law authorities.
Tan	2 months and 13 days. (Closed indefinitely after 12 Aug. 1944)	7	4 times by government 3 times by martial law authorities.
Vatan	7.5 months and 9 days (Closed indefinitely after 30 Sept. 1944)	9	5 times by government 4 times by martial law authorities.
Tasvir-i Efkâr	3 months (Closed indefinitely after 30 Sept. 1944)	8	4 times by government 4 times by martial law authorities.
Vakit	12 days	2	once by government once by martial law authorities.
Yeni Sabah	6 days	3	once by government twice by martial law authorities.
Akbaba	47 days	4	once by government 3 times by martial law authorities.
Son Posta	11 days	4	4 times by government
Haber	10 days	2	twice by martial law authorities.

Source: Cemil Koçak, 'İkinci Dünya Savaşı ve Türk Basını' (The Turkish Press in the Second World War), *Tarih ve Toplum*, No. 35, November 1986, pp. 29–33.

billed at one point by the British as 'friendly' and *Tasvir-i Efkâr* as 'not pro-German'.[35] Yet in October 1940 the *Review* had reported that *Cumhuriyet* and *Tasvir-i Efkâr* had been closed down by the government for articles which 'accepted the inevitability of German hegemony'.[36]

Although the men who controlled or wrote for Turkey's papers had their own inclinations, the government made sure they stayed within certain stated parameters. The *Review* concluded in its 31 October 1941 issue:

Neither of the extreme wings forms in any sense an Opposition Press. The whole press is united in its support of the Government's policy of neutrality, rearmament, defence of Turkey's frontiers in case of attack, the maintenance of the British alliance, and friendship and commercial relations with Germany. The difference between the two extreme wings lies in the degree in which the last two planks of the policy are emphasized.[37]

Many of the leading columnists were also Deputies in the Assembly; Ahmet Emin Yalman, Falih Rıfkı Atay, Ahmet Şükrü Esmer, Nadir Nadi, Hüseyin Cahit Yalçın, Necmettin Sadak, all held seats. Because of this the restraint shown in the press was to some extent self-imposed, although having the columnists in government helped İnönü to control them.[38] Also, according to the 1939 Regulation of the Republican Peoples' Party (article 160) the owners of major newspapers who were also party members were constrained to publish, 'within the principles of the party . . .' and not to 'disseminate views damaging to the general internal and external policies of the party . . .'[39]

Government sources, however, frequently proclaimed that there was freedom of the press in Turkey, and this was echoed in the papers. On 18 January 1940 the Prime Minister, Refik Saydam, told the Assembly: 'The liberty of the press is nowadays considered in many countries incompatible with the maintenance of internal order; we believe it to be the mainstay of that order. . .'[40] On 9 October 1939 *Yeni Sabah* and *Tan* protested at the insinuation in the German papers that the Turkish press was controlled. *Tan* proclaimed: 'In Turkey the press is free, there is no censorship. If the papers are united in defending the country's interests, that is because they are acting as the interpreters of Turkish public opinion . . .' *Yeni Sabah* declared, 'The free press is an institution for which the Presidency of İnönü will be gratefully remembered. . .'[41]

It particularly suited the government to emphasise freedom of the press when their official line seemed at variance with press statements. In this manner they were able to maintain an official stance of neutrality while intimating their true feelings through the press. Often when the Germans confronted the Turkish leaders with the unfavourable attitude of the Turkish press towards Germany, İnönü or Menemencioğlu could say that the press was free to say what it wanted. Similarly, when the British pointed to a seeming inclination to favour Germany they were told that the press was free, and reassured about the official position. This served to pacify the Germans while it reassured the British about Turkey's loyalty.

One can safely say that at all times during the war years the press broadly followed the government line. Nothing illustrates this better than the case of Numan Menemencioğlu. After the Cairo Summit in December 1943, the newspapers hailed his statement to the press as, 'The crystal clear words of a Minister who does not pursue hidden goals . . .'[42] Yet after his fall from favour he was criticised for his 'suspicious' and 'confused' policy.[43] Not one paper defended him, although some made excuses for his behaviour.

This book is divided into analytical and chronological sections. I have split my examination of the period into years purely for the sake of convenience and would not like to suggest that each year of the war constitutes a separate entity for study. In the first three chapters I have concentrated on the elements which formed the basis of Turkish policy making, and the men who were responsible for its formulation and implementation. In these chapters I have looked at how historical, social, economic and military factors influenced Turkey's leaders. In the chronological section I have examined the various phases through which foreign policy passed, as Turkey reacted to European crises.

1 . THE ECONOMIC BACKGROUND

GENERAL ECONOMIC PICTURE

Although sixteen years had passed between the inception of the Turkish Republic and the beginning of the Second World War, when war broke out Turkey had only just begun to show the most tentative beginnings of economic growth. This was largely due to the fact that in both industry and agriculture a long period of rehabilitation had to precede any actual growth or progress. 'To the extent that the government was able to mobilise economic resources, and administrative technical manpower, these were in the first instance directed towards repairing the damage caused by continuous wars.'[1]

The economic policies of the Turkish state in the years of its early existence and the years leading up to the war are both a reflection of its foreign policy and one of its determining factors. Turkey's early striving for economic independence parallels her striving for political independence. Mustafa Kemal repeatedly declared that political independence did not mean anything if it were not complemented by economic independence. İnönü declared at the Lausanne Conference: 'I refuse to accept economic slavery for my country.'[2] Turkey felt she had to seek economic self-sufficiency and self-determination if she was to shake off foreign domination in the economic sphere as she had done in the political context: 'Surrounded by hostile, or at least apparently untrustworthy powers, the Turks concluded that self-sufficiency in foodstuffs and basic industrial products was the answer.'[3] But they were working under a formidable handicap; the rehabilitation of the country represented an enormous task.

Economics was not exactly the forte of the Turkish leaders, who came from predominantly military and authoritarian backgrounds, and at Lausanne, 'İsmet's own ignorance of finance and economics handicapped him tremendously.'[4] An authoritarian and rigidly regi-

12

mented view of statecraft was simply applied to the economy. It did
not work. Per capita income was very little higher in 1945 than in
1929.[5] Although it is extremely dangerous to generalise about Muslim
aversion to profit-making and the preference for military rather than
economic achievement, as well as similar vagaries to do with 'religious characteristics', it must be taken into account that the leaders
of the new Turkey came from an Ottoman background, and this
background greatly emphasised authoritarian attitudes to power.
Although the new leaders were, unlike their ancestors, committed to
finding a lasting solution to their country's economic problems, they
lacked the necessary expertise. Not because of any so-called 'typical'
Muslim aversion to profit but because of a different specialisation
process which had caused them to become military men.

As a result, even on the eve of the Second World War, Turkey was
still an extremely underdeveloped and economically weak country.
Although progress had been made in some areas the Turkish leaders
failed to achieve economic self-sufficiency and independence. Even
with the étatist orientation after 1930 the backlog of underdevelopment proved too great. Turkey's leaders realised that foreign money
and assistance was unavoidable. The once despised foreign advisers
were called back to supervise the five-year plans, and foreign loans
were solicited. A situation of overwhelming dependency on Germany
developed. Self-sufficiency had proved impossible in the field of
economics.

This led the Turkish leaders to emphasise the political aspect of
their foreign policy even more. They realised that their economy was
in no state to compete in a total war with the major powers. Therefore
it became all the more imperative that Turkey maintain her freedom
of action to the greatest possible degree. From the first days of the War
of Liberation Atatürk had the economic problem in mind, and as
early as 1919 at the Congresses of Erzurum and Sivas the goal of
ensuring economic independence was stressed. The National Pact
emphasised this need. 'While leading the military front against the
Greek invader and the political struggle against the government in
İstanbul, Kemal simultaneously prepared political and economic
plans for the future state to spring up on the ruins of the defunct
Empire.'[6] The problems were immense, however, as not only had the
country been almost continuously at war since 1909, but the Greek
invasion had been particularly ruinous. There was widespread devastation, entire villages and areas of dense agriculture had been wiped

out. There was severe inflation, currency circulation rose from £T6.5 million in 1915 to £T161 million in 1919.[7] The importance Mustafa Kemal gave to economics was demonstrated in his words during the İzmir Economic Congress in 1923: 'This nation's survival and development depend entirely on its economy. This nation is not a warrior nation – it is an economic nation.'[8]

One of the issues on which İnönü was given the strictest instructions before he went to the Lausanne Conference was that of the Capitulations. These were arrangements of extra-territoriality, given by treaty to foreigners, enabling them to be beyond the ruling of Turkish law in matters criminal or commercial. The issue had become a symbol of Ottoman decrepitude for the Republican leaders. İnönü had been told to hold out for the abolition of these even at the cost of risking rupture, which actually occurred. Rupture was avoided over the Mosul issue, an oil-rich territory in northern Iraq that had become a matter of contention between Britain and Turkey, but it came over Capitulations. He was to refuse to accept these even if it were to lead to the breakup of the conference. It did lead to that. This is a measure of how strongly the Turks felt on the subject of independence in the economic domain. Lord Curzon, and G. Child, the American delegate, even threatened İnönü with blackmail by telling him that unless he agreed to the 'final proposals' in January 1923, 'not one American dollar, nor one English shilling would be forthcoming for the economic restoration of Turkey'.[9] This was just the wrong tack to take with a man who was already obsessed with the spectre of foreigners using economics as a tool to interfere in Turkish affairs.

Although the Lausanne Conference was a victory for the Turks in the political domain it was less so in the economic. Capitulations, it is true, were gone and the Turks were finally masters in their own home, but at least in the short term some of the provisions of Lausanne proved to be a heavy burden on their economy. One of these was the special commercial agreement whereby Turkey would be unable to change her customs tariff for five years from 1929, the tariff remaining fixed at the 1916 rate. Most of the foreign concessions remained in force, and were gradually nationalised over fifteen years.[10] The last foreign railroad concession was only recovered from the French in 1947.[11]

Foreign concessions for navigation rights along the shore were extended for two more years, Turkey acquiring the right of cabotage only in 1926. The Turkish share of the Ottoman debt had been the subject of protracted wrangling in Lausanne. Turkey's share of the debt was £T84.6 million. Although İnönü had succeeded in substantially reducing Turkey's share, even the annual target of £T7 million required to service it represented a heavy burden on the yearly budget. Payments only actually started in 1929 and in the thirties they amounted to as much as 13–18% of the budget, although this proportion was gradually reduced to 5%.[12]

In the domain of investment, although Zhivkova maintains that, 'connections between the national bourgeoisie and international capital started as early as 1927', foreign investors were wary of the new nationalistic Turkey. Although the Turks said they wanted foreign investment they wanted it on their own terms.[13] 'The liquidation of the Capitulations and the administrative difficulties put in the way of the concessionaries reduced the willingness of foreign capitalists to participate in the economic life of Turkey on its terms.'[14]

The attempt to set up a young state aiming at freedom from foreigners, cancellation of Capitulations, a revising of the status of foreign investments, and the liquidation of the Ottoman Debt on terms unfavourable to the creditors, 'these appeared as formidable threats to the vested interests of the Powers'.[15] The Turks were deeply suspicious of foreign intentions: 'The memories of the oppression and intrigues of the past, made the Turks hostile to any form of intervention or economic activity on the part of a western Power.'[16]

The French failed to obtain extensive communications, oil, and mining concessions after the failure of the American Chester Group to operate this concession. The Turks hoped that American capital 'free of imperialist stigma', could be recruited but they were disappointed.[17] The Turks' suspicion of foreign economic enterprise mirrored their suspicion of foreign intentions on the political plane. Another factor which adversely affected economic growth in the short term was the population exchange with Greece. During the twenties, 1,400,000 Greeks left Turkey.[18] As these people were mostly involved in specialised trade or skilled professions, and had considerable entrepreneurial ability, their loss was a loss for Turkey.

Turkey's economic development from the early days of the republic to the Second World War can be split into two stages. From 1923 to 1930 the government interfered little in economics, hoping private enterprise would rise to the challenge. When this failed from 1930 onwards the government developed its étatist orientation, taking a more direct hand in the economy, hoping in this way to make up for the backlog of underdevelopment. This was not easy. It was only in 1927 that the government recovered the lucrative tobacco, alcohol, and salt monopolies, previously held by the Ottoman Debt Administration. These combined represented an annual income of about £T40 million.[19] The government was also hampered by being deprived of its customs rights. The major move on the part of the government in the twenties was the 1927 Law for the Encouragement of Industry. Its aim was to promote real industrial enterprises, not small workshops. Many facilities were granted to these undertakings; these included grants of free land up to 100 *dönüms*, and the obtaining of additional land – if necessary by confiscation against the payment of compensation.

The government also reduced telephone and telegraph charges and cut taxes for such enterprises. It undertook to buy their products for its departments if the price did not exceed by 10% the imported variety of the goods provided. There is no doubt that economic enterprise was sorely lacking. In the Turkey of 1923 there were, all told, 341 mechanised factories, the definition of factory being that power came from a stationary source irrespective of the number of people employed.[20]

The government, however, lacking in economic experience, took the wrong course. Even Mustafa Kemal believed that the wealth of the country could be achieved by increasing the wealth of individuals. Both he and the People's Party wanted to transfer economic control from foreign ownership on to the shoulders of their local entrepreneurial class.[21] The local entrepreneurs made use of this opportunity, not by providing a valid industrial infrastructure but simply by seeking to replace the Jews, Greeks and Armenians who had left. They not only failed to provide the necessary energy for the beginnings of economic development, but made use of their country's weakness to enrich themselves by becoming importing agents for vitally needed goods, the flow of which could not be controlled because of the stipulations of the Lausanne Treaty.[22]

The local entrepreneurial class also outwitted the economically inexperienced officer class, which believed that national development was synonymous with the enrichment of the entrepreneurs. Thus those who understood 'business' would triumph over those who did not understand economics or sociology. To these people, who cannot really be called entrepreneurs, it seemed much easier to become the representatives of foreign firms rather than risk money and name in dubious economic ventures in the Anatolian hinterland.[23]

In 1938 only very few 'industries' in the true sense of the word existed, 90% of the factories being 'ramshackle affairs unworthy of being called factories'.[24] 'By reason of the obvious inability (or un-willingness) of native capitalists to finance the purchase of foreign-owned economic enterprises in the country . . . it fell to the State to buy out foreign owners.'[25] The failure of private enterprise to provide even some of the vital services, such as railroads, waterworks etc, led to the development of étatisme as the country's leaders realised that they needed to take a direct hand in economic development.

ETATISME

'Toward the end of the twenties the consciousness grew in Turkey that if the economy continued to advance at the existing rate, fifty or a hundred years would pass before Turkey would be on an equal footing as regards its income level and standard of living even with countries of no more than average development.'[26] Foreign capital adopted a 'wait and see' attitude towards the new Turkey and was put off by 'the drastic means taken by the Republic to safeguard its economic and political independence'.[27]

The government had already taken a hand in economic matters but laws such as that of 1927 had proved inadequate. The İş Bankası (Business Bank) had been started in 1924, as the nucleus for the providing of credit to potential enterprises. The Sümer Bank had been created in 1925 to provide incentives in mining and agriculture. But all these measures had proved lacking in scope; new managerial, financial and organisational measures were needed.

Several factors, external and internal – combined to bring about the adoption of an étatist policy. The Great Depression hit primary producers such as Turkey hard, due to the falling demand for agricul-tural produce and mineral raw materials. Even though Turkey was less dependent on its foreign trade than more industrialised countries, the catastrophic drop in world agricultural prices, greatly affected her export trade, 80% to 90% of which was in agricultural produce. Export returns fell from £T155 million in 1929 to £T92 million in 1934.[28]

This further delayed Turkish recovery. The western liberal model seemed to be bankrupt. But Soviet Russia, Nazi Germany and Fascist

Italy, all authoritarian states with apparently impressive economic records, furnished a different example. Leading politicians pointed out in the early to mid-thirties that state intervention took place in many economies and there seemed to be a need for more of it.[29] Soviet economic influence was on the increase in Turkey due to the good political relations existing between the two former outcasts. Accordingly, when Turkey announced her first Five Year Plan (1934–9) the Soviet Union made her an interest free loan of $8 million in gold to help pay for it. Soviet experts came to Turkey, Turkish students went to the Soviet Union, several Turkish plants were built by Soviet technicians, including the textile Kombinat in Kayseri, and a special institution was established in Moscow called the *Turkstoj* to conduct commercial relations between Turkey and the Soviet Union.

The primary internal cause for the adoption of étatisme was the fact that the government was in a hurry and private initiative had been too slow for its liking. It had to make up for a tremendous time lag and in the twenties it had only just begun to heal the wounds left by the First World War and the Greek War. Private enterprise was judged as too slow in view of all the groundwork which had to be completed before development actually began. 'Any efforts in the economic field were directed towards rehabilitation, i.e. the restoration of the pre-war *statis quo* rather then towards an increase of the economic potential . . .'[30]

The liberal economic regime of the twenties, therefore, failed to achieve any appreciable improvements. Until the end of the twenties the trade balance was unfavourable, capital was lacking, and the state needed money to finance its large security, military and police expenditures. Economic progress was therefore vital to Turkey, and it could not allow the economy to sag. Thus in the discussion of the second five-year plan, a Turkish Minister said: 'If we leave to private enterprises the execution of all the works necessary for the reconstruction of our country we may wait fifty years – and even then private enterprise may not be able to tackle them.' Fear, based on painful experiences of foreign financial exploitation, and the lack of private capital, made state control necessary.[31] The Lausanne stipulations came to an end in 1929 and Turkey issued a new customs law.

Etatisme of the Turkish brand aimed through industrialisation to bring about economic independence, more money for security, and a better balance of payments. This was to be achieved through direct legislation, recruitment of capital resources and five-year plans. The

Law for the Encouragement of Industry was widened, a State Office for Industry was established in 1932. The Ottoman Bank, which had really been an institution for the controlling of the Ottoman Debt by foreign creditors, was nationalised in 1931 and transformed into the Central Bank of Turkey. As can be seen from Table 2, in the 1930–9 period, revenues always lagged behind expenditure. There were no foreign loans and internal loans by public subscription to government bonds were not always well received by the public. The great increase in the budgetary deficit in the last years of peace and in the first year of the war reflects the great increase in military spending.

The Turkish economic blueprints during this time were the five-year plans. The first five-year plan began to be implemented in May 1934. It is significant that the plan was modelled on the Soviet example but that an American commission, headed by W. D. Hines and E. W. Henmerer, took part in its preparation.[32] Turkish suspicion of foreigners was beginning to give way to the admission that their skills were indispensable in view of the short supply of local expertise. The first plan had four principles, (a) preference for local raw materials; (b) fostering of a widespread textile industry based on local raw materials; (c) appropriate geographical dispersion of industrial centres; (d) priority given to the production of consumer goods while preparing the way for the manufacture of capital goods. It can be

Table 2. *Turkish Budgets: 1930/1–1939/40 (in £T millions)*

Year	Receipts	Expenditures	Deficit (−) or Surplus (+)
1930/1	196.3	210.1	− 13.8
1931/2	165.2	181.9	− 16.7
1932/3	182.5	174.0	+ 8.5
1933/4	170.2	173.6	− 3.4
1934/5	195.0	202.1	− 7.1
1935/6	218.3	223.7	− 5.4
1936/7	250.8	260.3	− 9.5
1937/8	275.8	303.5	− 27.7
1938/9	266.9	311.1	− 44.2
1939/40	273.4	398.7	−125.3

Source: T.C. Başbakanlık, İstatistik Umum Müdürlüğü, *İstatistik Yıllığı 1942–1945* (Statistical Yearbook of the General Directorate of Statistics), vol. 15, p. 393.

deduced from these goals that the aim was still self-sufficiency, although the need for foreign expertise had been acknowledged.

Financially, however, the plan proved to be much more costly than was at first estimated. Its cost, originally estimated at £T44 million, by the end of the five-year period had risen to £T100 million.[33] The necessity of finding these funds was what led to the Turkish governments' 'loan hunger' in the late thirties. The second five-year plan was also aided by foreign expertise, the *rapprochement* with Britain leading to the use of considerable aid from British experts in its drawing up and implementation. This plan also emphasised the drive towards self-sufficiency, stressing exploitation of local raw materials and food resources such as fish, fruits and livestock.

Although the two plans represent a herculean effort on the part of the government in the face of a tremendous task, it is arguable that they tried to do too much at once.[34] They were dealing with a largely pre-industrial society, industrial plants were seen to some extent sociologically as centres for education as well as profit. In some cases the educative aspect was more important than profit. In others, efforts were actually made to prevent the formation of industrial ghettos, by placing the plant in remote areas. The Karabük iron and steel works were therefore inconveniently located in relation to both the coal and iron supply.

In their paternalistic fashion the leaders of the new Turkey felt that industrial centres could transform peasants into a technically skilled work-force and thus reduce their dependence on agriculture. Although a small rise did occur in the number of persons employed in industry in relation to the rise in the total population (70% of which was occupied in agriculture) this increase was insignificant.[35] 'During the initial period from 1923–30, great economic inertia existed. Despite substantial investment and government-inspired prodding, little seemed to happen . . . it was not until after 1945 that per-capita real income began to register a steady rise.'[36]

There were some successes however, especially in import substitution. Textiles decreased from 44% of total imports to 27.5% at the end of the thirties; foodstuffs from 17% to 4.3%. On the other hand, there was an increase in imports of capital goods, machinery, cars, lorries, iron and steel.[37] The government was prepared to pay for these commodities even at the expense of local consumer goods. All factors considered, industry in Turkey, although it had freed itself from Ottoman-style submission to foreign domination, was still a long way from the strong self-sufficient position its leaders wanted.

THE PROBLEM OF AGRICULTURE

Agricultural policy was to prove the major difficulty for early planners. Turkey in 1939 was still a largely traditional agrarian society with 70% of the population engaged in agriculture. According to the 1940 census Turkey had a population of 17,820,950, of whom 13,475,000 lived in villages. Atatürk had always emphasised the vital importance of the peasantry. Agrarian reform aimed at redistribution of land started as early as 1923. Abandoned land, *Vakıf* land, and parts of large estates were considered for redistribution. In the twenties most of the benefits from redistribution accrued to the 'repatriated' Turks. There was considerable corruption, with much of the land abandoned by the Greek and Armenian community going to form large private estates. In all of this the smallholder and the landless were disregarded.[38] Although the reform movement was well intentioned at the top, lower-level administration was often corrupt and, of the public pastureland (40,000,000 *dönüms*) which was redistributed, only one-tenth went to the smallholder or landless peasant.[39] The *aşar* tax, often taken as symbolic of Ottoman oppression of the peasantry, was abolished, but only to be replaced with new inefficient and arbitrary measures such as crop confiscation.[40] The plots distributed were often not large enough for the recipients to grow enough to maintain themselves. 'The implementation of the law met with many difficulties and the distribution went on staggeringly until the end of the forties.'[41]

The major problem of the economy as a whole, that of finance, also affected agriculture. The peasant had enough difficulty in procuring his yearly hand-to-mouth subsistence; any progress depended on his finding additional capital. Capital available from the Agricultural Bank tended to go to the wealthy who could show collateral. After 1924 the Agricultural Bank was extended and its policy changed to aid the small farmer. The government also attempted to encourage agriculture, through model farms, experimental stations, agricultural schools etc. The result of all these measures, though discernible, was limited in extent. The cultivated area increased by about 58% during 1923–32, against the pre-1919 standards, but the population grew by

25–28%. The overall increase in production was due more to this overall increase in cultivated area than to the scanty improvements of yield per unit of land.[42]

The basic problem in agriculture, as in industry, was the sheer size of the task. As in industry there had to be a period of rehabilitation before progress could take place. 'Viewed against the background of destruction and neglect of the wars – especially the Greek war – this rise in yields represented rehabilitation rather than development if compared with the pre-war standards.'[43] Despite the efforts made in tobacco cultivation, for example, by the beginning of the thirties Turkey had only returned to its 1913 level.[44] The world economic crisis, which began in 1929, dealt a serious blow to Turkish agriculture, which lagged behind the standard even of eastern and southern Europe. When İnönü became President in 1938 the problem of transport was still such that Chinese rice was cheaper on the İstanbul market than Samsun rice.[45]

Z. Y. Hershlag argues that it was the overall depressed state of agriculture which caused the inertia in Turkish economic development. The preponderance of the agricultural sector and its low level of income, which did not improve until the late thirties, determined the overall income level of the population. 'The vigorous development of agriculture still furnished the key to any serious change in the level of income and standard of living . . . and the reforms introduced during the period of etatism failed to achieve the progress required in this field in a distinctly agrarian country.'[46]

Recent research has also indicated that the policy of land reform progressed unevenly. Çağlar Keyder and Şevket Pamuk have drawn attention to the fact that the aim of the étatist programme of the mid-thirties was to effect a transfer of the surplus from agriculture to industry, thus hopefully bringing about speedy industrialisation. This was unsuccessful as grain yields for 1932, 1933, 1934 and 1935 were below the 1929 levels. The war itself was to compound the problem with grain production decreasing severely during the 1938–45 period, with manpower and draught animals being put to military use.[47]

Nor was there any systematic approach to planning a war economy. The National Defence Law which was finally enacted on 26 January 1940 was widely criticised in the press and even among the ranks of the ruling single party, the Cumhuriyet Halk Partisi (CHP). This tardy measure alienated the producers with low fixed-price buying, and led to the enrichment of middlemen. Meanwhile increasing food prices and inflation completed the unhappy picture.[48]

It is also interesting that a certain anti-military sentiment was noticed in Turkey in those years. Although Atatürk always emphasised the need to be ready to defend the country, he deliberately played down the military orientation of the Turks who were now worn out by long disastrous wars. This created an atmosphere of unwillingness to approach the problems entailed by a war economy. 'For this reason Turkey entered the war years completely deprived of any war economic planning or organisation.'[49]

FOREIGN INFLUENCES

Turkish leaders had aspired, as much as possible, to avoid dependence on western loans, advisers etc. But this proved impossible in practice.

In considering wartime developments it is necessary always to keep in mind the austerity with which the drive for political and economic independence had been conducted since 1922, and the constant watchfulness against foreign domination in both spheres which had been so important a factor in the psychological heritage of the new generation of Turkish leaders.[50]

The emergence of Hitler and the economic expansion of Germany coincided with a period when Turkey was sorely in need of finance. Political relations had been normal-to-friendly; now economic relations came to have a primary importance. For the Germans, economic influence was a lever for political domination and in the mid-thirties Germany had set about transforming the Balkans into her economic hinterland. 'Germany's proximity to the countries in this geographical region enabled her to exert stronger economic and political pressure on them.'[51] The politico-economic link is evident in a German Foreign Office 'Brief for German–Turkish Economic Relations' complied in 1938. It emphasised that clearing and credit agreements must be stepped up, 'in order to obtain the desired objective of binding Turkey closer to Germany economically and thus strengthening our political influence in that country.'[52]

Turkey's foreign trade on the whole followed the variations of her foreign relations as the Turks tried to reconcile their foreign policy with economic needs. 'In fact the diplomatic struggle can best be taken against the background of markets and loans.'[53] By the mid-thirties the Turkish leaders became aware that economic dependence on Germany was not consistent with their foreign policy, and efforts were made to diversify foreign trade. In this they were not entirely successful. By 1937 Germany supplied 78% of Turkish wool yarns and tissues, 69.7% of her iron and steel, 61% of her machinery and apparatus and 55.4% of her chemicals. In return she took 75% of Turkey's new wool, 70% of her new cotton and chrome.[54] In 1939 Germany was still receiving half of all Turkish exports. The difficulty lay in the fact that nearly all Turkey's exports were agricultural raw materials (with the important exception of chrome ore) which Britain and France could purchase on more advantageous terms from their colonies and other long-standing trading partners, e.g., cotton from Egypt, sugar from the West Indies, tobacco from America and Rhodesia etc.[55]

Yuluğ Tekin Kurat has pointed out that for Turkey to withdraw from the German market could only be harmful to her. Germany was the only country which was willing to buy Turkish agricultural produce on a large scale as much of this produce was of lower quality than that usually demanded on the world market. In other words 'a large portion of the income of the agrarian sector was being provided by Germany buying Turkish agricultural products'. In purely economic terms Germany was Turkey's natural market and trading partner. Britain bought no cotton from Turkey during the 1940–4 period. By contrast Germany bought 1,318 tons in 1942, 1,580 tons in 1943 and 3,325 tons in 1944. According to Kurat the fact that Turkey still distrusted the Entente Powers and that this feeling was shared by Germany helped them to develop extensive ties; 'German Professors, technicians, and construction firms were finding openings in Turkey.'[56]

In addition to this the Germans were more often than not prepared to pay inflated prices for Turkish agricultural produce. These circumstances made it all the more difficult for Turkey to diversify her trade. Trade with Germany was also rendered more expedient through Hjalmar Schacht's 'clearing system' whereby an open account was kept in Germany for Turkish requirements which she paid for in the form of primary products. In the words of Hitler's 'economic genius':

Thus I had to look around for agricultural and raw material producing countries which would be willing to take German goods in exchange for the foodstuffs and raw materials they produced . . . Foreign countries selling goods to us would have the amount of our purchases credited to their account in German currency and with this they could buy anything they wanted in Germany.[57]

These seemingly accommodating words mask the fact that such agreements, although ostensibly convenient because they disposed of the need to pay in scarce foreign exchange, led to overwhelming dependency on the part of the raw material producer. Under such agreements Turkey forfeited her freedom to trade with other countries, as remuneration for her raw materials could only be in Reichsmarks which could only be used to buy German goods. In 1936 Schacht visited Turkey and proposed that German capital be given priority in financing large-scale irrigation projects. This would have meant the agricultural sector would also be dependant on German capital.[58] By the end of 1937, 78.2% of Turkey's trade transactions took place through clearing as against 17.8% with countries of free exchange currencies, and only 3.9% with countries to which Turkey was not bound by clearing or similar agreements.[59]

The other difficulty was the limited number of routes for Turkish trade. The rail link with Europe passed entirely into German hands early in the war, so did the Danube. After Italy's entry into the war in 1940 shipping in the Mediterranean became extremely dangerous. The only other link, the Basra railway, could not carry much trade. As the Germans conquered Greece and came to control the outlets to the Black Sea they were in a position to control all trade through the Straits.

In the mid-thirties, however, the Turks were attempting to bring their economic policy into line with the *rapprochement* with Britain. In 1936 the Turkish government accepted the tender of the British firm Brassert rather than Krupp for the building of an iron and steel works at Karabük. On 27 May 1938 the Anglo-Turkish credit agreement was signed for £16 million, £6 million of which was for armaments, the other £10 million for capital goods.

The Turkish leadership was also coming to realise the failure of their self-sufficiency policy. They fell back on hard bargaining, therefore, and on playing one side against the other. They tried by these means to make the best of the situation, attempting to draw the most favourable bargain possible from each side. Menemencioğlu went to Germany in July 1938; his tactics there and later in negotiations with the British serve as an admirable illustration of the Turkish attitude.

When the Germans confronted Menemencioğlu with the Anglo-Turkish credit agreement and told him that Germany could not allow herself to be forced into a secondary position, Menemencioğlu replied that he had come to Berlin to bring about a considerable increase in Turkish–German trade. He said it was understandable that 'some circles' in Turkey were trying to avoid an excessively one-sided orientation of Turkish trade, but that Turkey's need for capital goods was such that Germany still had a good market even after the agreement with Britain. 'He was also prepared to ensure that Germany would not be discriminated against in relation to England;'[60] but the truth of the matter was that the Turks were attempting to do just that, and to re-orient their economic policy towards Britain.

Menemencioğlu was trying to sow seeds of hope in German minds, by emphasising that Turkey had a clean slate, and thus hoping to secure the economic concessions Turkey needed so much. 'M. Numan then raised several economic questions also and inquired about the possibility of further deliveries of German war material, whereby Turkey would become more independent of England.' Menemencioğlu's tactics were the time honoured Turkish ones of bidding off one power against the other. During the same period Britain was being told that if she increased armaments and economic aid to Turkey, Turkey would be more independent of Germany. The memorandum summarising the Turkish–German trade negotiations said that despite the arrangements with England the Turks undertook to guarantee at least some deliveries of ore and wheat to Germany in 1938. 'In particular he [Menemencioğlu] would as soon as he returned, try to make possible an increase in the export of chromium from about 15,000 tons a year to about 100,000 tons during the coming treaty year.' Numan Menemencioğlu also told Clodius, the German chief negotiator, about the Anglo-Turkish credit agreement. 'Not only was Turkey prepared at any time to conclude a similar agreement with Germany, but for political reasons, she would even be eager to do so.'[61] It is possible that these 'political reasons' were a desire to be more independent of Great Britain.

Menemencioğlu's tactics paid off in January 1939; the Turkish–German credit agreement was signed granting Turkey 150 million Reichsmarks for fulfilment of orders including mining installations, an agricultural development programme, power plants, rolling stock, merchant vessels and war material to the value of 60 million Reichsmarks. This credit was to a great extent to finance the second five-year plan. But instead of increasing Turkish chrome exports to Germany in August 1939 as promised, the Turks refused to renew the Turkish–German trade treaty as a form of protest against the Nazi–Soviet Pact.

This created a serious problem in the disposal of surplus commodities;[62] 'It was as hard as ever (in 1939) for France and Britain to discover suitable exports from Turkey.'[63] The British feared that this would lead the Turks back to Germany; this fear the Turks ably exploited. Although on 26 October 1939, the Turks proposed to cease exporting chrome to Germany provided Britain undertook to buy no less than 200,000 tons a year, it was not in the Turkish interest to relax pressure on the British.[64] The British agreed on 30 October but now the Turks raised their terms. The British did not take kindly to this as they felt that they had 'already done quite well for the Turks', and pointed out that Turkey as an ally was under a moral obligation to withhold exports of chrome to Germany.[65]

Unfortunately, Turkish foreign policy implied a different attitude to morality, one of always putting the toughest possible case in furtherance of Turkish interests. In November 1939 during the Menemencioğlu–Halifax talks, 'The Secretary General Numan Menemencioğlu was to prove a resourceful and at times exasperating negotiatior.'[66] Menemencioğlu said Germany was refusing to buy categories of Turkish goods unless the goods included chrome. He said that unless Turkey found an alternative market for her goods some chrome would have to go to Germany. The Secretary General of the Turkish Foreign Ministry also said Turkey urgently needed armaments and he let it be known that they were prepared to supply 30,000 tons of chrome to Germany after outstanding orders on war materials had been completed. This had the desired effect of worrying the Foreign Office who said on 7 December that such an action would be considered a serious breach of faith. 'The Turkish Government was clearly out to make the most of the situation although it was genuinely concerned with the state of the country's defences.'[67]

Another one of Menemencioğlu's tactics was grouping Turkish exports so that the buyer of a high-demand export such as chrome had to agree to buy it in a package-deal which included such low-demand goods as dried fruit. In this manner the British were forced to accept a £T2 million purchase of dried fruit, Menemencioğlu having made this a *sine-qua-non* for an agreement. Menemencioğlu attempted to procure a contract whereby the British would undertake to buy all chrome production for twenty years. The British refused. But, 'later events showed that the British would have been well advised to tie-up Turkish chrome for a longer period: they were to pay heavily for their caution in January 1940'.[68] The French offered the Turks 105 shillings a ton for their chrome, the British called this 'outrageously and unnecessarily high', but as the demand for the strategic ore increased the price later soared to 270 shillings a ton. Overall the Turks gained markedly from what the British condescendingly called 'bazaar instincts'.

As the fortunes of war increasingly worsened for Britain she became more concerned about German influence in Turkey. There was no rationing of supplies to Turkey as there was for other neutrals. Every effort was made to provide the commodities needed for civil as well as military supplies. 'It was agreed that in certain cases Turkish products, even though expensive and not essential to the Allied war effort must be bought and paid for if necessary in materials and goods which the UK could ill afford to spare.'[69]

But by 23 June 1940 no chrome had yet been purchased under the January agreement, and the situation caused serious discontent in Turkey. In July 1940 the Turco-German commercial agreement was signed which provided for a volume of £T21,400,000 worth of exchange while it was in operation. In addition to this the Germans undertook the delivery of all goods purchased by Turkey. The Turks found that the overwhelming German military preponderance left them no choice but to increase their trade with Germany. G. L. Clutton of the Foreign Office noted on 1 May 1941 that as inflation and rising prices got worse Turkey would be tempted to move closer to Germany. 'In order to increase her imports and alleviate the position in that direction, Turkey might revert to her old economic relations with Germany, who with the whole of the European production behind her, would be able to offer the necessary increase in volume of consumption goods.'[70] This is exactly what happened as Turkey came to rely on Germany for her markets and capital products, neither of which the British were able to supply during the time of German ascendancy.

As the war dragged on the strain on Turkey's economy grew worse. To keep a large army constantly mobilised, and to apportion a large part of the budget to military expenditure became increasingly more of a burden. Taxation had always been heavy; with the war it became more so. Even the increased volume of taxation was not enough; income tax and property tax together only amounted to about 15% of the state income. The state monopolies (tobacco and alcohol) provided 20–25% with the remaining 60% coming from turnover and consumption taxes and from customs. But 'Expenditure on security, investments in development and payment of the public debt required constantly increasing funds.'[71] On 24 April 1941, the Turkish Ambassador in London told Eden that 'the position is now becoming difficult, for the army has been mobilized for some time and the pay of the troops was proving a heavy drain'.[72] The army also needed feeding and detracted from the effective agricultural workforce. In early 1941 Saraçoğlu asked Eden about possible financial help; regarding this, a Foreign Office memorandum dated 1 May 1941 stated: 'military expenditure has reached a higher level than Turkey can bear without recourse to loans and credits and other often unorthodox measures'.[73]

Just such an 'unorthodox measure' was the notorious 'Wealth Tax' which was widely applied in 1943. Although it reflected the genuine economic weaknesses of wartime and the Foreign Office felt it started as 'a draconian but equitable measure', it came to be a source of discrimination against racial minorities.[74] İnönü had intended it to be used as a weapon against war profiteers, some of whom were of foreign extraction. The Foreign Office admitted that many foreign businesses had done very well out of the war. G. L. Clutton wrote on 7 February 1943: 'many firms had in fact made a great deal of money out of the war, and transferred their profits abroad. Therefore the Embassy should be wary of defending them.'[75] But on the whole the tax was discriminatory and grave injustices did occur. Nonetheless, the fact that such a desperate measure was deemed necessary is an indication of the strain placed on the economy by war.

It is also interesting to note that the British Foreign Office, like the Germans, did attempt to use Turkey's need for industrial goods and technology to turn a political profit. On 5 December 1943 the Foreign Office suggested to Hugessen that he make clear to İnönü, 'that unless Turkey plays her part, there is no chance whatever of her receiving those industrial supplies in post-war years which are essential to the industrialisation of Turkey which was Atatürk's dream and is still İnönü's ambition'.[76] Ironically, this was precisely the tactic tried by Curzon in Lausanne in 1923. But this form of pressure could only be counterproductive. The Turkish leaders knew just how vulnerable 'Atatürk's dream' was. They were all too aware that the entire achievement of the past twenty years could be destroyed by one ill-considered move.

Therefore, in rapidly reviewing the Turkish economic situation before the Second World War we come to the following conclusions. In both industry and agriculture an extended period of rehabilitation had to take place before progress could be recorded. This imposed such a crippling time lag on the Turkish economy that when war broke out it was just showing the first stirrings of growth. The leaders of the new republic recognised that they were in no position to get involved in any total war as it was predicted the Second World War would be. Nor was there any consistent planning of a war economy. The Turks realised that their hopes of self-sufficiency had been in vain. This made them focus all the more on their foreign policy with the conviction that if they had to depend on foreign powers they would do so only on the best possible terms. In this they succeeded, although the failed to avoid a dependence on Germany, due to the advantages of trading with her, as compared to Britain. This remained the predominant influence on Turkish economic life.

2 . MILITARY INADEQUACY

It is a well-known fact that in total war it is not possible to divide a country rigidly into civilian and military sectors; the strength of one depends on the other. When the Second World War broke out Turkey was inadequately prepared in both sectors. Her inadequate industrialisation was reflected in her unpreparedness for technological warfare. 'One of the obvious pointers of the rather primitive stage of Turkey's industrialisation is her defence position.'[1] The realistic assessment of their country's military capabilities was a major factor influencing the Turkish leadership in their determination to keep Turkey out of the war.

Defence and security had always been central issues in the planning of the republic. Even in Lausanne, İnönü had emphasised the need to stay mobilised in order to back up his words with military muscle. This constituted one of the basic precepts of his foreign policy; understanding through negotiation and treaty was always welcomed, but alongside this it was of cardinal importance to make crystal clear that any aggression would be resisted by force. The lesson learnt in Lausanne was applied in the dangerous days of the Second World War: 'The Turks were able to impose circumspection on both the Germans and the British because they were intensely patriotic and fully determined to resist aggression, and because they had a substantial army, which though not modernised, was recognised as a valiant and formidable fighting force.'[2]

Although the Army was large and had a reputation for being valiant, the needs of modern warfare dictated that it be specialised and highly skilled. In these last two requirements the Turkish Armed Forces were sorely lacking. There were indications after 1923 that even the Turk could tire of fighting. Şevket Süreyya Aydemir has pointed out that there was a general lassitude regarding military matters, and a war weariness combined with a will to turn towards

31

reconstruction. Atatürk himself had deliberately avoided keeping the country subjected to a prolonged siege mentality.[3] At the İzmir Economic Congress he had specifically declared that Turks were not a 'warrior' nation but an 'economic' nation.[4]

Frey has also noted that during the thirties the Minister of Defence was no longer at the top of the 'ministerial pyramid'; that position having gone to the Minister of the Interior.[5] Consequently, although a large force was maintained for security reasons (and even this was a costly burden on the budget) military modernisation was not a top priority of the Turkish government.

As events in Europe took a more dangerous turn in the later 1930s the Turkish leaders began to focus more attention on defence. By European standards, however, Turkey was still markedly backward. In the Annual Report for 1937 the British Embassy in Ankara noted: 'policy of re-armament continues, but is by no means complete'.[6] The report noted that twenty-two divisions formed the manpower of the Army, but progress in mechanisation was slow. The shortage of tanks and armoured cars was noticeable, 'units are known to have been transported from Thrace to Anatolia and *vice versa* to participate in manoeuvres and reviews'. The total strength of the forces was given as 120,000 men of all ranks.[7] It is interesting to note here that the Turks still considered Italy as the major threat. Manoeuvres were held in the İzmir area with the intention of testing defence against the landing force of a hostile power 'tacitly recognized as Italy'.[8] Fixed defence works were erected on the west coast of Turkey. The 1937 Annual Report also mentioned the difficulty in getting information about the condition of any of the Turkish forces because of the official policy of secrecy on the part of the Turkish General Staff and government. The report concluded that Turkey's 'Defence programme will yet take several years to complete.' The events in Europe, however, were not to give Turkey several years. Aydemir notes that when war broke out the motorised transport of the Turkish Army consisted of a motley collection of old lorries of twenty-eight different makes.[9] This resulted in the situation where the 'army travelled on foot ahead of a supply train of horse-drawn carriages and wagons'.[10] Aydemir has indicated that even fodder for the horses was in short supply.

The lack of mobility displayed by the Turkish Army was also due to the gross inadequacies of the Turkish communications systems. Although İnönü had concentrated on the expansion of railways and building of roads, when war broke out there was still only one single,

one-track railway spanning the country from west to east. This mili-
tated against the quick mobilisation and concentration of troops. As a
result, Turkey was forced to maintain large armies on its frontiers.

The problem of lack of uniformity extended into the artillery and
hand arms. The artillery was equipped with a diversity of pieces
imported from Germany, Czechoslovakia, Sweden, Britain, France,
Russia and Switzerland.[11] The rifles used by the troops were a mixture including 'Mausers, Mannlichers, Lee-Enfields, Martinis, Le-
bels and others.'[12]

During the war Turkey felt the need to standardise rifle calibres by
shipping large quantities to Germany where barrels were bored out
according to a uniform calibre.[13]

In 1938 the Army consisted of 20,000 officers and 174,000 men
forming 11 army corps, 23 divisions, one armoured brigade, 3 cavalry
brigades and 7 frontier commands; 'primarily equipped with World
War I weapons'.[14] As late as February 1940 the Foreign Office noted:
'The Turkish Army is very short of rifles and has asked us to supply
150,000.' The Foreign Office stressed the importance of sending these
to Turkey. 'The fact that we have been unable to meet a large number
of Turkish requests for equipment has already had an adverse
psychological effect.'[15]

In the days preceding the Second World War air power had
become a vital factor. In 1937, Turkey had 131 first line aircraft,
which they hoped to increase to 300 by 1938. Of the 131 only half were
relatively modern. In 1937, purchases for the Air Force included 40
fighters from Poland, 20 'Martin' bombers from America, 10 out of an
order of 24 modern Heinkel bombers from Germany, 2 Bristol
bombers from Britain. The Air Force had 300 trained pilots. 'In a
Western European Air Force probably a good Turkish pilot would
only be rated moderate and with little ability to fly in bad weather.'[16]
There was a serious lack of skilled mechanics and no reserves of
aircraft and pilots. When Wing Commander Elmhirst visited the
Turkish Air Force in 1938 he reported, 'The Turks candidly admitted
the poorness of their officer training scheme, which entails five years
ground training before continuous flying instruction commences.'[17]
Even Ernest Phillips, in what is manifestly a propaganda brochure
printed in 1942, admits:

If the Germans were to stage an all out offensive in this area, they could bring
more planes into the air than the Turks could even gather, and if we were to

Fig. 3 Squadron of aircraft. *(Courtesy of İletişim Yayıncılık)*

send too many from Libya to help Turkey, the weakness there would be such that we should be in difficulties on the other side of the Suez.[18]

There were few airfields, and those that did exist were primitive and not suitable for modern aircraft.

The Navy was the weakest of the services. The British Naval Attaché reported in 1937: 'Judged by the standards of modern navies, however small, the condition of the fleet is far from satisfactory.'[19] It consisted of the outdated battle cruiser *Yavuz* (ex-*Goeben*), four destroyers and five submarines. These ships were 'sadly lacking in many essential improvements for offence and defence which had been added to other navies since the Great War'.[20] The Navy lacked all modern appliances for defending coasts and harbours, and the ships were defenceless against air attack. The Attaché concluded 'This rather depressing situation will no doubt be overcome when the navy starts to expand.'[21]

In 1938 there were signs of just such an expansion not only in the Navy but in all the services, with the government coming to realise that in the face of the looming world-wide threat, it had to focus more attention on defence than it had done hitherto. In February 1938, Sir Percy Loraine, the British Ambassador, reported from Ankara that a new law had been passed in the Assembly authorising the expenditure of £7,000,000 on aerial defences and £5,000,000 on military equipment.[22]

In May 1938 a credit agreement was signed with Britain which provided Turkey with £6 million for armaments credits. Before the armaments credit there had been doubts in British minds about Turkey's ability to pay for the military technology she wanted from Britain. Even at this early stage the British Ambassador realised the importance of assisting Turkey; he cabled Cadogan on 23 February 1938: 'It would seem dismally unfortunate if the financial difficulty stops their order being placed. Are we really debarred from using our tremendous money resources, one patent and tangible superiority that we possess over our European rivals for helping our friends . . . for building up in this instance a friendly navy in a region which represents for us a particularly high degree of political and strategical importance . . .' The Ambassador underlined that a strong Turkey would be less open to influence and military strength, would, 'strengthen her influence in the direction of peace and lawful behaviour throughout the Balkan peninsula and eastwards towards Iran and Afghanistan . . . The security of our friends contributes to our own security, a well armed and self-reliant Turkey will count at least two in a division.'[23]

On 25 May 1938, Loraine reported that a bill had been brought before the Assembly authorising the government to contract agreements up to a total of £T125.5 million in respect to the Turkish armaments programme. It is noticeable in this report that the Turks still felt Italy to be the primary threat, as shown by the priority they gave to heavy batteries for coastal defence in their armaments requirements.[24] In a dispatch a month later the Ambassador reported that the Turks wanted to purchase 64 medium tanks, 32 armoured cars, 350 lorries, 150 cross-country cars.[25] Indeed, the Turkish government gave the impression that they felt they had left modernisation too late, and had to make up for lost time.

S. D. Waley of the Treasury wrote to L. Baggalay of the Foreign Office on 22 July and related to him conversations with a Mr Lockhart-Lewis, of a firm acting as consulting engineers to the Turkish government regarding their armaments purchases. Mr Lewis said that the Turkish agent was difficult to deal with and had presented a programme of purchases which might cost £21 million. The Turks seemed to be inquiring about a much larger programme than that which their £6 million would allow. J. R. Colville minuted on this paper: 'The Turks are recklessly piling up orders for armaments, naval, military and aircraft, which cannot possibly be paid for out of the £6,000,000.'[26]

The sudden spurt in Turkish rearmament also took its toll financially. In his 1938 Economic Report Loraine pointed out that: 'National defence absorbs the greatest part of the budget estimates under any one head, amounting as it does to £T108,995,000 or 43.7% of total state revenue.' In the budget estimates for 1938–9 he noted that expenditure was up by £T35.1 million from £T260.2 million to £T295.3 million. This increase was reflected by various ministries as follows: 'National Defence got £T82.4 million, while Public Works got £T50 million.' The Ambassador noted that the gap between the two was significant and concluded: 'Turkey obviously does not feel that peace is upon them yet, and are spending on their security.'[27] The Turks certainly had come to feel very vulnerable.

Nonetheless, at the outbreak of war Turkey's preparations were extremely inadequate. As Turkey moved closer to Britain Germany refused to deliver various promised war materials. In mid-September

Fig. 4 Machinegun in minaret. (*Courtesy of İletişim Yayıncılık*)

1939 deliveries from Germany, German-occupied Czechoslovakia, and Poland ground to a halt. This left a big gap in Turkish armaments particularly since much of the expected material consisted of field guns, and other vital ordnance.[28]

During the Anglo-Turkish Treaty negotiations in September 1939 a military credit agreement amounting to £25 million was agreed upon. The sheer mass of the military material it was to provide for indicates that this was more a comprehensive military aid treaty than a standard clearing arrangement. For the Air Force, 258 fighter, bomber, training and reconnaissance aircraft were ordered complete with fuel, oil, photographic material, wireless, guns and bombloads. For the Navy, 2,500 mines of 2.5 tons charge each, 200 torpedoes, 700 depth charges, 36 assault craft, 25 patrol boats, 4 torpedo-boats, 3 coastguard boats, 6 minesweepers and 2 minelayers. For the Army an extremely detailed list was given ranging from tanks, through horse-shoes, to pickaxes.[29]

There is evidence that this near panic buying was a result of the realisation that the Turkish Armed Forces were having to face the Second World War with the technology of the First. According to a commander who served at the time: 'A new era had dawned in the techniques and tactics of war. We were just learning the rules of the First World War. Our arms, tactics and technique dated from that time.'[30] In another instance an artillery officer stationed in Thrace recalled:

We had guns which had served at Verdun in the First War. They weighed 48 tons. They were towed in two pieces with one ten ton tractor towing the barrel and another towing the carriage. The wheelbase of these was half a metre and they had iron wheels. Naturally these were not arms to be proud of compared to the panzers. What was worse was that we had difficulty in deploying them outside the base. We needed roads with a surface which could carry our guns . . .

As a result, for the said guns to travel to their destined deployment spots took two years.[31]

An exchange of letters between the Turkish Ministry of Defence and the Turkish General Staff which took place between March and May 1940 sheds further cruel light on the state of the Turkish Army. The Ministry of Defence letter dated 22 March stated that the Turkish Army was to be increased to 1,300,000 effectives forming fourteen army corps consisting of forty-one infantry, three cavalry divisions, seven fortified positions and one armoured brigade. The communication clearly stated that, 'the material resources of the nation were unable to provide for the provisioning and transport of this large number of effectives', and asked what measures could be taken to save on man and animal power.

The answering letter signed by Chief of Staff Marshal Çakmak took over two months to formulate and was dated 29 May 1940. It stated that the reason for the large number of men and animals was the condition of transport in the Army. If motor transport could be increased and conditions improved then, 'the pack-animal caravans will be turned to baggage trains using carts, thus representing a saving of one in three for animals and two in three for troops'.[32] Thus in the days of panzers and blitzkrieg the Turkish Army still had to make the transition from 'caravans' to 'baggage trains'. Also, as Aydemir indicates in the domain of Civil Defence: 'in nearly all respects the country was inadequately prepared to face the threat of war'.[33]

The entire capacity of the Turkish liquid fuel storage tanks was 100,000 tons. Nor were they capable of service at full capacity. During the war fuel supplies would drop to quantities sufficient for one week, sometimes less. In the event of war the meagre motorised transport the Army did have would be gravely short of fuel. The construction of the Çakmak defence lines in Thrace was hindered by the lack of cement and constructional steel. Of the former only 380,000 tons was produced a year. Both the cement factories were in İstanbul in vulnerable locations. The Karabük iron and steel works was not operational until 1939. Railway construction, although one of the few areas where genuine progress had been recorded was still gravely insufficient and lacking in rolling stock. This meant that even the minimum number of wagons for the needs of the General Staff could not be provided. Experiments in the evacuation of surplus population from İstanbul had yielded sobering results. 'It is possible to increase these examples. Everything indicated that if Turkey were to be drawn into a war, she would be confronted with immense difficulties. At all costs, we had to stay out of the war.'[34]

The few industrial centres Turkey did have could be destroyed within the first days of war. The coal mining area of Zonguldak could easily be bombed, as could the fuel storage tanks. 'Confronted with these possibilities all İnönü could do was to use all his intelligence and employ all means, without falling prey to sentimentality, in order to withdraw into a protective shell and look for ways of staying out of the war.'[35] Nor was this 'protective shell' very convincing. The natural defences of Anatolia were good but Thrace was indefensible. Despite all the money which had been lavished on them the defences there would at most have made possible a rearguard action. It followed that Turkey would lose a fair proportion of her population and her largest city in the first days of the war. Indeed the Turkish military authorities gradually pulled back their projected first line of defence from the Çakmak line at the border, to the Çatalca mountains just before İstanbul. Around March 1941 the projected line of defence was moved further eastward abandoning İstanbul and planning to meet the enemy in Western Anatolia.[36]

Although military weakness was used by the Turks as a stalling manoeuvre in the face of British pressure, there is little doubt that the Turkish leaders were genuinely concerned about their defensive strength. As a work written during the war years said:

It follows that Turkey is quite inadequately prepared for modern war. She must rely completely upon a powerful industrialized ally. If she cannot rely on such an ally, she cannot hope to fight with much more success than Holland or Yugoslavia. This radical insufficiency of arms and war material must be remembered whenever Turkey's foreign policy comes up for discussion.[37]

3 . PROCESS OF GOVERNMENT AND THE FOREIGN POLICY LEADERSHIP

In examining the decision-making process in the Turkish government during the war years two factors must be kept in mind; the government during this period was authoritarian, and power was very centralised. The Grand National Assembly, the Parliamentary Group of the CHP, the Cabinet and İnönü, in ascending order, formed the power structure in government. This power structure, included practically all the politically active elements in Turkish society. If any political activity were to be legitimately carried out, it had to be done within this framework. The system was as hierarchical as it was authoritarian, the authoritarian principle permeating all levels of the İnönü government. İnönü himself, as the authoritarian head of an authoritarian government, was at the pinnacle of power and the focal point of all this centralisation. Because real power was so concentrated, any pressure brought to bear on those who wielded this power also had of necessity to be concentrated. And as the leaders in question adhered consistently to a given set of values, then the chances of swaying the country's policy through the application of pressure on the leaders was very slight.

Power in the Turkish context had always tended to be authoritarian. According to Bahri Savcı, the principle of authoritarianism originated in the steppes of Central Asia, was further heightened by its coupling with Islam, and has been the most persistent characteristic of Turkish statecraft.[1]

This of course is the classical concept and growing political awareness has changed the Turk's attitude to the supremacy and non-approachability of all government. But coercion rather than conviction still remained the root of Turkish politics in Kemalist Turkey. 'Submission to the will of the ruler has been the fundamental principle of government not only in the ghazi society of the Ottomans but also in the Turkish society brought into being by Gazi Mustafa

Kemal.'[2] Since Kemalism was a movement dominated by soldiers and men in public service, it was a movement with an official and authoritarian character. 'In accordance with their official backgrounds the typical style of the Kemalists in achieving the national transformation they desired was that of command.'[3] Frey comments that the movement was instigated by a segment of the upper strata of society who were already in a position of social dominance; the Turkish 'revolution' was never a grass roots movement, but a movement imposed from above by the official and intellectual 'cadres'. 'The intellectualism, the imperiousness and the "tutelary" bureaucratic approach to national problems that typified Turkish government during most of the First Republic all would seem to accord with the modal social background of its members.'[4]

The Grand National Assembly, the Party Group, the Cabinet were all used as instruments for increasing the political will of the leader. Power was therefore extremely centralised. Until after the 1950 elections the Grand National Assembly was never really a theatre for genuine debate and decision making, but served more as an instrument of social control.

According to the Law of Fundamental Organisation (*Teşkilatı Esasiye Kanunu*), of 20 January 1921, all executive and legislative authority was concentrated in the Assembly as the supreme repository of governmental authority. Of the members of the Assembly Frey says: 'All signs are that national political life of Turkey revolved around these men.'[5] There was no constitutionalised system of 'checks and balances' or a separation of powers as in the American or British models. And 'close integration of top governmental organs' was the outstanding structural characteristic of Turkish government.[6] The President of the Republic was appointed from among its own members by the Assembly and the President in turn picked his Prime Minister from the same body. Also the Assembly selected from within its own membership: the President of the Assembly, the three Vice-Presidents, and the three administrative officers and six clerks who formed the Council of the Presidency of the Assembly (*Riyaset Divanı*). Thus all leading officials were chosen from its members.[7]

Whether or not any one candidate became a member was also determined by the Assembly through its control of entry requirements. Those under thirty, female, or illiterate were barred from the Assembly; this denied membership to about 90% of the population. Until 1946 the electoral system was indirect. Such a system was easier to control and manipulate. According to the code of the electoral law of 1942, one of the three provisions for the certification of the candidate, was the presentation of his name to the Provincial Inspection Committee by '*the* political Party'.[8] Since there was only one party, the CHP, this gave it control of all nominations of candidates to the Assembly. The candidate also, for all practical purposes, had to be a member of the People's Party. To be a member of the CHP he had to be of good repute and not have worked against the National Movement. Also he had to be without a 'negative political psychology'.[9] Tunçay has correctly noted that the authoritarian tradition continued under İnönü had its antecedent in the early days of Kemalism: 'Rather than defining the CHP as the leading party it would be more accurate to describe it as the party of the leader.' These provisions allowed the party to legally exclude from its membership all those it considered undesirable.

The Council of the Presidency of the party was the body which decided on the party's candidates for deputyship. This body was presided over by the General President of the party, who also chose its other two members: the General Vice-President and the General Secretary. This meant that real power over the selection of candidates for the Assembly rested with the General President. In the 1939–45 period this was İnönü. Although some influence was exerted on him by opinion in the area concerned, and by the General Secretary and others, this still meant that if İnönü disapproved of a candidate he did not have a chance. These were stringent conditions, but the opposite situation would also occur; when İnönü found someone congenial and wanted him in the Assembly he was hurriedly found a constituency and 'elected'. Sometimes appointments were made without even consulting the person in question. Ali Rıza Türel, who was later to become Minister of Justice, was asked by a reporter how he became a deputy. He replied, 'I was Assistant Prosecutor in İzmir. I saw my name among the list of candidates which was published in the newspaper, and so I learned.'[10]

Also general elections and by-elections were used to adjust the composition of the Assembly according to the President's requirements. After the foundation of the Republic, Mustafa Kemal sifted out all elements of actual and possible opposition (only 30% of the deputies from the First Assembly were re-elected to the second) in order to form a solid block of his supporters.[11] 'If election of a desirable element had not been secured at an election, he was elected through a by-election . . . The single party control was such that these by-elections were to a large extent devices for adjusting the composition of the Assembly to the demands of the existing leadership.'[12] Similarly in 1939 İnönü held elections to procure an Assembly that was more in keeping with his tastes.

Even though adjustments were made in the Assembly according to the demands of individual leaders, the main characteristic of the deputies was their uniformity. They nearly all came from middle-class to upper-class backgrounds, were much more educated than the population at large, and as central control increased, were devoted to the ideals of Kemalism. A significant number had been educated in prestigious schools such as the French orientated Galatasaray and St Joseph Lycées in İstanbul. These included Numan Menemencioğlu, Feridun Cemal Erkin and Necmettin Sadak. Mustafa Kemal, İsmet İnönü, Kâzım Karabekir and Ali Fuad Cebesoy were all graduates of the War Academy. Hasan Saka and Şükrü Saraçoğlu were among those who had studied in the Ecole des Sciences Politiques in Paris. The educational split between the people at large and their leaders is best noted by Frey: 'we see that in a society in which about three-fifths of the male population on average, could not read and write, at least three-fifths of the top level political leadership, on the other hand, was university educated'.[13] This was coupled with a situation where: 'The masses just are not active in what is going on; they never have been and they probably will not be in the present generation.'[14] This made for very effective central control by a dominant elite. The scene has now altered radically and there is much more involvement in politics.

It is sometimes suggested that the elite allowed their European educational backgrounds to influence their political behaviour, many having been educated abroad or in foreign language schools in Turkey. Even if this were true, the fact that the educational backgrounds were fairly evenly balanced must have made for equilibrium. Frey notes that the predominant cultural influences were French and German.[15] Foreign language, if taken as an influencing factor, also shows the same split on two sides. In the military group of deputies German was spoken by nearly one half. In the navy on the other hand the officers had been trained by the British and spoke English. It must not be forgotten, however, that the men in key posts were not making decisions on the basis of nostalgia about student days but by considering hard facts.

The Grand National Assembly, the embodiment of this elite, was therefore all powerful. There was no constitutional court empowered to review the constitutionality of legislation passed by the Assembly. Individual ministerial acts could be declared *ultra vires*, but within the framework of the constitution, which contained no limitation on the legislative power of the Assembly, 'the authority of the GNA was absolute'.[16]

İNÖNÜ AND MENEMENCİOĞLU

İnönü was thus the absolute ruler of an Assembly which had absolute power. The system of government which had already been rigid and authoritarian when he came to power, became even more so. 'After İnönü became President the political atmosphere became more illiberal.' There had already been a trend in this direction as Turkey, 'found models to inspire, if not to be closely imitated in the increasingly successful regimes in Italy and Germany'. In 1936 a labour law based on the Italian code forbade trade unions and strikes. In 1938 shortly before Atatürk's death other measures had been passed which prevented the creation of political parties and subjected the press to strict control. Police powers of arrest and detention were considerably extended.[17]

After war broke out, what responsibility there had been in the Assembly to approve state policy was shifted from the Assembly to the Parliamentary Group of the CHP. This was useful as the debates in the Assembly had to be open and public while the Parliamentary Group could meet behind closed doors. In this manner the Parliamentary Group, which was literally the Parliamentary wing of the CHP came to constitute a Parliament within a Parliament.

From the very start of his administration it became clear that İnönü wanted to establish his own brand of authoritarianism. This is not to say however that İnönü forced himself on the country. After Atatürk's death on 10 November 1938 it was apparently accepted by the majority in the highest echelons of the military establishment and by most of the CHP membership that İnönü was really the only successor. At the Parliamentary Group Conference İnönü got 322 of the 323 votes. (One vote, perhaps significantly went to Celal Bayar.) İnönü was thus nominated for the presidency. His election in the Assembly was a mere formality which was fulfilled on the same day (11 November) with the 348 members unanimously voting him in.[18]

As his principal biographer Aydemir puts it: 'Although İnönü had perhaps not always commanded the warm and wholehearted support of every member, they all united on the decision that he was the natural and logical choice.'[19] These polite words mask the fact that İnönü had none of Atatürk's charisma, and he was heartily disliked by some of Atatürk's closest advisers. There had also been a certain hesitancy on the part of Atatürk about his being elected President.[20] Although he was Atatürk's trusted counsellor they had serious differences. In the last year of Atatürk's presidency he had been removed from the premiership.

Cemil Koçak's recent study has indicated that İnönü did face real opposition among the leading cadres of the CHP over his nomination for the presidency after Atatürk's death. The fact that he was elected nearly unanimously was due largely to the fact that he still had a solid grounding in the party and moreover his opponents failed to produce a viable alternative candidate. The Atatürk–İnönü clash in the last days of the former's life stemmed from diametrically opposed views relating to economic planning, with İnönü favouring a much more étatist blend of economic policy.

İnönü also benefited from the fact that Celal Bayar, who had replaced him as Prime Minister, refused to be considered for the presidency.[21] The British Ambassador reported on 7 January 1939 that Fethi Okyar had been seriously considered: 'It was largely due to Fethi who made it clear that he did not want to be President, that the choice of İsmet as the unchallenged successor of Atatürk was reached.'[22] The 'old guard' of Atatürk, Sir Percy Loraine claimed, would have wanted 'an old soldier who would allow them to do as they pleased'.[23] By this 'old guard' the Ambassador presumably meant men such as Şükrü Kaya, Minister of the Interior, and Dr Aras, Minister for Foreign Affairs; by 'old soldier' he possibly intended Fevzi Çakmak. However, the Ambassador commented that all in all this was probably the best choice, as any other choice would have caused dissent.

The Ambassador had reported in a previous communication, announcing Atatürk's death and the election of İnönü:

General İsmet İnönü is just as incorruptible as his great predecessor. He is industrious and a sober liver, he has first hand knowledge of foreign affairs and a complete grasp of the administrative machine and of administrative problems . . . the transference of power and office thus took place with the utmost promptitude, with scrupulous regard for constitutional practice, without a ripple in the country's life. And the young Republic emerged with dignity and decorum from the first big test of its institutions.[24]

The Germans too had a high opinion of the man they were dealing with. A German Foreign Office memorandum written on 24 August 1941 described the reaction of Kroll, First Secretary at the Ankara Embassy, to von Ribbentrop's proposal that Turkish officials should be bribed: 'He questioned the Foreign Minister's remark that everyone in Turkey could be bought, pointing out that İsmet İnönü, the man who, in his opinion, was the one who alone mattered, could not be bought in any way.'[25]

The very report in which the British Ambassador referred to Fethi Okyar as a possible choice, goes on to say:

The fact that the machine went on without a hitch after Atatürk's death showed how natural and acceptable the choice was to all solid elements in the country. In point of fact, the Atatürk–İnönü combination had been ideal for Turkey. Atatürk supplied the large ideas, İnönü made them practical, was moreover responsible for everything else, and ran Turkey down to its smallest details. Atatürk's brain worked brilliantly for a few hours out of twenty four and was then submerged; but İsmet's brain if necessary, worked all twenty four hours. Atatürk was the more compulsive of the two; he was capable of calling a man a fool, and a few hours later, kissing him. But after İnönü considered a man a fool or a knave, there was never any subsequent osculation. The people knew İsmet's record and felt safe in his hands. They knew that İsmet had run the country to a great extent before Atatürk's death, and he would now carry on the lines he had already laid down.[26]

But in order to make progress along these lines İnönü knew he had to establish his own distinctive regime. Although he had been elected with seemingly reassuring unanimity, he had to take measures to insure against any challenge. The 'old guard' had to go. When Celal Bayar's cabinet resigned, İnönü was careful to avoid too sudden a break and requested Bayar to form a new government, with two changes from the previous one: Şükrü Kaya was replaced by Refik Saydam and Dr Aras by Şükrü Saraçoğlu.

İnönü had never liked Aras's flamboyant style and the Foreign Minister had been one of the instigators of the move to remove him from the premiership. Also İnönü felt that Aras had not followed instructions during the Nyon Conference and on several occasions the actions he had taken at Geneva were not in keeping with the instructions telephoned to him. As for Şükrü Kaya, İnönü was offended by some of his actions in eastern Turkey, where he ordered summary executions, and was allegedly involved in corrupt dealings. Both men had, so he believed, conspired against his election to the presidency. They had both been closely associated with Atatürk's 'drinking table' politics, a style of government which went directly against the grain with İnönü.[27] Although Bayar himself was not a 'İnönü-man', he had been kept in his position during the delicate transition period.

By the beginning of 1939, İnönü was ready to tighten his grip on the administration. New elections were held in January 1939. Celal Bayar resigned and was replaced by Dr Refik Saydam personally loyal to İnönü. İnönü used the election to pack the Assembly with deputies loyal to his regime. Tamkoç writes:

He appointed and dismissed prime ministers and ministers as he pleased and gathered around him those who were willing to submit to his dictates without any question . . . He intervened in the minutest details of administration . . . From the time of his election as president at least until the end of the Second World War, İsmet İnönü was, for all practical purposes, a dictator.[28]

Soon after Atatürk's death İnönü officially gave himself the title of 'National Chief' (Milli Şef). At the same time, the CHP Constitution was revised to make İnönü the permanent General President of the CHP.[29] The international arena was crowded with such 'national chiefs' and İnönü was no doubt inspired by this fact. But the foremost reason for his combination of the party presidency with the state presidency was the very real power vacuum felt in Turkish politics after Mustafa Kemal's death.[30]

During the İnönü administration it became clear that İnönü had made sure that a certain distance developed between the 'pinnacle post' which combined the governmental and party leadership and the nearest ministerial post. İnönü had been Atatürk's close associate, lieutenant and adviser. But İnönü himself did not allow anyone else to get so close to his pedestal of power. As Frey puts it, 'İnönü had no İnönü.'[31] He could not be criticised by the citizenry, the party or the press. Martial law and extensive police powers were introduced during the war years. 'He pursued a very cautious and prudent foreign policy which necessitated taking stern measures to control political activities in the internal arena.'[32]

Foreign policy became İnönü's priority area. Here especially, as E. Weisband notes 'İnönü fully controlled the instruments of government.'[33] His biographer Aydemir also remarks, 'The rudder of the Turkish ship of state was completely in the hands of İnönü – with all that implies.'[34] Officials of the Foreign Ministry held five or six sessions with İnönü weekly, when he set policy for the week. All diplomatic correspondence and cables were transmitted immediately to İnönü. He thus had an up-to-the-minute appraisal of the position on any given issue.[35]

Because of these factors it is essential, if an understanding is to be reached of the workings of Turkish foreign policy during these critical years, to understand, as far as possible, the workings of İnönü's mind. Any such appraisal has to be approximate at best, because İnönü was a secretive and very private man. As Weisband puts it 'one must outline those constant elements or considerations which İnönü brought to bear as he guided Turkey's course during the war'.[36]

If one had to choose one outstanding characteristic of İnönü's foreign policy, it would be its emphasis on caution. 'İnönü claims to have conducted foreign relations according to what he describes as the first principle of military strategy, the need to be prudent.' Weisband quotes him as saying: 'The one cardinal principle in setting foreign policy which I followed throughout the war was that an early mistake is hard to make up.'[37]

To avoid making such mistakes, İnönü very carefully considered each move. Aydemir stresses this when he writes that İnönü was always attempting to gain time by evaluating events from hour to hour. He quotes İnönü as saying, 'Let us first live through the night then let us live through the morning, and not by years, months or weeks.'[38] This is not to say that İnönü followed an opportunistic day-to-day path which ignored longer term considerations. He accepted the standards and aims of Turkish foreign policy and evaluated daily events with an eye to manipulating them accordingly. When this proved impossible, and circumstances forced him into a corner, then he started by stating that what was being asked of him was impossible, if the pressure persisted he would agree to talk about it, then during talks he would do all in his power to gain time, then and only then if all else failed he would make the least harmful concession. Weisband's assessment of İnönü is an accurate one: 'The fact that he worked prudently day by day does not mean that he possessed no long-term objectives. On the contrary, he operated with a commitment to one basic proposition: the preservation of Turkey for the Turks.'[39]

There is little doubt that he placed great importance on the gaining of time. An ex-Cabinet Minister, Suat Hayri Ürgüplü, who held office during the war years, stated that İnönü always reminded them of the importance of gaining time, and of playing the waiting game well. The Minister quotes him as frequently repeating the old Turkish adage: 'there is always safety in patience', and as often telling his Cabinet: 'If we wait long enough events will develop and then we may get another insight; if one waits long enough one of the three will die: either the rider, or the camel or the camel driver.'[40] Many of İnönü's manoeuvres make sense in the light of pronouncements such as these. 'Turkish neutrality, as guided by İnönü, was essentially a policy of waiting.'[41]

There was no room in İnönü's world for sentimentality and attachment to individuals. He was very much in control himself and he appointed and dismissed foreign ministers and prime ministers as it suited him, according to his judgement of the circumstances. He replaced Aras by Saraçoğlu. When he saw that he had to pacify the British at the nadir of Anglo-Turkish relations in 1944, he sacrificed the supposedly pro-German Menemencioğlu on the altar of British friendship.

Similarly, after the war when Turkey found herself isolated in the face of the threat from the Soviets who made a *démarche* to dispose of Saraçoğlu, who was disliked for his pro-Western and anti-Russian attitude, Saraçoğlu was allowed after a decent interval, to resign on grounds of 'ill-health'.[42] Recep Peker was appointed in his place. Peker became known for strong-arm tactics, and his inclination to muzzle all opposition was useful to İnönü.

But at this time İnönü had also been attempting to move closer to the United States, and when the United States took a poor view of the repressive nature of the İnönü regime, Peker as representative of illiberal attitudes also retired on grounds of 'ill-health'. One reason why İnönü could dispose of ministers so easily was that he never allowed them to develop a following of their own. Recep Peker, a strong man, who could possibly have constituted a threat, was denied the customary appointment as Deputy Leader of the party when he was appointed Prime Minister.[43] Nihal Kara has also pointed out that İnönü's shift to multi-party politics after the war was also largely a move designed to win favour with the 'Democratic Front' who had recently defeated totalitarianism.[44]

The nature and extent of his power is demonstrated by what happened to Menemencioğlu. Suat Hayri Ürgüplü was present at a dinner party soon after İnönü and Menemencioğlu returned from Cairo in December 1943. At this gathering İnönü publicly fêted Menemencioğlu as 'victor of the negotiations', publicly embraced him and toasted him for having 'checkmated Eden and Hopkins' and having 'relentlessly driven home the Turkish case'. All present had then raised their glasses in a toast to the victorious Foreign Minister, who was much overcome by his chief's effusive praise.

Yet a few months later he was summarily dismissed, because the trend of events required a *rapprochement* with the British. This time, again at a dinner party, İnönü raised his glass in a toast and told those present, 'I feel as though a millstone has been lifted off my chest. For two years I put up with Menemencioğlu's caprices. So the man was an able negotiator, so what? Now I feel much better for having disposed of him.'[45] All were expendable, and examples such as Menemencioğlu illustrate that İnönü did not allow anyone to become too close to him. He suspected that Menemencioğlu was beginning to feel indispensable, and had to prove that no such person existed under his regime.

At this juncture it would indeed be useful to look at Numan Menemencioğlu, seen by some as the brain in foreign affairs: 'Among those who served in a decision making capacity as a result of İnönü's discretion, the most important was Numan Menemencioğlu.'[46]

Menemencioğlu was commonly regarded as a brilliant intellect and a top class diplomat. Massigli, the French Ambassador referred to him in his memoirs as 'The most brilliant man in that team . . .' (The Turkish Ministry of Foreign Affairs).[47] Even while Saraçoğlu was the Foreign Minister, Menemencioğlu was really the brain providing the ideas at the ministry. As a first-rate career diplomat he moulded the Ministry of Foreign Affairs and improved the calibre of its officials. Those who knew him personally admit that he was more versed in foreign affairs than Saraçoğlu who was a newcomer to the field.[48] He was the moving force in improving the standards of the Foreign Ministry even while working under Dr Aras, Atatürk's Foreign Minister. 'In any event Menemencioğlu played a more significant role and deserves greater credit than Aras for the growth of a well-trained diplomatic corps in Turkey during the 1930s.'[49]

The Germans also had the impression that Menemencioğlu was the moving force behind the scenes. Von Papen told Ribbentrop on 28 March 1941, that 'M. Numan takes a much more realistic and waiting attitude than the Foreign Minister . . .' In a later telegram he stated: 'Numan always sees the political realities much more clearly than his Foreign Minister.'[50] But the German documents also show that this 'realism' did not necessarily favour them.

Menemencioğlu himself wrote in his memoirs that his appointment

as Minister was simply a change in the outward form of his responsi-
bilities. 'I had no apprenticeship to serve in this post as already for the
past 13 years I found myself at the head of matters at the Ministry and
thus involved in directing Turkey's foreign policy. My responsibility
had simply taken another form.'[51]

Menemencioğlu kept tight control on the workings of the Ministry.
Weisband suggests that he developed an over-possessive attitude to
the Ministry and that this was what eventually caused his downfall.[52]
In view of İnönü's extreme suspicion of any powerful minister this
remains possible. Menemencioğlu came to be the most prominent
among the ministers, or as Weisband puts it, *primus inter pares*.[53] Frey
has also stated that during the war years the Foreign Ministry 'moved
to the apex of the ministerial pyramid'.[54] Menemencioğlu's office
became the focal point for unofficial meetings with ministers from
other departments and Saraçoğlu would start his day by going to see
him.[55]

Menemencioğlu and his policies have been the subject of much
controversy. To some he was decidedly pro-Axis and favoured closer
co-operation with Germany. To others he was first and foremost
Turkish, and as such entirely ready to be completely realistic and
pragmatic in taking care of what he considered to be Turkey's vital
interests. Anthony Eden himself came to be convinced that Menemencioğlu was favourably predisposed to the Axis cause.[56] In examining the operation of Turkey's foreign policy during these years it is
essential that we have an understanding of this man and his policies.
On one thing most sources agree, Menemencioğlu's first aim was to
keep Turkey out of the war: 'Menemencioğlu's primary aim as Foreign Minister was to keep Turkey out of the war.'[57] Mrs Streater has
also said: 'The main pivot of his foreign policy was maintaining
Turkey outside the war.'[58]

To accomplish this aim Menemencioğlu was prepared to employ
the most pragmatic of means. It was this pragmatism which led to his
coming to be seen as 'pro-German' in British circles. By his adroit
manoeuvring he gained Turkey the crucial breathing space she
needed. Turkey's strategic importance made it difficult for her to
maintain a simple stance of straightforward neutrality. Her location
made her valuable for her 'powerful friends' but when these 'friends'
became too domineering Menemencioğlu saw nothing wrong with
keeping his options open by moving into a closer relationship with
their enemies. 'He [Menemencioğlu] saw nothing inherently wrong

in a policy that maintained an alliance with Great Britain and a friendship pact with Nazi Germany.'[59] This was his way of maintaining what he called Turkey's 'active neutrality' which was designed to safeguard Turkey's integrity while preventing either Germany or the Soviet Union from becoming over-powerful.

At the same time he tried to keep Turkey from linking her fortunes too closely with Britain in order to maintain her freedom of movement. This freedom of movement could only be maintained in a world theatre in which the players had approximately the same importance. A total and crushing victory making one side all-powerful was totally against the Turkish interest. Menemencioğlu told the German Ambassador von Papen and Anthony Eden the same thing: 'We wish this war was not to end with a total defeat either on the one side or the other . . . Turkey's interest is in the direction of a negotiated peace.'[60] Even Turkish authors such as Tamkoç regard Menemencioğlu as pro-German.[61] It is however unfair and inaccurate to judge this immensely capable official as pro-German simply because he saw no inconsistency in dealing with Germany to preserve Turkey's best interests. In many instances where the British accused him of being pro-German, it was simply a case of his not being pro-British enough to satisfy their requirements. For the British, Turkish entry would have shortened the war. Turkey was a tool to be used towards this end; it was *their* interest which demanded that she come in. Menemencioğlu seems to have been branded as pro-German merely for having recognised this fact and acted accordingly. As Massigli put it: 'Numan Menemencioğlu . . . saw the game of international power balances, so dear to Turkish diplomacy, as the most reasonable path.'[62]

Menemencioğlu, although he might have admired the economic and military efficiency of Germany, was deeply mistrustful of Germany's motives. He feared unchecked ambition on the part of Germany, as he feared such ambition on the part of the Soviets. While the Germans were still at Turkey's gates he told von Papen: 'We do not want much to do with the New Order. For us, every state has its right to independence and its own existence. Too little is known about the aims of the New Order propagated by the Axis.'[63]

In this conversation, held on 28 March 1941, von Papen told Menemencioğlu that Hitler had opted for Turkey in the choice between Turkey and the Soviet Union and stated that this must bring forth a more favourable attitude from Turkey towards Germany, who had after all, denied the Russians the Straits. Thus: 'Turkish thinking must get rid of the suspicion that we were trying to encircle Turkey by way of Rumania, Bulgaria and Greece.'[64] Von Papen stated that Menemencioğlu was in fact more realistic than Saraçoğlu. He was certainly realistic enough to tell von Papen that Germany's attitude was not born out of a feeling of benevolence to Turkey, as it would not be in the German interest to let the Soviets come down to the Straits and reach the Mediterranean.

The option [of allowing Russia to reach the Straits] would mean that Russia would reach the Straits and the Mediterranean through Rumania and Bulgaria, i.e. that Germany would be encircled from the south. If the Germans are willing to pay this high price, then they will presumably lose the war and we Turks will profit in a different way. The Führer's decision not to let the Russians get to the Straits is therefore very wise and is in the German interest.[65]

In response to von Papen's appeal that something should be done to put German–Turkish relations on a basis of greater trust, Menemencioğlu replied: 'You know that we are allied with England. We want to keep honourably the few obligations which we have, and if you Herr von Papen, now expect a kind of "benevolent neutrality" on the part of Turkey, then I must tell you that such political acrobatics appear hardly possible to me.'[66] Menemencioğlu stated that each case that came up between Turkey and Germany had to be judged on its own merits and declined to make any blanket commitment. He also told von Papen that 'although we are allied we will not let ourselves be misused in any way to the advantage of any third power'. On the one hand, Menemencioğlu told the Germans that he had not been fooled into thinking that they were doing Turkey any favours, that he mistrusted the idea of German hegemony, and that Turkey had to keep her obligations honourably. On the other he made it clear that Turkey would fight if attacked, but that she was not prepared to allow Britain to push her into anything which was not in her direct interest. Also he told von Papen that Turkey had always been in favour of a strong Germany in the centre of Europe. Thus he staved off a German 'friendship offensive' but without closing the door on any unpredictable future developments and without hardening his line and thus risking German aggression.

Von Papen reported to Ribbentrop that 'one cannot today predict what stand Turkey will take in a question that does not affect her immediate security' and implied that the use of the Soviet option in favour of Turkey had been wasted. 'Perhaps it would have been more expedient not to let the option in favour of Turkey become known and to use the question of the option as a means of pressure in any difficulties that may arise.'[67]

Menemencioğlu therefore succeeded in keeping the Germans guessing. From the very outset even before the actual outbreak of war Menemencioğlu was against Germany having a dominant influence in Turkey. 'Menemencioğlu did much to prevent Turkey from becoming too dependent, economically or militarily, upon Germany.'[68] It was Menemencioğlu who informed Ribbentrop in 1938 that Turkey wanted a neutral policy and that consequently she would not purchase most of her military equipment from Germany and would use the RAF as a model in redesigning her airforce.[69] Menemencioğlu has described how during this same visit to Germany he was treated with much pomp and circumstance by Ribbentrop. His treatment he noted, was much more in keeping with the status of a political envoy and not one who was primarily interested in economic affairs (he was chief of the Turkish trade delegation). Soon afterwards he was to find out the reason for this when Ribbentrop asked him 'point blank' about more comprehensive talks with a view to forming an alliance. Menemencioğlu reported: 'I told him in the nicest possible manner that our experience of 1914 had not been brilliant . . .' and he contrasted German foreign policy with Turkish, telling Ribbentrop: 'I see no harmony between it [German policy] and the modest policy followed by Turkey.'[70]

Knatchbull Hugessen believed that Eden was convinced Menemencioğlu was pro-German.[71] On 6 July 1944 after Menemencioğlu's resignation Hugessen commented: 'Nor would I go so far as to say that Numan is pro-German and certainly not that he is pro-Nazi . . .'[72] Hugessen also said that Menemencioğlu was not against the Anglo-Turkish alliance:

But I know from experience that he did all he could to secure it on the best possible terms for his country. I remember well during the negotiations in the summer of 1939 that after M. Massigli and I had secured rather unexpectedly favourable terms from M. Saraçoğlu in Numan's absence, the latter returned from leave and applied the brake severely, whittling away much that M. Saraçoğlu had been prepared to accept. This indeed has been Numan's role all along, but I am convinced that he was activated by his conception of Turkish interests and not by any predisposition to favour Germany.[73]

In other words Menemencioğlu, being an able and professional diplomat, was only doing the best for his country and even Hugessen admitted that Saraçoğlu had given away rather a lot. Hugessen went on, 'I should be inclined to say that without any special feeling of favour towards Germany, Numan has throughout been influenced by two main ideas, to keep his country out of the war altogether or at least for as long as possible . . .'[74] Massigli the French Ambassador concurred in this estimation of Numan Menemencioğlu. Although he makes a pointed reference to Menemencioğlu's 'Germanic education' (which is erroneous as he was educated at St Joseph, a French *lycée* run by Jesuits, and later studied law in Lausanne, Switzerland), he goes on to say:

With us Numan Bey was known as a germanophile; no doubt he admired the economic power of the Reich and took the measure of the germanic machine; many reports kept in the archives of the Wilhelmstrasse testify that Berlin felt it could rely on his sympathies; however many other documents in the same archives prove also that in decisive crises these hopes were dashed.[75]

Sympathy was not a valid criterion for making a judgement where Menemencioğlu was concerned: 'Menemencioğlu was not guided by what he regarded as false sentimentality. If İnönü brought a prudent style to bear in foreign policy decision-making, Menemencioğlu exercised a strict pragmatic realism.'[76] Together with his chief they made a formidable team. It must not be forgotten however that although Menemencioğlu's influence was supreme at the Foreign Ministry, this was still at the discretion of İnönü, and when İnönü felt he was running the risk of alienating the British too far, Menemencioğlu had to go.

What emerges from this brief look at the machinery and personnel of decision-making in the Turkish government during the Second World War is an extremely centralised power structure with a solid grip on the country as a whole. It could be said that İnönü effectively held the monopoly of real power, although he did rely on advisers and placed some importance on putting on a show of legitimate democratic procedure. The legislature although consulted by the executive for the sake of form, could only acquiesce in the executive's decisions, 'the power as well as the authority to commit Turkey to a policy decision shifted far in favour of the executive'.[77] Menemencioğlu and Saraçoğlu would present decisions before the Assembly knowing already that it was not a question of approval but of fulfilling the 'rubber stamp' function the body had come to acquire.[78] The Committee for Foreign Affairs in the Assembly was symbolic as it only followed İnönü's directives. Weisband cites Professors Esmer and Armaoğlu as his authorities when he states: 'It was essentially a committee that consistently followed the line set by the Government, that is İnönü.'[79]

The fact that power was so concentrated and absolute made it extremely difficult for outside elements to bring pressure to bear effectively. A situation such as that which arose in Yugoslavia, where there were pro-German and pro-Allied factions in government, was not possible in Turkey.[80] Even if Menemencioğlu *had* been pro-German, it is unlikely that Germany could have swayed Turkey to her side as long as İnönü remained in power, and the Allies were not totally defeated. The fact that İnönü and the close circle around him and subordinate to him, had clear standards and goals from whose essentials they refused to budge, is central to understanding their success.

In a nutshell, the warrior diplomats were masterful diplomatic bargainers because they were patient and persistent in their positions and because they displayed deep insight into the intricacies of diplomacy and they were aware of the strength and weaknesses of their opponents. They were also capable of making accurate and realistic assessment of the forces at work, and balancing their objectives and their means.[81]

4 . THE HISTORICAL CONDITIONING
OF A GENERATION

The small body of men who wielded power in Turkey during the Second World War were largely of the generation which had lived through the Young Turk Revolution, the First World War, the Turkish War of Liberation and the founding of the Turkish Republic. The circumstances and events of these years conditioned the thinking of the Turkish foreign policy elite. The cumulative effect of their experiences would greatly influence decision-making in later days and mould the men who shaped and applied foreign policy.

Suat Hayri Ürgüplü had this to say on his generation's historical heritage: 'Most of the leading cadres of the 1939–1945 period had lived through the hardships and humiliations of the First War. Therefore the foremost consideration was: how could Turkey find a way to stay out? We were mostly of the generation which had lived, known and suffered the First World War.'[1]

1908–18

In 1908 İnönü was a young captain with the Edirne Army. It was against the background of the disintegration of Ottoman power in the Balkans that he joined the Committee of Union and Progress (CUP), the secret society of the Young Turks. It is interesting and significant that he did so at the suggestion of a trusted friend and schoolmate from the İstanbul War Academy, Fethi Okyar.[2]

Fethi Okyar was to become Member of Parliament, Minister, Ambassador to London and Prime Minister. That İnönü acted on his suggestion illustrates the closely interwoven nature of the Turkish leadership within itself and with the times, to the point where relating the events of these years amounts to tracing the careers of the men who would hold critical positions in the 1939–45 period. E. Weisband quotes Professor A. Suat Bilge as saying that Fethi Okyar was 'the only person İnönü really did listen to regarding foreign policy'.[3] The same author states that it was Okyar who played an important part in convincing İnönü of the need to align himself with Britain before the Second World War began, and facilitated the signing of the Tripartite Treaty with Britain and France. It was this same person, then a young officer attached to the General Staff of the Thessaloniki Army, who convinced İnönü of the need to join the activists of the CUP.

Aydemir calls the young officers of the CUP a 'generation in preparation'. İnönü himself was deeply impressed by this circle of dedicated young officers: 'When we gathered together in our rooms, we would examine the position as though we were the ones responsible for the defence and high level politics of our country . . . as if the solutions were all in our hands.'[4] It was this generation which was to attempt to find the solutions, though their respective stars were to shine at different times.

After the Young Turk Revolution in 1908, the Ottoman Empire was plunged into yet another series of wars. The high hopes of the CUP were soon dashed by internal and external events. The Balkan countries united in an alliance and marched on İstanbul, horrifying the Turks by advancing up to the Çatalca lines before İstanbul. In 1911, profiting from this weakness, Italy attacked Ottoman Tripolitania, an act the Turks considered one of extreme treachery and were not to forget.[5]

Meanwhile Mustafa Kemal and İsmet İnönü were diverging from the CUP which was coming increasingly under German influence. 'Advancement in the Society (the CUP) was for those willing to become tools of German policy and Mustafa Kemal never made any secret of his contempt for those who did not put Turkey's interest first.'[6] Mustafa Kemal's and İnönü's dislike for Germans and their heavy-handed methods dated from this period, and in İnönü's case would have a very significant influence in the 1939–45 period. In 1913 a Military Reform Committee of forty-two arrived from Germany. By the end of the First World War the number of German advisers rose to 800 officers.[7] A German was put in charge of the department of General Staff Headquarters of which İnönü had been head, and İnönü was relegated to acting as his assistant.

İnönü's recently published memoirs covering the First World War years are very enlightening as regards his attitude in the Second

World War. Here İnönü openly declares 'if they [the Germans] had won a victory of the scale they desired it would not be easy to be rid of them'. He gives an interesting account of a conversation with Bronsard Paşa, the German officer who was acting as Chief of General Staff which occurred just as the German armies marched into Belgium. İnönü asked the German officer:

> 'So now you are at war, let us say you win, what will be your gain? What will be the reward of such great sacrifices?'
> 'Belgium! Belgium!' he answered.
> I asked again:
> 'What is Belgium, it is only a small country?'
> Bronsard Paşa replied.
> 'Yes it is small but very valuable.'
> I persisted in my questioning.
> 'What will happen after the war?'
> He finally let the cat out of the bag.
> 'Turkey!' he said.
> I had fully understood that by this he had meant that they would gain Turkey. I was very struck but contained myself.
> 'Well,' (I said) 'how is this to be?'
> 'We will work together' (he answered).
> 'I don't think we will work together after the war.'
> At this point Bronsard Paşa gave me an answer which showed his true intentions.
> 'I see, you do not think so, but how many are you? How many are you to pursue this idea?'
> 'There are enough of us.' (I answered)[8]

Many actively objected to this 'Germanising' and those like Kâzım Karabekir (who was later to play a crucial role as a leading general of the Nationalist forces) who saw that Germany was going to drag Turkey into the war and said so, were condemned to oblivion in obscure posts.[9] These memories were to be of significance during the Second World War years. Koçak has pointed out that in 1941 the Germans complained of anti-German statements in Turkish school history textbooks. These stated that the German generals in Turkey during the First World War had sacrificed Turkish troops for the sake of their own national aims, and had behaved as dictators towards the Turks in their own country. No mention was made of the 'brotherhood in arms'.[10] Although major scholars like Trumpener and Howard disagree on the extent to which Germany did manipulate the Turks into war, even Trumpener admits that Liman von Sanders, the head of the German Military Mission, had to exercise care 'so as not to assign German Officers to offices controlled by Turkish commanders who were inimical to Germany'.[11] The same author notes the feelings of Ambassador Wangenheim who feared the growth of what he called 'intransigent Turkish nationalism', which was 'a growing danger to our present and future task in Turkey'.[12]

Although İnönü did not get personally involved in internal army quarrels he did notice that the Germans were given unprecedented authority over much of Turkey's affairs: 'Anything that could be called a State Secret in the military and political domain was delivered into the hands of foreign officials, representing a power commanding one of the two camps in world politics. The German Reform Committee was in a position enabling them to follow everything that went on, on a day to day basis.'[13] This situation left its mark on İnönü and is reflected in much of the Turkish reluctance to divulge information to foreigners between 1939 and 1945 when the Turks were extremely secretive not only with the Germans but also with their allies the British.

It must be noted however, that in the final instance much of this secretiveness proved futile. D. C. Watt has pointed out that the German listening and code breaking service, the *Forschungsamt*, intercepted and decoded communications between the Turkish Embassy in Moscow and Ankara. D. Irving has also indicated that Dr Paul Schmidt, the director of the German Foreign Minister's personal office, received all the confidential data concerning decoded cables of foreign missions in Germany and elsewhere. Schmidt later told his American interrogators, 'The intercepted messages of the Turkish Embassy in Moscow and the American Embassy in Berne were deemed of particular value.' This information was circulated to Foreign Minister Ribbentrop, State Secretary Wiezsäcker, and State Under-Secretary Woerman. On the same subject, D. Kahn has stated that Turkey was among the thirty-four countries whose secret communications the German codebreakers were reading.[14]

It is also interesting to note that of the players who would have great significance in later years it was not only İnönü and Atatürk who were present on the stage at this time. Franz von Papen who was later to become German Ambassador to the İnönü government was Operations Officer with the Falkenhayn army group in Mesopotamia: 'My experiences and the contacts I made with leading Turkish

Fig. 5 Numan Menemencioğlu in Ottoman garb.   *(Courtesy of Hürriyet)*

soldiers and officials were by no means unimportant when, more than twenty years later, I returned to Turkey as German Ambassador.'[15] Von Papen also experienced the difficulty of transporting an army and supplies over the Taurus mountains, the valour of the Turkish soldier in last-ditch defence, and Mustafa Kemal's distaste for Germans:

At Abu Chuff, a water hole in the hills south of Hebron, I met Mustafa Kemal on his way south with the 7th Army. He was in a fearful temper and seemed to have had a misunderstanding with Falkenhayn over the measures to be adopted. It was a most regrettable situation which led to his recall and replacement by General Fevzi Paşa.[16]

Marshal Fevzi Çakmak was this 'General Fevzi' and he had no better opinion of the Germans. Von Papen also met General Ali Fuat whom he called 'one of the most brilliant officers in the Turkish Army', later to become one of the leading commanders in the War of Liberation and a key figure in the General Staff during the Second World War.[17] Other prominent figures of the Second World War also appear in the pages of the history of these years. Recep Peker (Prime Minister and later Minister of Interior in İnönü's governments), and Hüsrev Gerede (Turkey's Ambassador to Berlin), both served as officers on the Russo-Turkish front with the Erzurum army.[18] In a significantly different context, perhaps, nothing illustrates the Ottoman connection better than the fact that Numan Menemencioğlu was a close aid of the last Ottoman Grand Vezir and Foreign Minister, Ahmet Tevfik Paşa.[19]

The lesson of German meddling in Turkey's affairs was not lost on Mustafa Kemal and İsmet İnönü and the experience of those days would persist in influencing the governing elite. On 22 August 1926 the Ankara Tribunal of Independence was to say:

The whole Turkish nation was dragged into war as a result of a *fait accompli*, the work of a German Admiral who received his orders from the Kaiser, and whose very name was unknown to the Turkish people. The Turkish ministers who submitted to such steps look more like obedient submissive servants of the Kaiser than ministers responsible for the welfare of Turkey.[20]

Ürgüplü confirmed that İnönü was suspicious of the Germans due to his First World War experiences. The same source indicated that this also held true for leading soldiers such as Marshal Fevzi Çakmak who had lived during the days when German officers had commanded members of the Turkish officer corps as members of the military of a vassal state.[21] Ahmet Şükrü Esmer – distinguished Turkish political historian and informed journalist of the Second World War years – emphasised the same point. He stated that İnönü was of the school of military who did not trust the Germans as a result of their treatment of the Turks in the First World War.[22] So appeals by the Germans to these Turks as 'former comrades in arms' fell on (in İnönü's case literally) deaf ears. From this emerged one of the basic tenets of Turkish foreign policy; the avoidance of 'senior' and 'junior' partners in alliance. As much as possible, it became the Turkish practice to seek equality as the basis of any alliance. For as long as it was feasible the Turks avoided military alliances in the 1930s, preferring friendship and non-aggression agreements.[23] As circumstances made it necessary to obtain military help in the thirties they hoped to purchase security through the close association of a number of powers of equal strength such as the Balkan Entente.

1918–23

The Ottoman Empire collapsed at the end of the First World War. Nationalism and its growth in many of the subject peoples had been a major factor in bringing about the collapse. Strangely enough Turkish nationalism was one of the last to develop. But when it did it carried the War of Liberation to its successful conclusion. This struggle was carried on on two parallel fronts; military and diplomatic. 'Victory could not have been achieved without an astute foreign policy which paralleled the military campaigns.'[24] Most foreign and Turkish sources agree that this is so: 'The War of Independence consisted of two fronts; one military, the other political . . . In order to achieve success in the military fronts the Ankara government placed great importance on the diplomatic front.'[25] The Turkish Nationalists' paramount aim was to create an independent and sovereign Turkey. In furtherance of this aim they evolved a set of 'limited but almost rigid' demands with which they confronted the western world.[26] In this fight for survival the main elements of Republican foreign policy crystallised. The importance of bargaining, of self-reliance, and of flexibility when needed, were all driven home in those formative days.

When Mustafa Kemal arrived in Samsun on 19 May 1919 he faced a country in ruin. Nor was he under any illusions about help from any quarter. Even the so-called liberal American press showed itself to be ruthless when it came to Turkey. The *New York Tribune* stated the Turk was, '. . . the pirate of the Bosphorous whose hands are dripping with blood . . . The Turks have always been a parasite and a stench in the nostrils of civilisation.'[27] Another American newspaper declared:

'the sentiment of the whole civilised world is against letting the Turk retain Constantinople. He has shown neither a desire nor a capacity for civilisation, let there be no temporising with him.'[28] Similarly, in November 1914 Lloyd George had called the Turks, 'A human cancer, a creeping agony in the flesh of the lands which they misgoverned . . .'[29] With tender sentiments such as these to contend with Mustafa Kemal realised very early on that Turkey could rely only on herself.

The western powers had already succeeded in 'cutting up Asia Minor as though it were a cake'.[30] During the war a series of secret agreements had already divided Turkey among the powers. The Constantinople Agreement between France, Britain and Russia had settled that Russia would get İstanbul and the Straits. The treaty of London of 26 April 1915, gave Italy rights in the Antalya region. These were further extended in the Treaty of St Jean de Maurienne in April 1917. The Sykes–Picot Agreement of May 1915 had shared out more of Turkey between France and England giving Adana to France, as well as extensive holdings in the Turkish interior. After the collapse of Russia in 1917 these secret treaties were publicised by the Bolsheviks who denounced them. Thus Atatürk found out just what the Entente powers had in mind for the Turks.

At this point the worst disaster occurred, and paradoxically provided the spark that saved Turkey. The Greek Army invaded the İzmir region in May 1919 under cover of British, French and American warships. This development fanned into flame the dormant cinders of Turkish nationalism. The Turks, though prepared to admit defeat to vastly superior forces belonging to the victorious Allies could not bear this adding of insult to injury:

> The cession of remote provinces inhabited by alien peoples could be borne, even the occupation of the capital could be suffered, for the occupiers were the victorious Great Powers of the invincible West . . . But the thrust of a neighbouring and former subject people into the heart of Turkish Anatolia was a danger and a humiliation beyond endurance.[31]

Mustafa Kemal had been provided with his most valuable raw material; popular outrage brought about by this ill-considered move on the part of the Entente Powers.

The aims of Kemalist foreign policy and its intentions for the future, were set out in the Erzurum and Sivas Congresses during the summer and autumn of 1919. During these gatherings the Nationalists took great care to stress that they were legitimate bodies acting in

the name of the Sultan who was under duress. In the Sivas Congress
the delegates took steps to counter the machinations of the Entente
Powers who were making use of antiquated geographical terms such
as Cilicia and Mesopotamia which had been put in the Mondros
Armistice, to occupy larger areas of Turkey. A clear statement of the
minimum acceptable boundaries was called for. The Sivas Congress
laid down the principles which would become the *Misak-ı Milli* or
National Pact, which the Nationalists claimed was the legitimate
expression of the national will and their minimum desiderata. A rigid
instrument, it acquired 'an aura of sacrosanctity' as it became more
and more synonymous with the Nationalist Movement.[32] 'The principles embodied in the National Pact were the foundation of Turkish
foreign policy not only during the National struggle but also in
subsequent years.'[33] This instrument declared clearly to the world
that the boundaries it laid down consisted of the maximum sacrifice
the Turks were willing to make for the obtaining of a just peace. All
the territories contained in the National Pact constituted a formal and
non-divisible whole.

From the very earliest stages of the War of Liberation Mustafa
Kemal kept up diplomatic contacts with the western powers. It was
during these days that bargaining, that invaluable tool for the application of foreign policy, began to come into its own. Kemal actively
cultivated the divisions between the powers. When the British ar-
rested the Ottoman Chamber on 16 March 1920, the French and
Italians hurriedly sent M. Kemal deputations making clear that
British policy was not theirs. 'The Turks . . . knew that the Allies were
not solidly united on the Turkish Question, and so they began to
prevaricate, in their time-honoured way with a view to gaining valuable concessions.'[34] The dissolution of the Ottoman Chamber only
added grist to the mill of the Nationalists who could now proclaim
with added authority that they were the only legitimate government.

It was clear to Atatürk that another bargaining lever was Soviet
Russia, an outcast among nations, just as Turkey herself was. On 18
March 1921 the Treaty of Moscow was signed, and the Soviets
became the first nation to give the Ankara government diplomatic
recognition. By mutual agreement the date of the signing of the
Moscow Treaty was changed to 16 March, the anniversary of the
British occupation of İstanbul. The Nationalists were fully aware that
this development would be viewed as ominous by the Entente
Powers.[35] The British did view this development as dangerous and a

General Staff memorandum dated 7 December 1920 explored the possibility of giving the Turks more lenient terms than those of the severe Treaty of Sèvres. The General Staff hoped to constitute a Turkey which could be used as a buffer zone against the Soviets.[36] Twenty-four years later, in 1944, and 1945, Turkey was to be seen once again by Britain as a buffer against Soviet Russia.

During the February 1921 London Conference, Bekir Sami, the Nationalist delegate, only attended after the Nationalists had secured an invitation as an equal party not subordinate to the İstanbul government. This insistence on parity would be echoed in later years when İnönü would only go to Cairo in December 1943 after he was assured of being invited as an equal, not summoned as a subordinate. In London a series of secret agreements were concluded with the French and Italians, further isolating the British.[37] 'If the Angora Government was proving its prowess on the field of battle, its conduct in the field of diplomacy was superb. Early in 1921, Turkey settled her relationships with her neighbours, renewed friendships with France and Italy – thus separating these two powers from England – and became friend and ally of Soviet Russia.'[38] On 21 October 1921 the Treaty of Ankara was concluded with France who had to come to an agreement with Turkey as her occupying troops were now desperately needed in Europe. The Treaty of Ankara was 'essentially a separate peace with France behind Britain's back'.[39]

The Turks conclusively defeated the Greek Army on 9 September 1922. But Mustafa Kemal was to be confronted with one more major crisis before the end of hostilities. The British were still in occupation at Çanakkale, the strategic town controlling the Dardanelles, which was included in the territories claimed under the National Pact. This small bridgehead was to bring Britain and Turkey to the brink of another war. For some time Mustafa Kemal was engaged in a war of nerves with the British. In the end his realism won the day. He had to 'struggle with victorious generals breathing fire against their enemies'.[40] Atatürk also realised that Lloyd George and a handful of his followers saw the issue as a matter of prestige and 'face' in the context of their eastern empire. The matter was settled by negotiation.[41]

Indeed, Atatürk's greatest asset was knowing where to stop. Falih Rıfkı Atay draws an interesting and illustrative comparison between Atatürk and Enver Paşa: 'Enver's special quality was boldness, Mustafa Kemal's was insight . . . Had Mustafa Kemal been Minister of War in 1914 he would not have pushed the country into the First

World War; had Enver entered İzmir in 1922, with the same *élan* he
would have turned back, marched on Syria and Iraq and lost all that
had been won.'[42] This self-imposed constraint was to form another
basic principle in foreign policy for the succeeding generations of
policy-makers.

LAUSANNE – FINAL SETTLING OF ACCOUNTS

İsmet İnönü's tactics and character during the Lausanne Conference
display much of the tenacity and dogged determination which was to
become his hallmark in the critical days of 1939–45. At Lausanne the
western powers confronted Republican Turkey with the bills of the
Ottoman Empire. Atatürk made this quite clear in his *Nutuk* (speech),
a marathon speech delivered to the Assembly in 1927. 'The issues
discussed at the negotiating table at Lausanne were not confined to a
recent period involving three or four years. The Conference was
dealing with accounts dating from past centuries . . .'[43]

İnönü's first task was to drum into arrogant men such as Lord
Curzon that Turkey and the Turkish delegation 'were not so many of
his Indian subjects, but a nation free, sovereign, and equal to any
other'.[44] The position was difficult, the British in the person of the
imposing Lord Curzon saw Turkey in the position of supplicant.
Turkey saw herself as a victor, having won by arms victories she had
no intention of losing through diplomacy. The conference dragged on
for eight months largely as a result of İnönü's obstinacy. İnönü had no
experience in the 'thrust and parry of extempore debate' so instead he
developed his own methods: 'He dug himself in. He contested every
point, however small, he pleaded deafness, consulted interminably
with his colleagues; read out long prepared statements.'[45] Curzon's
splendid oratorial skills were lost on this little man who infuriated him
by constant interruptions. At one point after Curzon gave him the
draft of the proposed treaty, İnönü asked for eight days to study it,
while Curzon had his train prepared and threatened to leave.

This effort to gain time, stalling by plunging into minutiae, ad-
journing to consult with experts or colleagues, always cautious, never
precipitate; this was the İnönü style in diplomacy which was to
exasperate Anthony Eden and Churchill just as it exasperated Lord
Curzon. 'The same old tune, sovereignty, sovereignty, sovereignty'
commented an irritated Curzon.[46] 'Yours is not the only sovereignty
in the world,' he mocked on another occasion.[47]

İnönü replied unperturbed: 'There are complaints that we talk too much of sovereignty . . . We came here as the representatives of a nation which has grasped the meaning of independence, taken it by force, and come here to achieve a just peace . . . If we have had to mention our sovereignty frequently it is because we find ourselves obliged to do so by proposals damaging to it.'[48] Atatürk had refused to walk on a Greek flag when he entered İzmir in triumph, commenting: 'that is the sign of the country's independence.'[49] The fact that the Turkish leader had such regard even for the independence of his recent and bitter enemy demonstrates the value he and his representative in Lausanne put on sovereignty.

Sovereignty was also to be the key issue in the discussion of Capitulations, the subject which was to prove the thorniest one of the conference. The Capitulations, the series of economic, judicial, financial and social concessions given to foreigners living and working in the Ottoman Empire, had, to a great extent, put much of the control of the Ottoman world of economics and commerce in foreign hands. Now, the western powers who were the beneficiaries of this system, saw no reason to change the economic structure in Turkey because of any change in the political structure. But to the Turks the Capitulations were the last strings attaching them to the Ottoman Empire, and as such they had to be broken. In some ways they were even more important than border disputes. The question of the Straits had been settled relatively simply with Turkey accepting a guarantee under the government of the League of Nations. The status of the territory of Mosul was to be discussed separately. 'To the patriotic Turk, the expulsion of the foreigner from his doorstep availed little without his expulsion from within his house.'[50] In a very real sense the Capitulations had created a series of foreign states within the state. Particularly on judicial Capitulations İnönü proved unyielding.

He refused to accept the jurisdiction of any court in Turkey, other than Turkey's own courts. İnönü came under tremendous pressure from the British, French and Italians, who made it look as though he was personally responsible for a possible breakdown of the negotiations. 'Bombarded by the Allied delegations with appeals and menaces', İnönü held firm.[51] It was largely this intransigence which caused the rupture of the negotiations in February 1923. Atatürk put the blame squarely on the shoulders of the Allies, and declared on 17 February: 'The Entente Powers do not realize that the Ottoman

Empire has passed into history . . . The Turks cannot dispense with their natural, legal and logical rights.'[52]

But time was in favour of the new Turkey, and when the conference met again on 23 April, the Allies proved considerably more pliable. Agreement was reached on a reduced share of the Ottoman debt for Turkey, and abolition of judicial Capitulations.

The Treaty of Lausanne was signed on 24 July 1923. In almost all of its provisions it represented a victory for the new Turkey. 'It was the epilogue of a defeated and apparently shattered nation which rose from its ruins, faced the most powerful nations of the world on terms of absolute equality, and won from them almost all of its national demands.'[53] It also represented the end of İnönü's apprenticeship, along with that of many of the generation who had seen the new Turkey emerge from the ashes of the Ottoman Empire; a tired, poor, but independent country badly in need of a period of prolonged peace.

5 . TURKEY AT THE OUTBREAK OF WAR

The period from the conclusion of the Lausanne Treaty up to the signing of the Anglo-Franco-Turkish Treaty of 19 October 1939, saw Turkey go from a position of non-alignment to one where she had to admit the need for 'powerful friends'. In the early post-Lausanne days this role was filled by the Soviet Union. But the Soviet Union was primarily a land power and the rise of Italy as a major threat led Turkey to seek the friendship of a naval power as well. This started the Anglo-Turkish *rapprochement*. Therefore Turkey sought for some time to balance these two 'powerful friendships'. Zhivkova points out an interesting interchange between the British Ambassador in Ankara, Sir Percy Loraine, and Kemal Atatürk which took place on 17 June 1934. Atatürk openly told the Ambassador that Turkey wanted to move closer to Britain. The Ambassador in return, pointed out that Turkey's 'most intimate friend was Russia'. At this the Gazi expressed displeasure and indicated that if the Ambassador considered the two friendships mutually exclusive there was nothing more to be said. 'Atatürk's talk with the British Ambassador shows that the wish of the Turkish government in 1934 to establish closer relations with Britain was not prompted by any intention to restrict Turkish contacts with the USSR.'[1]

In the late thirties, although Anglo-Turkish relations improved there was a marked reluctance on the part of Britain to give Turkey concrete assurances which might be provocative to Italy, who they still hoped to wean away from Germany. A telegram sent to Sir Percy Loraine dated 14 February 1938, instructed the Ambassador to suggest some statement that would allay Turkish doubts about British reliability while stopping short of giving a formal guarantee.[2] The Foreign Secretary made clear that 'this is a question about which we can take no risks'. Ironically this situation was an exact reversal of the British and Turkish roles during the war years. Both Britain in 1938,

71

and Turkey in 1943, wanted the benefits of support without risking its obligations.

The Italian factor was thus the major consideration in Turkish foreign policy planning during the mid 1930s. Admittedly, the Italian threat proved something of a non-event when Italy actually joined in the hostilities during the Second World War, but it must be kept in mind that she was the major factor in the evolution of the Anglo-Turkish *rapprochement* of the mid and late thirties. Also in terms of historical precedent, memories of Italian enmity were very recent and the Turks had not forgiven the attack on Ottoman Tripolitania in 1911, and the long cherished Italian dreams about expansion into Anatolia. In 1934 the Italians had heavily fortified the Dodecanese islands just off the Turkish coast. Indeed Italian propaganda was very active. Bari radio, the broadcasting arm of Mussolini's propaganda, frequently made Turkish broadcasts.

These did not fail to raise an echo in the Turkish press. The Turkish columnist, Z. Sertel wrote on 10 March 1939: 'Why does Bari radio speak Turkish? We are not a colony. We are not involved in hostilities against Italy, we do not need Italy's Turkish broadcasts. Nor are we particularly interested in Fascist Italy's domestic affairs. In that case, why these Turkish broadcasts?'[3]

It was after the Italian invasion of Albania on 8 April 1939, that Turkey openly aligned herself with Great Britain. For a significant time Turkey managed to carry on both British and Russian friendships simultaneously. The Soviet Union was a power factor in Europe like Great Britain, France and Germany, and because of her geopolitical position a more vital power factor for Turkey. Also, relations with the Soviets had been good since the early days of the Republic. Atatürk was enough of a realist to appreciate the value of friendly relations with so powerful a neighbour at a time when distrust for all things western was at its height in Turkey.

In reality Republican Turkey conducted her foreign policy practically since her inception in the 1920s, leaning upon and with the support of one of the Great Powers, although she avoided formal affiliation with any one of them until 1939. Indeed until 1936–39, the Turkish foreign policy decisions likely to affect the USSR were taken in consultation with the Soviet Union, as a result of good neighbourly policy initiated by Lenin and Atatürk, although Turkey maintained friendly relations with the West.[4]

In fact Turkey only gradually drifted away from the Soviet Union, leading to the state of distrust prevailing after the unexpected Nazi–Soviet Pact of August 1939. Zhivkova speaks of a 'gradual and carefully phased-out withdrawal of Turkey from the Soviet Union'.[5] But it was more a realisation in Turkish decision-making circles that Turkey would not be able to act as a bridge between the western powers and the Soviets, as she had hoped. Kemal Karpat calls the worn out view of 'arch-enemies', 'The Western stereotyped concept that Turkey's fear of the Soviet Union is so deep as to make her ready to undertake any sacrifice in order to assure her survival.'[6]

Some schools of thought are now emerging which argue that contrary to the 'historic rivalry' concept of Turco-Russian relations, it has been more profitable for Turkey to have good relations with the Soviet Union. 'One of these schools claims that Turkish modernisation and political progress in terms of national self-assertion has been more rapid during the periods of *rapprochement* and friendship with the Soviets.'[7] By 1939 although the Soviet Union was no longer 'the only pebble on the Turkish beach', relations were still good.[8]

The British, too, appreciated the value of Turkey as a possible connecting link with the Soviets, although British distrust of Soviet Russia was strong. 'To reach Moscow the British leaders took two paths: the southern route to Turkey and possibly through her, to Russia, and the direct road to Moscow.'[9] In fact, although British relations with Turkey continued to draw closer during the last days of peace and first days of war, two things became abundantly clear; Turkey would drive an extremely hard bargain, and she would try to maintain her ties with the Soviet Union.

Turkey could afford to name her price as both the power blocks fully appreciated the value of her strategic position. On 12 April, Halifax wrote to his Ambassador in Turkey, Sir Hughe Knatchbull-Hugessen that, 'His Majesty's Government consider of the first importance that the Turkish Government collaborate in any project of common defence . . .'[10] On 10 April, Halifax told the Cabinet Foreign Policy Committee, 'that Turkey was much the most important country to us of the countries of south-east Europe, and it was imperative that we should do nothing to queer the pitch with her'.[11] Watt has also drawn attention to the 'Key position of Turkey' in the Balkans as the most powerful member of the Balkan Entente. Britain was hoping that Turkey could draw Bulgaria into the Entente thus creating, 'a bloc which Germany could clearly only tackle by outright military aggression.'[12] Similarly, after the Anglo-Turkish Declaration of 12 May, the German Ambassador in Ankara, von Papen wrote to Berlin: 'If the position we occupy [in Turkey], is taken over in the future by Britain and France, our relations with the countries lying beyond Turkey, Iraq, Persia and the Arabian world will be mortally hit.'[13]

After the Anglo-Turkish Declaration of 12 May stating that they would oppose any aggression in the Mediterranean area, the Soviet attitude remained favourable. *Izvestia* called it 'a valuable investment in the cause of world peace'.[14] Indeed, the Soviets had been kept informed of the development of Anglo-Turkish relations, and on 27 April 1939, Potemkin, the Vice-Commissar for Foreign Affairs, had visited Ankara. 'He (Potemkin) had listened with pleasure and approval to the account of the negotiation undertaken with Britain and France and expressed hope that the edifice of peace in progress now between Turkey and the West would be completed in Moscow by Russia joining it.'[15] It is interesting that according to Zhivkova, İnönü told Potemkin at this meeting that the western powers had hoped that Germany would turn against Russia and tire herself out, but now they were realising that the situation was becoming very dangerous for them and were seeking to form alliances.[16] Later Saraçoğlu, the Turkish Foreign Minister told Hugessen that the Soviets felt isolated and were suspicious that they were intentionally being kept at arm's length. 'This feeling even amounted to a considerable degree of mistrust.'[17] But there are also indications that both the Soviets and the Turks were putting up a brave front. After the Anglo-Turkish Declaration had been made public on 12 May, on 13 May the Turkish Ambassador in Moscow, Apaydın, reported that the Soviets kept a guarded attitude about the whole affair, and *Tass* only published it after Turkish prompting.[18]

However, relations between Turkey and the Soviets seemed close enough for the Romanian Foreign Minister, Gafencu, to request Turkish mediation between Romania and the Soviet Union. 'The relations between Moscow and Ankara seemed so good and so helpful that M. Saraçoğlu offered me his good offices to assist me in any way that I wished in establishing a closer contact with the Soviet Union.'[19] However, the truth of the matter was that Turkey's Balkan allies looked none too eagerly upon the *rapprochement* between Turkey, a key member of the Balkan Entente, and Britain. They feared this would prove provocative to Germany.

In fact, a problem which kept recurring during the Anglo-Turkish talks before the Declaration was Turkey's commitment to the Balkan Entente. Britain wanted Turkey to undertake concrete commitments in the form of guarantees similar to those given by Britain to Greece and Romania. 'The British Government was hoping that if Greece were attacked, Turkey would be involved in the war due to the obligations undertaken with the Anglo-Turkish Declaration.'[20] But Turkey had always been wary of any commitment which might involve her in problems in circumstances beyond her control. When the Declaration was read in the Assembly, Saraçoğlu emphasised that it stood independent of any commitments to the Balkan Entente. Therefore, even before negotiations for a treaty proper began, Turkey was making sure she did not give herself up into British hands. Furthermore, Turkey wanted to avoid giving any guarantee to Romania which would involve her in problems with the Soviet Union. Thus the Turks, although providing for their security, sought to keep their options open.

ANGLO-TURKISH TREATY NEGOTIATIONS

It must also be emphasised that during the earlier part of the war, until late in 1943, Turkey was seen as a source of manpower, which the British hoped could be tapped and actively employed in hostilities. It was only in late 1943, due to American and Soviet reluctance to see full Turkish deployment in the Balkans, that Britain come to insist on the use of Turkish territory for airfields and bases. In 1939, 'Britain relied on substantial military help from Turkey rather than from the other Balkan countries.'[21]

The copies of memoranda supplied to the British delegations at various stages of staff talks with the Turks in June 1939 are interesting from several points of view. Firstly, they show the importance given to the Turkish alliance by Britain and the Turkish reluctance to show their hand. Secondly, the Soviets were still considered close to Turkey. Thirdly, these memoranda show to what extent the British were unprepared for a war of speed and attrition: 'The Allied position in the Mediterranean will be considerably strengthened from the outset by the intervention of Turkey as an ally. She is the most powerful member of the Balkan Pact and also the Saadabad Pact.'[22] Turkey was thus seen as the connecting link between the two. British officers, however, complained that they found most of the Turkish answers to their questions 'lacking in detail' and that the Turks were generally reluctant to give precise information regarding strategic matters.

It is also interesting that the British saw Turco-Soviet relations as close enough to suggest the basing of Soviet air forces in Turkey: 'In view of the close relations between Turkey and Russia there would presumably not be the same political objections to the employment of Russian air forces from Turkey as there are reported to be against them being based in Poland and Rumania.'[23] Nor were the Turks mistaken in 'making a point of insisting that immediate necessities be sent them as soon as possible . . .', in view of the total lack of preparation on the part of the British for the events that were to follow.[24] The British instructions bear out this view: 'If German and Italian forces were to overrun Greece, Yugoslavia and Rumania, and join in the attack from Bulgaria, Turkey might be forced to withdraw from her frontier, but she would be able to hold-out almost indefinitely on the line of the Bosphorous, Sea of Marmara and the Dardanelles.'[25]

The British obviously were not informed about what blitzkrieg warfare could do. The British delegation was instructed to tell the Turks that they need not worry about the Dodecanese as 'their reduction to an innocuous state in a future war will only be a matter of time . . .'[26] But in 1943 Rhodes proved to be an impossible nut to crack, even at that late stage. According to the same instructions the British and French navies could easily control the Italian navy, thus protecting the Turkish coast. The British talked about the 'moral effect' of being at war, with France and Britain enormously increasing the strain on Germany's resources. The Poles were expected to relieve pressure on the West, by staging, 'some form of offensive in the East . . .', 'The whole of the French frontier opposite Germany is covered by the Maginot Line which consists of probably the strongest fixed defences now in existence. In these circumstances a direct attack on France is most unlikely.'[27] The whole tenor of these instructions indicates how far the British were from the facts. The French navy had to be destroyed by the British themselves because France collapsed, Maginot Line and all. The Poles did not stage any offensive because they were destroyed in three weeks. All during the military talks France was considered as a very real factor. The Turks, comparing statements like these with the way events turned out were all the more firmly convinced that they did not want any part of it.

THE NAZI–SOVIET PACT AND ITS EFFECT ON ANGLO-TURKISH RELATIONS

It was against this background, at a time when Turco-Soviet relations seemed to be good enough for Turkey to offer air force bases for Soviet use, that the news of the Nazi–Soviet Pact exploded in Turkey. The news was received in Turkey with surprise and apprehension. At first, however, the Turks tried to put as good a face on it as possible. F. R. Atay commented in the official *Ulus*:

The news of a Non-Aggression Pact between Soviet Russia and Germany had led everywhere to profound amazement. Everyone's attention was turned to the staff talks in Moscow. The news that was expected these days from Moscow was the result of the military and political negotiations between the Great Democracies and the Soviets . . . Because of this the telegram announcing the signature of the Pact of Non-Aggression has had quite the effect of a blow . . . It is not yet time to express conclusive views on this subject.[28]

The Turkish press showed a mixture of disillusionment and caution. Asım Us wrote in *Vakit*: 'The last ten years of European history had showed us that words like promises, principles, and ideology are only useful in fooling naive nations; in practice there is no belief, principle, or ideology that cannot be sacrificed for material advantages . . . In this case the whole matter depends on Soviet intentions.'[29] Z. Sertel in the pro-Soviet *Tan* stated that the democracies were unable to give the Soviets the security she wanted and therefore she was forced into seeking it in an agreement with Germany. Now war was inevitable: 'We are confronted by a *fait accompli*. The peace front has lost its most important element. And this loss will strengthen Germany.'[30]

Yunus Nadi in *Cumhuriyet* used stronger language, although even he implied that the Soviets might have had peace in mind:

The statement of these non-aggression obligations without any condition or regulation, so openly and unconditionally is beyond comprehension. In that case one is forced to believe that there are hidden motives behind this move. To accept that the Soviets who split hairs over the little Baltic States, should give the Third Reich freedom of action all along their western and southern frontiers, is not just difficult, but inconceivable . . . It is because of this that it is necessary to wait to see the realities of the situation . . .

Nadi pointed out that the Soviets did not hesitate before the danger of appearing to the world as having relinquished their major principles. This led one to believe that there was no faith that could not be sacrificed to urgent interest. He concluded: 'Given that we have been confronted with the most incredible surprises, we shall certainly see in time its even stranger developments. Let us remain calm and await the events to come.'[31] Nadi echoed the sentiments of Asım Us in his disbelief of fine words and promises. In another *Cumhuriyet* article he reiterated the conviction that the world was still ruled by self-interest and greed:

Poor Collective Security . . . ; One cannot be sorry enough that this League (League of Nations) was never able to function effectively and actively, and has finally fallen into the weak and near-dead state it is in now. One can only come to the conclusion that hidden conceit in people's thoughts has rendered impossible their development to a level where they would be able to unite around an ideal of peace and justice. The error lay in the attitude of most of the Nations joining the League, who joined it as a token gesture, and thinking that they would find there a source of strength without having to sacrifice anything of themselves. But the strength of the League of Nations could only be the strength that its members themselves invested in it.[32]

The Nazi–Soviet Pact certainly deeply disturbed and surprised Turkey, whose orientation in foreign policy now entered a new phase.[33] She found herself isolated with the two western democracies. This dealt a very damaging blow to her relations with the Soviet Union. Even after the Nazi–Soviet Pact, however, the Turks still did not give up hope of being able to bridge the gap between the west and the Soviet Union, and Saraçoğlu went to Moscow early in September 1939 with this aim. The Germans and Italians now hoped that the new situation would cause Turkey to shift from her pro-western policy. The British were in fact very afraid that this would happen. The Turks, although now more than ever dependent on the British, drove a hard bargain in treaty negotiations and stalled until the most favourable conditions could be torn from their prospective allies.

Nor were the British wrong in assuming that Hitler would use this new situation to draw Turkey away from them. Hitler wrote to Mussolini on 25 August, 'Even Turkey under these circumstances can only envisage a revision of her previous position.'[34] Mussolini replied, 'A new strategy on the part of Turkey would upset all the strategic plans of the French and English in the Eastern Mediterranean.' The Germans were indeed also hoping to use Turkey's good relations with the Soviets for their own benefit, just as Britain had done. The German Ambassador in Moscow reported on 5 September that he had again asked the Soviets 'to work on Turkey with a view to permanent neutrality'.[35] 'Molotov replied that the Soviet Government had considerable influence with Turkey and was exerting it in the sense desired by us.'[36] When, on 17 September, Molotov suggested a Pact of Mutual Defence should be proposed to the Turks including a clause which would absolve the Soviets from any involvement against Germany, Voroshilov added that 'such a Pact would be a hook by which Turkey could be pulled away from France'.[37]

This was exactly what the French were afraid of. The British Ambassador in Paris telegrammed the Foreign Office on 26 August, that the Quai d'Orsay had informed him they thought the situation in Turkey, since the conclusion of the Nazi–Soviet Pact, extremely delicate. The arrangements with Turkey were not solid. They feared that the Germans would dangle the same sort of 'share in the spoils' in front of them as they had done with Stalin.[38]

In the same vein the British Ambassador, Sir M. Palairet, reported from Athens on 25 August 1939, that the Yugoslav Minister in Athens stated that he was worried by the change of attitude of the Turkish Chargé since the signature of the Nazi–Soviet Pact. He had previously been almost aggressively anti German and was now decidedly moderate. Palairet added, 'I trust that this attitude is not significant.'[39] If so insignificant why did the Ambassador pass on a second-hand impression? The fact that the British were watching so closely surely indicates that they too did not feel that they could fully trust the Turks. The fact that even so small a factor as this was reported to London suggests strict official briefs about keeping eyes and ears open.

The British Foreign Office and its French equivalent, the Quai d'Orsay, were in fact very sensitive during this period to the slightest hint of possible change in the Turkish attitude. After the Nazi–Soviet Pact the British desired to push through a firm treaty as soon as possible as war loomed nearer. The Turks, however, opposed this with caution and stalling tactics. 'On the very eve of war, the Turkish Government still awaited the development of international events and was not in a hurry to sign a treaty. Therefore it made high financial and economic demands, hoping that this would delay the signing of an Anglo-Turkish treaty.'[40]

On 24 August, Halifax wrote to Hugessen saying that in view of the deteriorating international situation the treaty should be signed as soon as possible:

Please impress upon his Excellency the necessity of making rapid progress so that we should be in a position to afford the world proof of the solidarity of our governments in face of the common danger. It is for this reason and not of course, that I doubt in the remotest degree Turkish good faith, that I am so anxious to publish our agreement.[41]

The British were extremely anxious at this juncture to appear accommodating in the face of all Turkish demands, as Germany stepped up her pressure after the Nazi–Soviet Pact. Halifax again wired Hugessen on 25 August, 'Retention of Turkey in the peace front is obviously vital at this stage and His Majesty's Government are ready to make great sacrifices to attain this end.' He said that if the Turks made any suggestion which did not appear wholly impossible the Foreign Office should be informed immediately: 'In the present circumstances and those that may shortly develop, have no doubt that His Majesty's Government would be prepared to go to great lengths . . .'[42]

The Turks could hardly fail to make use of such an accommodating attitude. Turkey insisted on a credit of £35,000,000 for war materials, a gold loan of £15,000,000 for solving the country's pressing economic problems and about £2,000,000 for liquidating the clearing deficit.[43] The Turks, in their best bargaining tradition, knew they were needed desperately by Britain and thus exploited their position of strength between the two sides. The Germans, immediately after the announcement of the German–Soviet Pact, put heavy pressure on Turkey to cancel all existing contracts for war material with Germany, saying they found it unsuitable to ratify the credit agreement, particularly since the credit provided for war material. Saraçoğlu told Hugessen that he found himself unable to resist this pressure.[44]

Halifax, on 25 August, asked Hugessen's advice on any means by which such pressure could be counteracted, and wanted to know if there were any means which could induce the Turkish government to an early signature of the treaty: 'Could it in any way be made more palatable for them in the light of the new Russian development? . . . Or do you hold that the only reason for their holding back is our failure until now to meet them on economic and financial issues?' The Foreign Secretary went on to say that he was in close touch with Mussolini and that the latter would do his utmost to avoid being dragged into war over the Danzig issue. However, the Foreign Secretary felt that it would not be a good idea to tell this to the Turks for it might incline them to compromise with Germany and Russia: 'You should report at once any indication coming to your notice of any change of attitude on part of the Turkish Government . . .'[45]

This document reveals that the British still considered Italy to be a determining factor in the Turkish attitude, and that the Foreign Office was noticeably unsure of the Turks, although they tried to give the opposite impression. On 26 August, Hugessen asked for urgent instructions regarding Turkish demands for bullion and purchase of their tobacco crop, and requested full powers. He also said that a military mission sent to Turkey now would give the impression of mistrust, and added that if the Turks were to reverse their position a mission would not arrive on time.[46]

On 25 August, the British Ambassador in Athens reported that the 'fantastic rumour' had reached him that the German–Soviet Pact had been arranged in Ankara by Papen with the corollary that Turkey would defect from the peace front.[47] There were also rumours that Britain had made concessions to Italy at Turkish expense. The Ambassador in Turkey was instructed to make clear that the Anglo-Turkish alliance was 'the basis on which the whole of our Mediterranean policy rests'.[48] These days immediately after the Nazi–Soviet Pact seemed rife with sinister rumours and a general air of worry cum panic pervaded relations. Ambassadors requested instructions urgently and surprise pacts were sprung. One gets the impression that there was a general aura of mistrust, although official denials and reassurances were not in short supply.

The Foreign Secretary was also worried that there were indications that the Turks preferred to have Italy in the opposite camp, rather than as a neutral conserving her energy or an ally with dubious intentions. 'They [the Turks] will fight if Italy does', summed up Hugessen on 26 August, adding, 'I have heard vague rumours of neutrality talk . . . but have not seen any reason at present to take them seriously.'[49] To the Turks the Italian threat was still very real, and the British attempts to wean Italy away from Germany into a neutral position or into the position of an ally were not liked. The Ambassador wired on 5 September, that the Turks were much more inclined 'to try conclusions' with Italy.[50] In the drafting of the treaty therefore, the Turks were insisting on the wording, 'as a result of aggression in the Mediterranean area', making the treaty operational. The British felt this was needless provocation. The British Ambassador said that Turkey felt 'quite sure of herself in a duel with Italy'.[51]

In the last days of peace and immediately after the outbreak of the war, the Turks tightened up on their bargaining. They were aware of the unsettled frame of mind of the French and British. A Foreign

Office minute of 27 August stated: 'The Quai d'Orsay are much impressed with the necessity of making every sacrifice to keep Turkey on the side of Britain and France and to hasten the conclusion of the agreement . . .'[52]

On 2 September, German forces invaded Poland and thus started the Second World War. The western powers were alarmed that the arrangements with Turkey had not yet been concluded. As the tension increased the Turks became more adamant in regard to their requirements were they to conclude a treaty. The Ambassador reported on 3 September, 'The Secretary General's remarks tonight suggested that there will be more pressure for larger gold loan and further credits for war material . . . it seems most unlikely that they will sign the Treaty until they have at least obtained more than we have so far offered.'[53] The Turkish negotiators insisted on a 'suspensive clause' whereby treaty obligations could only become operative when the stipulated demands had been met in full. The Embassy reported on 15 September: 'The Minister of Foreign Affairs sticks to his proposals under which Turkey will carry out her engagements from the moment when provisions in special agreement (i.e. regards financial and economic points) have been entirely executed.'[54]

On 4 September, the War Cabinet were informed the Turks were increasing demands for financial assistance and that they were unlikely to sign any agreement unless their demands were met. The Cabinet agreed that it was of the utmost importance to conclude the agreement with Turkey as soon as possible.[55] On 5 September: 'Reference was made to dangers and difficulties we had created for ourselves in the last war by not securing Turkey's friendship or neutrality beforehand. There was no difference of opinion that at this juncture it would be worth paying a stiff price to avoid a repetition of similar dangers and difficulties.' The Cabinet stressed on 6 September the need for agreement with Turkey because of the deteriorating position in Poland. The Turks were still demanding a gold loan of £15 millions. The Cabinet believed that the failure to grant the loan was the main reason for failure to reach an agreement. They then agreed that because the situation in Europe was working against Britain it would be desirable to secure a treaty with Turkey as soon as possible.[56] The Turks were well aware of this and consequently once again demonstrated their aptitude for using the European situation as a bargaining counter to secure the best possible arrangement. The Turkish negotiators were also aware that Saraçoğlu's forthcoming visit to

Moscow raised fears in Britain that Turkey might come to some understanding with the Soviets. So the European situation, plus the possibility of an agreement with Moscow were artfully exploited by the Turks. The Ankara Embassy reported that it would be possible to secure agreement immediately if the British Government increased the armaments credit by £11 million. The Cabinet agreed and concluded on 18 September: 'It was vital to bring the negotiations to a successful issue, because there was a danger that if not brought to a head, Turkey might sign a Pact with the USSR.'[57]

Hugessen's letter to P. B. Nichols on 22 September sheds considerable light on British reaction to Turkish demands. Although the Ambassador was prepared 'to bet his official and personal shirt' on Turkish loyalty he conceded that they were being difficult on some points which he stated were 'worrying'. He said, 'they have been very sticky in their financial and economic demands, but I attribute this to bazaar instincts'. Even Hugessen, however, saw that the Turkish insistence was also due to 'a feeling that they are in a position to push us hard, which they certainly do'.[58] He reported that the hardest bargaining occurred with Menemencioğlu, which he said could be due to his 'hard bargaining tactics' or 'a desire to slow things down until the situation becomes clearer'.[59] On the suspensive clause he asked 'Was it put in to provide a way of escape by facing us with impossibilities, or does it represent genuine (and I think justifiable) anxiety about their state of military preparedness.' The answer to Hugessen's question was both; the Turks did feel that they needed time while things were uncertain with the Soviets, but they also knew that they were hopelessly unprepared for war, which even Hugessen was ready to admit as he insisted on early arrival of military supplies. 'It is no use asking the Turks in their present state of defence in Thrace to come in and face a mechanical attack. They have seen the disasters which have happened in Poland . . .'[60] Yet only recently the British had spoken in terms of a Polish 'offensive'.

In the Cabinet discussion on the Turkish negotiations on 23 September, it was felt that Turkey was making 'unreasonable demands' in asking for £15 million in gold in return for a treaty which would be rendered inoperable by a suspensive clause. 'The Turks appeared to contemplate that we should hand over the bullion practically unconditionally. After this we should be requested to supply them with war materials in large quantities, despite the fact that it was urgently required by our own troops.'

The Turkish Minister of Foreign Affairs was now on his way to Moscow and it was possible that on his return things would be more disadvantageous for Britain. There was the belief, prevalent in Cabinet, that it was now more urgent than ever to have Turkey on Britain's side, even if only in name, rather than on Germany's side: '£15 millions in gold was a heavy price, but it was not too heavy a price to pay for Turkish neutrality'. The failure to reach an agreement with Turkey would be a serious diplomatic defeat, just as an agreement would be seen as a great success.[61] Even at this stage the British still half expected a Turkish defection as a result of Soviet pressure. Menemencioğlu correctly estimated what price the British were prepared to pay and set his figure accordingly. He was not mistaken in thinking that the Allies would be quite prepared to grant most of what he asked.

Hugessen said, in a telegram on 20 September, that it was better to sign a treaty with a suspensive clause rather than waste time with details; the French Ambassador, he said, was in agreement. They both felt that the Turks would be reasonable and not make impossible demands. Both Menemencioğlu and Saraçoğlu had told them that they were under pressure from their General Staff who, in the light of the late arrival of help for Poland, were seriously worried about the defence of Thrace. The British and French Ambassadors also agreed that Thrace was in no state to resist mechanised attack.[62] By pointing to the plight of Poland the Turks justified their demands for the delivery of armaments prior to any undertaking on their part.

On 28 September, P. Nichols of the Foreign Office wrote to the British Ambassador in Paris that the French Ambassador in London was worried about the delay in initialling the treaty. He was afraid that Ribbentrop and the Soviets might put pressure on Saraçoğlu.[63] The French were in favour of working out details later, which gave the Turks the advantage of using just those details as part of their strategy. Hugessen seemed to have been quite taken in by Menemencioğlu's tactics. The Secretary General told him on 21 September, that pressure might be put on Saraçoğlu in Moscow and that it would look bad if the British looked as if they were holding back now. Hugessen in turn, emphasised to London that the delay might cause the Turks to 'yield points in Moscow'.[64] Menemencioğlu, using the possibility of pressure on Saraçoğlu in Moscow, ably and subtly accelerated the process whereby the British accepted his position.

This is not to say that the Turks were not genuinely concerned that pressure would be brought to bear on Saraçoğlu. This is why they wanted to keep the news of the initialling of the Treaty on 30 September quiet, in order to avoid prejudicing Saraçoğlu's chances while he was negotiating. Hugessen derived the impression from Menemencioğlu that, 'He attaches the greatest importance to leaving the Turkish Minister of Foreign Affairs every possible opportunity for ascertaining definitely what is the true policy of the Soviet Government . . .'[65]

The Turkish Minister of Foreign Affairs wanted to make use of this trip to determine whether the Nazi–Soviet Pact was a measure only for the partition of Poland, or if this move had only been a prelude to further conquests. 'This was a revealing example of the vigilance with which the Turkish government guarded and attempted to further good relations with its Northern neighbour . . .' Thus Turkey found herself in the position she had so long sought to avoid: boxed in between two contradictory friendships.[66]

Saraçoğlu therefore went to Moscow to bridge the gap between Britain and the Soviets. Despite the Nazi–Soviet Pact, Turkey still hoped to be able to forge the crucial link that would join the Soviet Union to the 'peace front'. As late as 7 October, the Turks still hoped for a satisfactory outcome. Aras, the Turkish Ambassador in London told Dr Jackh of the Ministry of Information that he expected a Turkish–Russian agreement compatible with the Anglo-Franco-Turkish alliance, both to be signed at the same time. Dr Aras said the ultimate Turkish aims were 'to be a bridge between Great Britain and Russia' and to isolate Hitler.[67] But this proved to be an impossibility. As seen above, even in August it had been feared that the Soviets would exert pressure on Turkey to draw her away from the Allies. This was the Soviet aim in inviting Saraçoğlu to Moscow. 'The Turkish and Russian reasons for negotiating were therefore fundamentally opposed.'[68]

Ribbentrop wrote to von Schulenberg, the German Ambassador in Moscow, on 2 October telling him that he was, 'particularly anxious for the Russian government to proceed in that direction (pressure on Turkey) in order to dissuade Turkey from the final conclusion of assistance pacts with the Western Powers, and to settle this at once in Moscow'.[69]

The extent to which the Soviet negotiators followed German instructions demonstrated the difficulty of the Turkish position. On 7 October, von Schulenberg again received instructions from Ribbentrop. The Minister was worried that a Soviet–Turkish agreement would be arrived at and he stipulated that if the Soviets could not

avoid making such a pact, 'we would regard it as a foregone conclusion that she should make a reservation in the Pact whereby the
Soviet Union would not be obligated to any kind of assistance aimed
directly or indirectly at Germany'.[70] The demands made on Saraçoğlu by Stalin reflect the German desiderata:

(a) Turkey would change the article in the Tripartite Pact whereby she
promised to give the western powers 'all the aid and assistance in her
power', if they had to activate their guarantees to Greece and Romania, to 'consultation' only with the powers.
(b) An addition to Protocol 2, which absolved Turkey from taking any
action which would involve her in war with the U.S.S.R. The
addition desired by Stalin went: 'And moreover these engagements
cannot oblige Turkey to support Great Britain and France if these
countries go to war with the U.S.S.R. In this case for the duration of
the said war the Anglo-Franco-Turkish Pact would remain inactive.'
(c) The Soviet Union wanted an 'exclusion clause' analogous to Protocol
2 which would absolve her from intervention to aid Turkey if this
country were attacked by Germany.[71]

Ribbentrop had written on 2 October: 'In my opinion, as already
stated several times, it would be in the Russian interest, on account of
the question of the Straits, to forestall a tie-up of Turkey to England
and France.'[72]

Accordingly, Stalin's proposals at his first meeting with Saraçoğlu
contained a detailed list of changes he desired in the Montreux
Convention. These included a joint Turkish–Russian approval for
passage through the Straits of warships of a nonriparian power, in
peacetime or in war. Also the Soviet Union demanded the rights to
approve passage for all warships of powers acting under the League of
Nations. They also included the reduction of the permitted tonnage
by one-fifth. Saraçoğlu replied that any alteration in the Tripartite
Pact was beyond his power, the treaty had already been initialled and
the French and British would rightly object to any amendment. As to
the 'German Clause', Saraçoğlu vehemently declared that such a
clause would deprive the pact of its *raison d'être*. As for any revision of
Montreux, Saraçoğlu strongly denied any possibility of bilateral revision of a multilateral convention and said Turkey would never allow
another Treaty of Hünkâr İskelesi.[73]

How much importance the Turks placed on a satisfactory outcome
of the negotiations is demonstrated by their efforts to get France and
Britain to modify the article pertaining to Romania and Greece.
Saraçoğlu summoned the French and British Ambassadors in

Moscow and asked them to support an appeal he was making to their governments. He talked about the disastrous effect a break in the negotiations would have, and Stalin was not renowned for his patience.[74]

When talks began again on 14 October, Saraçoğlu could inform Molotov that the British and French had agreed to change to 'consultation' the article in question. The Soviets then immediately brought up the German reserve clause. In the face of Saraçoğlu's repeated and unequivocal refusals to consider it, Molotov always returned to the charge with the statement that this was a promise he had made to Ribbentrop.[75] This indicated to what extent the Soviets were committed to Germany. Saraçoğlu again refused to consider any illegal revision of the Montreux Convention.

During the final session on 16 October, Molotov insisted on the German reserve clause and on the revision of Montreux. Saraçoğlu's intransigence obliged both sides to concede that the talks had ended in failure. But there is evidence that as early as 9 October, the Soviet negotiators had given up sincere negotiations and no longer desired a satisfactory conclusion. Schulenberg wrote to Berlin on 9 October: 'Molotov expressed the view that in all likelihood a mutual assistance pact with Turkey would not be concluded.'[76]

While Ribbentrop was in Moscow Stalin deliberately ignored Saraçoğlu and the latter was shunted from opera to ballet to football match, until he refused to go anywhere unless Stalin saw him. This humiliation left its mark on Saraçoğlu who became renowned for his anti-Soviet attitude. On 17 October, Sir S. Hoare, the British Ambassador in Bucharest, reported that the Turks were very angry at the way they had been treated, and if the Turkish Ambassador reflected in any way the feeling of his government 'they will at the first available opportunity make manifest their resentment at the insolence of the Russian demand'.[77] But the Turks did nothing of the kind. Quite the contrary, they made placatory statements about 'useful talks'. The prominent journalist, Y. Nadi wrote in *Cumhuriyet*:

It is our sincere belief that Turkish–Russian friendship is strong enough not to be affected by the signature or non signature of any document, for this or that reason. . . . During all these tremendous events, all of Turkey's attention has been focused on avoiding doing anything which would harm others, especially her neighbours. She has done nothing more than look to her own security, nor can she do otherwise in future.[78]

These words, however, disguised the deep unease felt in Turkey during those days. Saraçoğlu's failure in Moscow to reconcile Turkey's two big friends marks the end of the period during which Turkey attempted to juggle the two relationships. This heralds a new phase in the development of Turkish foreign policy with the Soviet Union now becoming a major worry. But Saraçoğlu's Moscow negotiations are also revealing of some lines of thinking in this policy.

Saraçoğlu was prepared to give ground on Turkish commitment to aid Britain if she had to activate her guarantees in Romania and Greece. But this was really no sacrifice for Turkey as she had been reluctant to agree to involvement in someone else's problem which ran counter to her foreign policy. The points on which Saraçoğlu stood firm indicate the issues which Turkey considered vital to her wellbeing. The German reserve clause would have taken away her very reason for seeking an alliance with the Soviet Union. Saraçoğlu's attitude when faced with Soviet demands for the revision of Montreux also illustrates how far relations had deteriorated since 1936 when Turkey had proposed an agreement whereby she would not allow ships hostile to the Soviets to pass through the Straits. And although Zhivkova maintains that 'the Turkish Government failed to seize the opportunity of signing a treaty of mutual aid with the Soviet Union', it was more a case of the Turkish government finding themselves confronted by impossible demands on the part of a power they had hitherto considered a friend.[79]

The treaty signed on 19 October gives further indications of the Turkish outlook. Although Turkey had to put Article 3 concerning Greece and Romania back into the treaty, on other points she resisted admirably. The British wanted complete reciprocity of commitments, but Paragraph 1 of the treaty which committed Britain and France to aid Turkey if she were attacked by any European state did not contain any element of reciprocity. Although Britain insisted, the Turkish government refused to enter into such obligations toward the western powers. Paragraph 3, giving Turkey obligations to Greece and Romania had long been a bone of contention. A new element was introduced in the form of Article 4 which committed Turkey to maintaining benevolent neutrality towards Britain and France if they were attacked by a European power. The Turks also insisted on the inclusion of Protocol 2 which absolved them from any action likely to lead to war with the Soviet Union.

In a special agreement on financial matters, Britain and France granted Turkey a credit of £25,000,000 for war materials, a gold loan of £16,000,000 and a loan of £3$^{1}/_{2}$ million for the transfer of Turkish credits.[80] The Turks therefore had secured a treaty very much in keeping with their foreign policy aims. They would become actively involved only if attacked, in the meantime they would be given large sums of money, great quantities of arms, and if their Allies were attacked in the west they only had to promise benevolent neutrality. Nor did they have to undertake any action at all until all the war materials promised had arrived.

TURKISH REACTIONS TO THE OUTBREAK OF WAR

At this stage it would be useful to examine Turkish public opinion at the outbreak of war. Initial caution about the Soviet attitude eventually gave way to the admission that the Soviets had been instrumental in encouraging Hitler to act. But Turkey was still very much preoccupied by Italy and her attitude in the conflict. A. Daver wrote in *Cumhuriyet* announcing that war had broken out and added: 'War was a certainty ever since the German–Soviet Pact had been signed. History will place the responsibility for this war on Germany and partly on Russia who gave her encouragement and thus increased Germany's impudence.'[81]

The same article mentioned that for now Italy was outside the conflict. This signalled the departure from the cautious attitude of 'wait and see', which the Turkish press had first adopted to the Nazi–Soviet Pact. The official *Ulus* columnist F. R. Atay commented: 'The Non-Aggression Pact between Germany and Russia did not save peace as was thought in Moscow, quite the contrary, it provoked war . . . If Russia had joined the peace front, it is unlikely that Germany would have launched herself on this terrifying game of chance.'[82] When Italy maintained her neutrality, some tentative hopes were raised in Turkey. Sadi Ertem in *Vakit* generally encouraged Italy to stay out:

The Peninsula is surrounded by sea dominated by the allied fleets, leaving it open to bombardment and blockade . . . The result will be that her coasts will be ruined, she will go hungry, she will lose her islands, and become cut-off from her Colonies. Will the Italy coming to the peace table in this condition be more effective than the victorious Italy of 1918?[83]

Not all assessment of Italy was positive however, Asım Us wrote in the same paper that when the Germans, having disposed of Poland, began their expansion into the Balkans, Italy would then find it

expedient to discard her mask of neutrality and emerge as a belligerent.[84] Germany got more stern treatment than Italy. H. Ocaklıoğlu
wrote in *Yeni Asır* that the German methods of invasion and aggression had continued to swallow smaller nations, but warned Germany
that there were countries which would resist her to the end; he then
went on to say about Italy: 'If Italy shows sobriety and intelligence by
remaining neutral, the holocaust might be contained between four
nations. To prevent the fire from reaching the Balkans or the Mediterranean remains Italy's responsibility. If Mussolini shows the reason
and judgement which Hitler failed to show, the spread of the great
catastrophe will be limited.'[85]

Italy was in fact the major point of interest in much of the press of
this period. E. İ. Benice wrote in *Son Telgraf*: 'Whether Italy remains
neutral, in relation to the position resulting from the British and
French declarations of war is of very great importance. It is in fact the
major issue today. If Italy remains neutral there is no chance that war
will spread to the Mediterranean . . . There is a definite need for the
complete clarification of Italy's intentions . . .'[86] N. Sadak in *Akşam*
voiced suspicion and cynicism when he wrote: 'Is Italy going to
remain neutral or will she come in at the moment most advantageous
for her? This is the question occupying most minds today. We are in
an age when neither promises given nor documents signed have any
value. The only factor determining nations' decisions is the profit
factor as it appears at any given moment . . .'[87]

The nervous glances cast in the northern direction were also evident in some writers' articles. F. R. Atay in *Ulus* wrote that negotiations failed with the Soviets because of the clash between
obligations to Britain, the Soviet position, and the Montreux Convention. But he stressed that this did not mean the end of the Turkish–
Russian friendship. He underlined that any undertaking Turkey went
into would be to preserve peace and security in its own area: 'This
unchanging principle of Turkish foreign policy is sure to be appreciated by our friends the Soviets.'[88] H. C. Yalçın in *Yeni Sabah*, said that
Turkey had tried hard to reconcile Anglo-French views with those of
the Soviets, unfortunately this had proved impossible.[89]

The views of the press on related subjects in this period are also
enlightening. On the subject of the Russian–Finnish war, which the
Turks closely followed, R. Emeç wrote in *Son Posta* that the Soviets
had made claims on Finland and negotiations were in progress. Of the
Finns he said: 'Because they are a long way from nourishing illusions,

while negotiating with the Russians on one hand they have been taking the precautions necessitated by circumstance . . . Finland wants to live in peace with the world. But nor does she seem at all likely to make sacrifices of her national integrity and freedom.' Emeç hoped negotiations would lead to a satisfactory solution.[90] The Turks obviously saw a potential parallel between Finland and themselves.

As the long-expected war came to Europe the Turks found themselves solidly placed, on paper, in one of the belligerent camps. They had nourished strong hopes of including the Soviet Union in this arrangement, but now they found her not only outside but also in a position of co-operation with Germany.

6 . THE YEAR OF SURPRISES: 1940

1940 was a year of severe crises and unforeseen events for Turkey. 'When the Turks, the French and the British signed an alliance it was impossible to foresee either the German successes in Western Europe and the developments which brought the Axis to the very doors of Turkey, or the threat of complete hostile encirclement . . .'[1]

In the previous year during the treaty negotiations the British had spoken in terms of the 'Maginot Line' and the French having 'the best existing land defences in the world', this making 'a direct attack on France most unlikely'. They had also spoken of a 'Polish Offensive in the East.'[2] In view of what actually happened it was hardly surprising that the Turks kept themselves aloof.

It is no more surprising that Turkey, 'was not even ready to allow the indispensable naval and air bases to be prepared in her territory'.[3] The British and Turks approached the Alliance with completely contradictory viewpoints. To the Turks it was an insurance policy to be put into practice only in case of dire need, while for the British it was a means of effective action in the Balkans and Middle East. Barutçu quotes İnönü as saying at the time: 'The aim of Turkey is (in the case of British entry into the war . . .) to remain out as long as possible. For us this is ideal . . . Turkey is now no longer alone, she has insured herself with the world's strongest insurance firm . . . For us war is out of the question unless we are left absolutely no choice . . .'[4]

This contradiction did not become obvious until later in the war, because the Turks managed to obscure the issues with what were ostensibly credible arguments of military weakness, which the British had to take at face value. Faced with a situation in which they found themselves powerless to insist on Turkish compliance, the British had to acquiesce none too willingly in the view that they approved of Turkey's actions.

The Germans, on the other hand, like the British, seemed to fail to appreciate the true nature of the Anglo-Turkish Treaty. To them (no doubt due to British design), the Anglo-Turkish Treaty seemed to pose a very real threat. They sought therefore to restrict its scope. On 14 March the German Ambassador, von Papen, proposed to İnönü a German–Turkish treaty including a statement from the Turkish government that Turkey would defend its neutrality, 'even with the force of arms' against the Allies.[5] The British Foreign Office felt that the Germans feared the Allies would be granted facilities in Thrace, the Straits or the Caucasus even when Turkey was not a belligerent.[6]

THE BAKU AFFAIR AND SOVIET–TURKISH RELATIONS

This question of 'facilities' was also prominent in what was one of the most ambiguous episodes of the early war years: the projected bombardment of the Russian oilfields at Baku in the Caucasus. The Russian gains in Poland, the Baltic States and Finland worried the French who now looked for some way of crippling Russia's war potential by opening a theatre of war geographically distant from France. Also, Baku oil was being exported to Germany. Between January 1940 and June 1941, the Soviets delivered 16 million barrels of oil to Germany. The Germans had hoped to share in the exploitation of Soviet oil but Stalin was not willing to go so far.[7]

The French felt Baku could only be hit by aerial attack. A study of the problem, commissioned by Edouard Daladier and prepared by General Weygand and Admiral Darlan, was completed by 22 February 1940. The study entitled 'On the eventual intervention for the destruction of Russian oil' concluded that such an attack would seriously disrupt Soviet organisation.[8] It soon became obvious however, that Turkish co-operation was essential to any undertaking of this nature. When the French studied the question in conjunction with the British at the Supreme War Council meeting of 28 March 1940 it was decided that, 'Action by the Allies would necessarily depend on the attitude of Turkey.'[9]

Churchill, as First Sea Lord, was strongly in favour of the project, and urged the Foreign Office to secure Turkish collaboration over the use of the Straits for the venture. But, 'Halifax knew this was hopeless' and Cadogan minuted, 'it is most unlikely that Turkey if nonbelligerent, will tear up the Montreux Convention for our convenience . . .'[10] Although Paul Reynaud felt the Turks would not countenance a naval action in the Black Sea, he put forward evidence that aerial attacks would not be subject to the same objections. This evidence consisted of a report from René Massigli, the French Ambassador in Ankara, in which the latter recounted a conversation with Foreign Minister Saraçoğlu on this matter.[11] The Ambassador reported that Saraçoğlu had 'spontaneously' broached the subject and said the Russians were worried about such an attack. Massigli, upon being requested to comment, had pointed out that any such operation would involve Allied aircraft flying over the territory of Iran or Turkey. To this Saraçoğlu replied by asking: 'Do you fear a protest from Iran?' The Ambassador therefore concluded that there would be no objections from Turkey but that it would have been indiscreet on his part to press the Foreign Minister further. He recommended that if such an attack were planned it should be undertaken without Turkish authorisation, no request being made to Ankara, thus enabling Turkey to plead a *fait accompli* in the face of Russian reproaches.[12] Although the sequence of events remains a murky affair, it seems fairly clear that Turkey was sounded as to her intentions. The view which Van Creveld infers from Massigli's memoir, which is that 'Turkish consent was never asked', is not accurate.[13]

On the whole the British were at best lukewarm on the idea. Although a Foreign Office report dated 25 March mentioned that a way had to be found 'of disabling Germany's only ally', and the Chiefs of Staff saw Baku oil as the 'Achilles heel' of the Soviet Union; Chamberlain felt the plan had too many flaws.[14] The major consideration for their lack of enthusiasm was the Turkish attitude. Alexander Cadogan wrote on 23 March, 'The weak point in the scheme . . . is that so far as I can judge we should forfeit the assistance of Turkey. Turkey might wink at us flying over Turkish territory but if we "aggress" in this way that will give her a splendid excuse (which I think she would be glad of) for not coming into the war . . .' Halifax wrote to Cadogan on 25 March that Britain would be doing herself a 'great injury' if she 'fell foul' of the Turks on this issue, he felt that the French report was 'painted in rather attractive colours'.[15] His own information from his Ambassador in the field, Hugessen, did not tally with the French version. Hugessen reported that Turkey was not yet ready for such a move.[16]

Indeed the British were extremely aware of Turkey's importance for them. During the meeting of the Chiefs of Staff with the Ambassadors to the Balkan countries on 26 March it was decided that, 'Turkey is the northern bastion of our position in the Middle East . . .' The same men stated on 8 April, 'It is of vital importance that we retain Turkey as an ally . . .'[17] These considerations plus the German success in Norway and its consequences ruled out of practical consideration the project of an attack on Caucasian oilfields.

The true nature of this episode remains unclear. It is unlikely that a man as cautious as İnönü would have approved such a venture. Yet Professor Fahir Armaoğlu states, 'Although Turkey did not oppose the plan (of bombing Baku) she did not give official authorization to overfly her territory. In other words, the Allied planes were to have flown over Turkish territory without her knowledge.'[18] The evidence tends to imply that Saraçoğlu who was somewhat given to making off-the-cuff remarks, and whose recent humiliations in Moscow still rankled, may have given Massigli the impression he got, which the latter as a dutiful career diplomat reported to Paris.[19]

Aydemir likens this episode to the First World War situation when an ill-considered bombardment of Russian ports by the battle cruisers *Yavuz* and *Hamidiye*, formerly *Goeben* and *Breslau*, involved Turkey in war with Russia. The bombardment of Baku, he maintains would have given the Soviets reason to invade Turkey.[20] The position was exacerbated by the publication of the German White Book which alleged on the basis of captured French documents, that Turkey had been party to a plan to attack the Soviet Union.[21] But the Soviet reaction was surprisingly measured. This sheds some light on Soviet–Turkish relations at this stage. The truth of the matter was that as the situation in Europe began to look more favourable for Germany, particularly after the invasion of Romania, the Soviets pursued a policy of hesitant *rapprochement* with Turkey.

It is interesting to note that both Germany and Great Britain used Turkish wariness of the Soviet Union for their own ends. Germany used the Soviets to frighten the Turks away from a more active co-operation with Britain while the British sought to convince Turkey that they were her only real hope of avoiding Soviet intimidations.[22] On the whole the British approved of the Soviet–Turkish *rapprochement* hoping to use Turkey to draw the Soviets away from Germany, while they still feared a Soviet–German understanding at Turkey's expense. One deterrent to any German move through the Middle East was the fear that this would bind the Soviets to Britain.[23] On 1 August von Papen explained to Hitler that the situation between the Soviets and Turkey should be kept 'fluid' so that Turkey could not become the connecting link between London and Moscow.[24]

It is interesting to note that the British Ambassador in Moscow, Sir Stafford Cripps, cabled on two occasions on 2 August and 30 October 1940 that Turkey should forestall any Soviet–German ultimatum by making concessions to Moscow on the Straits.[25] The Foreign Office had no illusions, however, and felt that Cripps should be told that it would be wrong and 'extremely ill advised' to try to force sacrifices out of Turkey which would be contrary to her vital interests. A minute by O. Sargent dated 20 August stated that, 'We are not in a position to dictate to Turkey in this matter and the latter has made it quite clear that she does not intend to make the attempt at buying-off Russia.'[26] Nonetheless relations seemed to be improving and on 2 November Hugessen reported that Menemencioğlu had told him Turkey was looking into the possibilities of acquiring war material and petroleum from the Soviet Union.[27]

On the occasion of Molotov's visit to Berlin, Yunus Nadi of the *Cumhuriyet* reviewed Nazi–Soviet relations since the Nazi–Soviet Pact. He said this pact, which many had considered 'impossible' had proved profitable for the Soviets: 'Those who said this possibility did not exist have been proved wrong by events. However, arrangements and agreements between states are always calculated on interest, and are always temporary. Even those treaties put on the market having been stamped 'eternal' are only temporary and transient.'[28] Nadi certainly seemed to be leaving the door open for potential realignment.

The Soviets, however, in the meantime showed their hand to Germany. On 13 November, barely ten days after Menemencioğlu had talked of procuring arms from the Soviet Union, Molotov told Hitler that they considered the Straits vital to their security and wanted to give Bulgaria, the country nearest the Straits, a guarantee similar to that given by Germany to Romania. Hitler was extremely suspicious of such a move and asked if Bulgaria had asked for such a guarantee. He also stressed that he would have to consult Mussolini before approving any such undertaking. Molotov was adamant and insisted on a guarantee 'not on paper but in reality'.[29] Before the Soviet Union would agree to join the Axis she would require 'a base for light naval and air forces on the Bosphorus and the Dardanelles' and recognitions that the area south of Batum and Baku in the direction of the Persian Gulf was the 'centre of the aspirations of the Soviet Union'.[30] Once again, the extreme strategic importance of the Straits saved Turkey. The Soviet demands showed the Germans that there was no further hope of co-operation with Moscow. Like the Soviets, Germany had no intention of sharing the Straits with anyone. On 18 December, barely three weeks after Molotov left Berlin, Hitler ordered the preparation for operation 'Barbarossa'.[31]

THE FRENCH COLLAPSE

The French catastrophe came as a deeply felt shock for Turkey. It further confirmed their belief that they wanted no part in the European conflagration. France had been judged by the Turks to have the best armies in Europe, and İnönü himself had believed that the war in the west would be fought on the Maginot Line and would last four or five years.[32] The British also, believed war would be a long, drawn-out affair. When France caved in within the space of a few weeks the Turks reacted with a mixture of shock, fear, and anger at what they considered to be the extremely irresponsible manner in which France had been pressuring them to join in the fray when she knew her own end was approaching.

There was also an element of relief in the Turkish attitude, as they saw that their policy of caution had paid off, and their realism and pragmatism in putting Turkish interest first was vindicated by events. The entry of Italy into the war had made their treaty obligations operational but they had managed to parry the Anglo-French call to duty. France signed an Armistice with Germany on 22 June: 'How could a country withdrawing from the war force another to join in it?'[33] As the Allied military reverses multiplied in Europe there had been increasing fears in some quarters in Turkey that they had, once again, joined the weaker side. As the battle raged in Sedan, Turkish MPs had their doubts: 'It was possible that we were once more fated to join the weak side. We began to feel the vociferous presence of those opposed to the Anglo-Turkish Alliance.'[34] In June and July von Papen reported that German victories had caused extensive soul searching among the Turkish parliamentarians, and that there was talk of replacing Saraçoğlu with Hüsrev Gerede, Turkey's Ambassador to Berlin, who had close contacts with Hitler and the Wilhelmstrasse.[35] After Dunkirk the Assembly was extremely active in its examinations of the situation. There were those like Fazıl Ahmet (Elazığ) and Hikmet Bayur (Manisa) who felt Turkey had to go to the aid of the Allies and that public opinion should be prepared for war.[36] There were also those who felt Turkey had acted with undue haste in concluding the Alliance. All were worried about the attitude of Italy. Kâzım Karabekir asked Saraçoğlu what the meaning was of joining a war on the losing side, as Italy would only join after the Allies were clearly seen to be losing. Saraçoğlu made a non-committal reply, and added that it was not true that Turkey was about to enter the war, and public opinion should not be unnecessarily alarmed.[37]

There was a general aura of awe in the face of unfolding German military might as the Germans rolled back the French armies, 'fighting shoulder to shoulder like their Teutonic ancestors'.[38] This was accompanied by a general feeling of anger that the democracies should have allowed themselves to be caught out to such an extent. 'The whole French Army collapsed in 23 days. This is the end of a government and nation whose infrastructure had completely rotted away . . . The Democracies showed themselves to be entirely unprepared. Why, in this condition, did they declare war on Germany? It is incomprehensible . . .'[39]

There were calls in the press at this time for Germany to be reasonable and not repeat the mistakes of 1919. The press urged a compromise peace and moderation, as Turkey saw the balance of power in Europe begin to look dangerously lopsided. Y. Nadi wrote in *Cumhuriyet* that now the 'scenario' of the French surrender in the same rail carriage used in 1919 for the Germans was over and out of the way – let Germany turn to constructing world peace:

The belief of a society of nations can only take root if nations allow each other the right to exist. Europe could have achieved this in 1919 if the men claiming to set up a new order had sufficiently understood the needs of our century. Military and economic hegemony only serve as files to sharpen the hatred of oppressed masses.[40]

Esmer took a more anti-German line. Commenting on Hitler's speech of 21 July, he said things were not as Hitler painted them. Germany had been in the right when she repudiated Versailles but she had now embarked on the path of aggression and conquest. Germany invaded the smaller countries in Europe on the pretext that they were being forcibly pulled into the British orbit:

The small nations of western Europe have met their present fate not because they tried to assume an aggressive posture towards Germany, but because they believed in Germany's word and followed a policy they called neutrality and were unprepared . . . Let us see if Hitler, if he is victorious, is able to give Europe a system more just than the system of Versailles, which he has criticised so severely. If he can, and only if he can, he will prove himself justified in making these criticisms. But if present developments are any indication this seems unlikely . . .[41]

Even in this anti-German article, it was possible to discern emphasis on compromise and balance in Esmer's reference to Germany's justifiable claims. It is interesting to note that he criticised neutrals, considering Turkey's status very different. Not all the press was pro-Allied however, and E. Velid in *Tasvir-i Efkâr*, reputed to be pro-German, followed quite a different line and criticised Chamberlain for offensive language against Hitler, referring to his calling Hitler 'a Mad Dog that should be destroyed'. He invited both sides to be more moderate and told them to stop insulting each other. 'We see no advantage at all in the persistence of the two sides in this violent provocation. . . . Give up these harsh words and take advantage of any talk of peace, sincere or insincere . . .'[42]

On 23 June Velid in *Tasvir* attacked the exaggerated news stories about 'thousands of aircraft sent by America to Britain' etc . . . He said exaggeration and provocation in the press had got France to where she was now. The losses of the last few months on the Western Front had occurred precisely because too much time was spent writing words such as these. 'One side spent its time drawing sarcastic caricatures while the other went without butter to construct guns. The horrifying results we now witness occurred because of this.'[43]

Turks had always admired military success and the weakness and defection of France filled them with distaste. There were even suspicions that France had ulterior motives in forcing Turkish entry. A. Ş. Esmer believed that France, although she knew she was losing, was pushing for Turkish entry hoping to use this as a counterweight to secure more favourable armistice terms from the Germans.[44] Suat Hayri Ürgüplü told this writer that when it became known that approximately two weeks prior to making their official *démarche* through Massigli, the French had already made it known in London that they were planning surrender, this raised a general outcry against France.[45] Even Massigli, who claims he was not informed, admits that the Turks were quite right to be enraged at what they saw as an attempt to push Turkey forward at a time when France was beyond helping even herself. The Ambassador also admits confessing to Sir Knatchbull Hugessen on the way to their interview with Saraçoğlu to ask him to fulfil Turkey's treaty obligations: 'To remind Turkey of a promise given was one thing, but to invite her to rally to our cause on the very day of the evacuation of Paris was another . . . "I feel something of an assassin" I told my colleague during our trip . . .'[46]

There was also a feeling in the Assembly that if it was not too late, a new opening should be looked for in the direction of Germany. Turkey, it was said, should make use of her unique strategic position in this new European balance. Kâzım Karabekir maintained the need for a Turkish-German agreement in the face of a mutual Russian danger. He said this did not mean the scrapping of the Anglo-Turkish alliance but a realistic appreciation of what other possibilities existed which could combine with it to safeguard Turkey.[47]

There was also a feeling amongst some of Turkey's leaders that it was not such a bad thing if Britain were weakened. Barutçu quotes Rauf Orbay as saying that he hoped that the Allied forces in Belgium would be made prisoner; Orbay went on to say: 'The British will not be beaten. There is no doubt that an Empire capable of raising 45 million soldiers will gain the final victory. But the more they are weakened beforehand the better it is for us. If they win an outright victory, we also are in trouble.'[48]

The Turks saw the French defeat as the destruction of the delicate power balance in the Mediterranean. They were particularly worried about the French fleet, as if this were to go over to the Axis Turkey would be gravely threatened from the sea. Britain's position was considered so precarious that on 5 June the British Ambassador reported that Churchill's speech in which he sought to underline British determination to resist ('we will fight them on the beaches . . .') had a very bad effect on Saraçoğlu.[49] When the British and the French Ambassadors emphasised to Saraçoğlu on 11 June the good effect a Turkish declaration of war would have in the Balkans, the Minister retorted that a French victory would have an even better effect.[50]

When the British suggested that Turkey insert 'for the present' into the wording of their statement of non-belligerency, the Minister for Foreign Affairs told Hugessen on 18 June that the British wording had been approved and the declaration was about to be made when news was received of Pétain's armistice request. The declaration had been postponed as a result.[51] On 19 June Hugessen reported that the Greek Ambassador had told him that there was very strong feeling in the Turkish government against the French for having tried to bring Turkey into the war at a time when they must have known that they themselves could not go on. The Greek Ambassador assured him that the Turks felt they had chosen the wisest course in the general interest.[52]

Although Hugessen reported on 25 June that there was no change in the Turkish attitude, he admitted that the two questions being asked continually were: (a) What will happen to the French fleet? (b) Is the aircraft strength in the United Kingdom up to dealing with the expected attacks? Saraçoğlu had told him that if the French fleet was able to surrender to the Axis, 'it would be the greatest mistake in history'.[53] The British hold on Turkey during this time seemed tenuous even to the British themselves. A Foreign Office minute dated 1 July 1940 and written by Sir O. Sargent underlined the

enormous importance the Turks attach to this issue [French navy]. It is, in fact, abundantly clear that on the answer to the question whether or not we are to lose the French fleet depends our ability henceforward to hold the Turks. If we lose the French fleet, we may be able to argue that it was not our fault. But this will not cut much ice with the Turks . . . The Turks may well take the loss as finally disposing of our sea power in the Mediterranean, and as depriving us of any value as an ally. It might even afford them the occasion to make terms with the Germans . . .[54]

The Foreign Office were also worried that Turkey would decide that Britain could no longer protect her against the Soviets and thus turn to Germany (there had in fact been stirrings in this direction, as we have seen). Sargent expressed his concern in these terms: 'The seriousness of such a *volte-face* on the part of Turkey need not be stressed, and it is for this reason that we ought I am sure to do our utmost to hold Turkey where she is . . .' He wondered:

what means we have of convincing Turkey that it is in her own interest to continue to collaborate with us? . . . The first thing is clearly to convince her that if she refuses to compound with Germany and Italy she is safe from being attacked by sea . . . It all depends, therefore on whether we can assure her that the Germans and Italians will not be able to use the French fleet to establish a complete preponderance in the E. Med.[55]

All this evidence points to the fact that securing Turkey's loyalty was a major factor in the British decision to destroy the French fleet. The Turks heartily agreed with this action, according to Hugessen's 18 July report: 'Turkish civilian opinion highly approving of forceful action easily interpreted by their mentality.' Although the Ambassador reported that the press had been 'fearfully understanding of our dilemma, and favourable . . .', there were indications that the Turks saw these latest developments as only confirming their convictions that when it came to questions of national survival, friendship came a very poor second.[56]

Selim Sebit wrote in *Tasvir* that the French–English friendship was always thought to be one of the strongest ever. Now, he said, the old friends had become deadly enemies. The British destroyed the French fleet and the French bombed Gibraltar. He stated that this enmity between two powers who had formerly been good friends was terrifying:

Now we have begun to examine our closest friends with suspicion – after all one is never sure, and cast complying regards at our enemies, if we have any, – after all, one never knows . . . While there are such poignant examples before our eyes, it has become a matter of necessity for us to observe caution in our actions, and adopt a very prudent attitude.[57]

Developments, therefore, seemed to justify the Turkish leaders' political cynicism, and the poet M. P. Yahya Kemal voiced their feelings with a traditional verse: 'As soon as are seen the beginnings of collapse and decay, the friends will race the enemies to the plunder . . .'[58]

ITALY COMES INTO THE WAR

On 10 June 1940, Italy declared war on the Allies. This rendered operational Turkey's obligations under Clause 1 of the second article of the treaty with Britain.[59] But the Turks had decided well in advance that they would try by all means at their disposal to stay out before admitting any obligations.

The view is frequently put forward by a number of students of this period, that the Allies, Britain in particular, did not want Turkey to come in at this time as it would bring the war to the Balkans and endanger the Middle East.[60] But a more realistic interpretation is that Britain could not do much about Turkish entry. Faced with Turkish determination to uphold their interests, as they saw them, coupled with their own precarious position, the British *had* to accept Turkey's terms as putting more pressure on her might have been counter-productive and pushed her towards Germany. We have seen above how tenuous the British felt their hold on Turkey had become. In this position the British had to give the best possible interpretation to Turkey's attitude, and reluctantly they put about the story that they agreed with the Turks. There were, however, undeniable elements of logic in the Turkish position and as events progressed the British actually became convinced by the Turkish arguments and, rather ignominiously had to recant their previous position.

Although there were some in the Assembly who felt that Italy's entry gave rise to an immediate and automatic state of war between Italy and Turkey, the majority favoured caution and advocated finding a way to stay out. There were fears that the Soviets would take advantage of the situation and Saraçoğlu spoke of a Soviet build-up of air power in the Crimea. 'We had to consider conditions, the position of our allies and ultimately the defence of our nation. There was no question of being swept into adventures for the interests of others as in the First World War.'[61]

Turkey decided to apply Protocol 2 of the treaty which absolved her of any action which might lead to war with the Soviet Union. This was considered a blatant 'pretext' by the British who were gravely disappointed by the Turkish action. When Saraçoğlu told Hugessen about the government's decision he greatly emphasised the Soviet danger which the Ambassador attempted to play down. Saraçoğlu said that during the interview between the Turkish Ambassador in Moscow and Molotov regarding this issue, Molotov's manner had been 'most menacing' but admitted that there had been no official Soviet *démarche*. Hugessen and Massigli kept the pressure on Saraçoğlu:

We repeated that we could not believe in the seriousness of the Russian danger, and it seemed clear that Russia and Germany had hit on Protocol 2 as a convenient means of paralysing Turkey. We were convinced that the Turkish Government had allowed themselves to be bluffed . . . In general we made no attempt to minimise the deplorable effect which the decision would create in Allied countries and we expressed the greatest possible disappointment with the Turkish reply.[62]

Hugessen said Turkey's attitude to the Soviets was based almost entirely on practical considerations and that as long as the Allies were unable to furnish direct assistance Turkey would not run 'the supposed risk'. The Ambassador reported on 14 June that it was 'impossible to resist the impression that the Turkish application of Protocol 2 is a pretext'.[63] He attributed the Turkish attitude to the unfavourable military situation. G. L. Clutton of the Foreign Office remarked in one of Hugessen's telegrams on 16 June: 'The evidence in favour of the conviction that Turkish invocation of Protocol 2 is merely a pretext is very strong.'[64] The paper went on to say that the British had been informed that when the Turkish Ambassador had told Molotov of Turkey's intention to mobilise if Italy came into the war, Molotov had said something like 'do what you like'. Saraçoğlu's version of this was that Molotov had said: 'Turkey could choose which country she wanted to be wiped out by.'[65]

On 14 June Hugessen saw İnönü. İnönü told him that it would be no good to provoke the Soviets now as they could in the course of time come around to the Allies' side. Hugessen stressed the bad effect the Turkish move would have on the attitude of the Balkan states. İnönü countered that it would have quite the opposite effect, 'any Turkish involvement now would encourage the Balkan states to pull away from her. Whereas if Turkey remained as at present and continued to build up strength, Balkan countries would be drawn towards her.'[66] On 15 June Halifax instructed Hugessen to stress with the Turks that the present decision of the Turkish government could only have the most deplorable effect on the Allied governments. He was told to remind the Turkish government of the Allied conviction that it was necessary to continue to struggle to ultimate victory: 'If Turkey falters now she may well have cause later to regret her decision.'[67]

There never was, therefore, any question of the British approving of Turkey's decision to stay out. When Saraçoğlu told the British of his intention to make a declaration about Turkish non-belligerency, the British suggested the Turks put 'for the present' in the wording. Also when Saraçoğlu asked the Allied Ambassadors if he could say in the Assembly that Turkey had taken this step with the approval of the Allies, their reply was categorically negative.[68] The French Ambassador in London wrote on 25 May that if Italy attacked Greece and the Allies had to go to her aid Turkey should be asked to concert all measures with the Allies, but 'this would not necessarily mean a declaration of war', it could be in the form of military and naval facilities.[69] When Hugessen inquired what was meant by the above the Foreign Office told him in instructions dated 2 June:

The point is that if the Allies implement their guarantees to Greece as a result of an Italian attack on Greece a state of war will exist between the Allies and Italy, and it is essential that in these circumstances a state of war should also exist between Italy and Turkey. Turkey should adopt the same attitude as the Allies with regard to any formal declaration to be made . . .[70]

On 26 June Turkey issued her declaration of non-belligerency:

The Government of the Turkish Republic has considered the situation which has arisen from Italy's entry into the war and have decided on the application of Protocol 2 . . . Turkey will preserve her present attitude of non-belligerency for the security and defence of our country. While continuing on the one side military preparations, we also have to remain more vigilant than ever. We hope by this position of watchfulness and by avoiding any provocation, we shall preserve the maintenance of peace for our country and for those who are around us.[71]

R. Bowker of the Foreign Office, Southern Department, commented on 28 June that the declaration was 'unsatisfactory on all points'.[72] G. L. Clutton outlined its defects from a British point of view: (a) omission of any reference to an agreement with Britain; (b) statement of Turkish military preparation falling far short of notification of mobilisations; (c) no hint that non-belligerency was only provisional. 'The declaration, in short, gives the impression of a move towards strict neutrality.'[73] Von Papen in fact reported to his Ministry that, 'the game has been won'.[74] The British, even in this situation, made an attempt to salvage what they could out of Turkey and suggested to Hugessen on 21 June that he inquire whether they would 'turn a blind eye' to their territorial waters being used to interrupt enemy shipping.[75] The Ambassador replied on the next day however, that this was highly unlikely: 'I think they are mainly guided by a desire to avoid anything likely to get them into difficulties.'[76] Turkey had in fact shifted into a much stricter neutrality than she was to observe in 1943, for instance, when she allowed the British to supply their campaign in the Aegean islands from Turkish soil, gave haven to escaping troops, and actually helped evacuate them. On 1 November 1940 İnönü declared that Turkey's position as 'out of the war' precluded any use of her sea or air space by any of the belligerents.[77]

There was in fact a feeling in some Turkish quarters that any declaration at all was redundant:

The situation of the Allied front was clear. France had collapsed. Britain had gone into this war unprepared. According to Marshal Pétain Britain would not last long. In this situation, to make a declaration implying commitment to the alliance would be a grave mistake . . . As far as I was concerned the alliance was annulled *de facto*. It was not necessary to explain this.[78]

Barutçu claims that even Saraçoğlu admitted the declaration was 'politically weak' though grounded on legality.[79] Therefore, although Turkish foreign policy was applied with seeming unanimity to the outside eye, there were those who disagreed with the government and felt an even stricter neutrality was called for. Similarly there were those like Recep Peker and Şevket İnce who considered Turkey automatically at war. But the majority backed İnönü in his cautious policy, although they may have believed that a different emphasis would have been preferable in parts of their foreign policy.[80]

Therefore the British who on 11 June had instructed their Ambassador to tell the Turks to take immediate action against Italy, and 'not delay awaiting any hostile act', as there was 'no excuse for further delay', now realised that Turkey would not be moved by anything except her own interest.[81] Indeed, it had become doubtful whether she still considered herself bound to Britain. The British decided to cut their losses and make what they could out of the situation: 'The Foreign Secretary could see no remedy for this unfortunate situation.'[82]

Halifax told the Cabinet on 15 June that in discussion with the Prime Minister on the previous evening: 'It had been agreed that the best plan was to make the best of a bad job. The Turks were to be informed that Britain was not happy with them and were to have pointed out to them the deplorable effect of their action on world opinion.'[83] In a Foreign Office minute, R. Bowker commented on 19 June:

Her [Turkey's] use of Protocol 2 is a pretext, the real reason for her unwillingness being the very unfavourable development of the war for the Allies in France. We have decided to put the best face on Turkey's attitude. Nevertheless if the occasion arises for Turkey to appeal to us to carry out our obligations under the treaty we shall no doubt have at least a moral justification for determining our action in accordance with the circumstances of the moment.[84]

The British felt so strongly about their failure in Turkey that they were even prepared to look upon Turkish intransigence as an excuse absolving them of their obligations to Turkey.

The Turkish press at this time tried very hard to impress upon the Allies that Turkey was still loyal and was in fact acting in their interests. On 17 June 1940 Sadak outlined the Turkish predicament in *Akşam* by stating that although Turkey was still loyal to the treaty with Britain, 'Unfortunately our geographical position is unlike any of the great democracies . . .' Sadak stressed that Turkey found herself unable to help her ally although if she could, 'no man would hesitate to bear the difficulties'. He went on, 'But for Turkey to leave her position outside the war in the present unsure world conditions would only bring the war to the Mediterranean, which is as yet peaceful. This would only increase the burden on the Allies by enabling war to spread to the Balkans, the Middle East and beyond.'[85] The article voiced the recurring argument which the Turks were to use on the British; that Turkey should save her strength. Saraçoğlu told the British Ambassador on 6 September, 'But surely, you do not want to waste Turkey?'[86]

It is interesting to compare the article above with an article written by the same man on 21 October 1939 concerning Turkish obligations to enter the war if Romania or Greece were attacked. Sadak emphasised at the time that Romania and Greece as 'Balkan Allies', were of vital interest to Turkey:

In this situation when England and France are fighting for the security of the Balkans and consequently of Turkey, to help them will be an act dictated by our vital interests. Nor is it necessary for war to be actually taking place in the Mediterranean. Even in a war to be fought in Europe that by one way or another spreads to the Mediterranean there is a mutual obligation to assist.[87]

Only eight months after this article was written France collapsed and precisely this situation occurred. Turkish decision-makers thus used two absolutely contradictory situations to further a consistent aim. In October 1939, they felt in danger and by stressing the obligation to help Britain and France (hence the wide interpretation of the Mediterranean clause in the Sadak article) insured themselves with them. In June 1940, the Allies were in danger yet the Turks managed to avoid any commitment, squirmed out of the same Mediterranean clause, justified their actions by the same treaty (Protocol 2), and emphasised that by staying out they were avoiding placing additional burdens on the Allies. In two contradictory situations the result was the same, Turkey was preserved.

Leading Turkish journalists underlined that although Turkey was outside the war she was not neutral and was determined to fight if attacked. Again, Sadak proclaimed in *Akşam*, 'Neither neutrality nor fear has ever saved any nation.' He said the countries which had been invaded had only wanted peace, but had made too many concessions in order to have it: 'The first policy to go bankrupt in this war was neutrality...'[88] Y. Nadi of *Cumhuriyet* mentioned that Turkey had, 'no designs on the territory or rights of any country', but that she would, 'do her duty to the end' if the need arose.[89] F. R. Atay in the official *Ulus* stressed that the Turkish homeland abounded with natural defences. He also made it clear that, 'We have frequently repeated that we are not after any adventures. But no one can guarantee that adventure will not one day come after us . . .'[90]

Despite such strong official language Turkey took great care to pursue a balanced policy at this time. On 12 June a German–Turkish trade agreement was decided upon. The fact that this agreement was reached so soon after Italy's entry into the war was interpreted by Papen as a demonstration of Turkey's desire to continue to maintain relations with the Axis.[91] The agreement, however, excluded chrome and did not have much long-term significance (it was formally signed on 25 July).[92] The Axis themselves seemed to have been taken aback by the extent of Turkey's reserve. The Italians had been expecting at least a rupture of relations and had even sent their families home.[93]

Even though the British had been gravely disappointed by the Turkish decision to announce non-belligerency, events showed the Turkish arguments to be correct. As the full extent of the damage done by the collapse of France became known, and Britain's position in the Middle East and India became threatened, Turkey's value as a friendly neutral at the crossroads was more than appreciated. But the British also saw that Turkey's position was precarious. On 17 July Major General Cornwall-Evans estimated that the Germans could conquer Turkey and reach the Iraqi border in sixteen weeks. Once the Germans were across the Straits, the Turks he said, could offer little resistance.[94] This contrasts markedly with the British attitude in the days before the conclusion of the treaty when they thought Turkey could 'hold out indefinitely' on the Straits.[95] He also estimated that if Turkey were threatened by Germany and Russia at the same time she would not offer any resistance. R. Bowker commented on Cornwall-Evans' information, 'We conclude from it that the Germans would not have any difficulty in forcing their way through Turkey.'[96]

The British were therefore forced to recant, and now adopted the position that the Turkish treaty had negative value in as much as it denied Turkey to the Germans. The Foreign Office now stated that they 'had hardly expected Turkey to do otherwise' when she declared non-belligerency and 'fully recognized the difficulties in which she found herself'. The treaty was valuable as a potential rather than actual asset. It was feared that any other attitude would force Turkey 'to throw herself into the arms of Germany'.[97] We have seen above that the British *had* expected Turkey 'to do otherwise'.[98] Hugessen somewhat grudgingly admitted on 21 August that, 'Turkey at this stage would prove more of a liability than an asset.'[99] The War

Cabinet Chiefs of Staff Committee agreed that to force Turkey would be counter-productive and 'might jeopardise Turkey's own security and through Turkey our whole position in the Middle East'.[100]

ATTACK ON GREECE

When Italy attacked Greece on 28 October, this brought into force Article 3 of the Anglo-Turkish treaty. It also rendered more blatant the contradiction between the previous British position and the latter-day one. It will be recalled that on 25 May the British had declared that if they had to implement their guarantee to Greece as the result of an Italian attack, 'it is essential that a state of war should also exist between Italy and Turkey'.[101] Yet on 9 September the Foreign Office were of the opinion 'that no great advantage would accrue to us from a Turkish declaration of war against Italy, should the latter attack Greece'.[102] The run of events had enabled the Turks to make such a convincing argument that the British were fully pre-pared, when Greece was actually attacked, to ignore Article 3 of the treaty.

It must be noted that at this stage in the war Turkey's potential was assessed in terms of manpower. As a reserve or actually fighting, the British saw Turkey primarily as a provider of troops and secondarily, a provider of bases. This situation would last until it was reversed in late 1943. In September 1941 Churchill was to write to Stalin: 'In the south the great prize is Turkey, if Turkey can be gained another powerful army will be available.'[103]

A Foreign Office telegram sent to Hugessen in Ankara and Palairet in Athens on 22 May suggested that the Turks might be prepared 'to carry out the duty of protecting Greece' as they 'had a large number of troops and were not directly threatened'. The telegram went on: 'Such a duty, if suggested to them by their allies under the Treaty of Mutual Assistance might also appeal to their vanity.'[104]

Although Hugessen never made this suggestion, the fact that the Foreign Office felt Turkey might be swayed by 'vanity', amply il-lustrated how much they misjudged the situation. On 28 May the Foreign Office boldly instructed Hugessen in Ankara that, in the case of a direct Italian attack on Greece or the Allies, Turkey 'should declare war on Italy and occupy the Dodecanese'. On 31 May the British Ambassador Sir R. Campbell, reported from Paris that the French were anxious for Turkey to 'show Italy danger in her rear' by taking military measures in conjunction with her Balkan Allies.[105] It was hardly surprising for the French to be so out of touch with the realities of the situation, considering they disastrously underestimated the danger to their own 'rear'. Even if the Balkan Allies had not been too worried about even angering Italy, let alone taking military measures, it is doubtful whether Turkey would even have asked them at this stage, to adopt a more forward policy.

On 18 August Hugessen was instructed to draw the attention of the Turkish government to the threatening attitude of Italy towards Greece. He was asked to suggest mutual consultation to the Turks and was given discretion as to whether he was to invoke specific treaty obligations or just mention the treaty in general terms only. He was also instructed to inquire 'in as discreet a manner possible' whether the Turks would give any 'effective cooperation' if Britain had to implement her guarantee.[106] When Hugessen saw Saraçoğlu on 20 August the latter said he could make no categorical statements beforehand and added that he did not want to put any further strain on Soviet–Turkish relations. 'My impression is that the Minister of Foreign Affairs was leaving door wide open for eventually avoiding anything beyond consultation.'[107] The British, although they had decided to tread lightly, had not completely given up on Turkey. Hugessen wrote to the Foreign Office on 21 August that the Germans might make political capital out of a second default by Turkey of her treaty obligations if she did not help Greece. Hugessen reported that Turkey, 'will certainly not send troops to Greece'.[108] It is worth noting here that the question asked on 28 May about whether Turkey would send some of her large number of troops to Greece, was finally answered.

In their meeting of 23 August the Chiefs of Staff Committee stressed that the failure to support Greece and a consequent Greek capitulation would have a very bad influence on British credibility in Turkey. Also: 'The Committee were informed that there was a danger of Turkey endeavouring to find a way out of her treaty obligations if Greece was attacked.'[109]

The impression derived from the above is that the British were still sounding Turkey as to any move they might induce her to make. On 6 September Hugessen asked Saraçoğlu what he felt about Romania and Greece. The Ambassador got the impression that Turkey, although she was watching both situations closely, still maintained the same reserve. 'I think that they have taken no decision beyond one to lie low as long as possible and hope for the best.'[110] The Ambassador again mentioned the disastrous effect a Greek collapse in the face of an attack from Italy would have on Turkey if she allowed this to happen.

The British Ambassador in Athens, Sir M. Palairet felt very strongly about the Turkish attitude. On 23 August he wrote:

If we cannot prevent Turkey from refusing to enter the war if Greece is attacked are we ever likely to be in a position to get her to play her part? If Turkey would be a liability as argued by Hugessen then, why were we at such pains and expense to obtain Turkey's alliance? . . . and will anyone be taken in by Turkey making Russia a good excuse for evasion in this case?[111]

On 30 August Palairet lamented that if Turkey, 'is always allowed to repudiate her engagements on grounds of Russian danger, I can see no use in alliance'. He called the Turkish policy 'pusillanimous' and 'evasive'.[112]

On 2 September Palairet reported that the Greeks, although hopeful of Turkish help, were discouraged by the Turks' evasive attitude. Koliopoulos points out that the British government made a reluctant effort to get Turkey to promise to help Greece in the event of an Italian attack. The Turks, he says, refused to make such a commitment, and only promised to make a statement in the National Assembly to the effect that Greece's fate was of 'vital' interest to Turkey.[113] A. Cadogan felt on 4 September that: 'We have decided two things, not to nag them [Turks], but at the same time to let them understand which way our mind is working.'[114]

Palairet's repeated appeals prompted Halifax to cable him on 3 September that it was necessary, 'to exercise caution in urging Turkey to go any further than she is prepared to go . . .'[115] However, on 11 September the Foreign Office instructed Hugessen to point out to the Turks that any weakness Turkey showed in regard to an Italian attack on Greece would be merely likely to encourage Stalin and Hitler to deal with Turkey in a like manner.[116] It would seem that although direct pressure was not being applied at this juncture the Foreign Office still used any opening to keep Turkey up to the mark.

On 7 October German troops began to enter Romania. This rendered completely operational Article 3 of the treaty whereby Turkey was obligated to give 'all aid and assistance in her power' if Britain had to implement her guarantee to Greece and Romania. Yet Hugessen wired London on 12 October that it would not be wise to ask Turkey to implement Article 3, as Turkey would ask for concrete support and general statements of goodwill would not sway her. The

British, aware of their weakness, had decided that the best they could do was aim at 'maintaining Turkey as a benevolent neutral rather than an unwilling belligerent'.[117]

Although the official Turkish government position was one of caution, the Turkish press, while echoing this line to some extent, were allowed to be more outspoken. This is one instance where a government-directed press let some of the government's true feeling show, under the mantle of freedom of the press. Faik Fenik wrote in *Ulus* that now there were German and Italian troops in Romania: 'In this way the Axis have set about creating the New Order in Europe according to the blueprint in the Tripartite Pact. They have started in Romania.'[118] F. R. Atay wrote in *Ulus*: 'German–Rumanian co-operation has finally led to the establishment of German control on the whole of the Danube basin down to the Black Sea coast. Today's Romania is nothing but a piece of living-space unable to decide her own destiny, and under political, economic and military control.'[119] In relation to the effect of this situation on Nazi–Soviet relations, A. Ş. Esmer wrote in *Ulus*: 'Now the Soviet lands from north to south are neighbouring lands under German occupation. If the Russians take one step anywhere at all they are bound to tread on Germany's toes.'[120] This was an obvious warning to Moscow of the dangers it was now facing.

Turkey was also an important factor in Italian calculations. On 17 October Ciano estimated the time to be ripe for a move against Greece even though Badoglio was against it because, 'Greece is isolated. Turkey will not move . . .'[121] Ciano also agreed with Mussolini that 'If we leave the Greeks too much time to reflect and to breathe, the English will come, and perhaps the Turks and the situation will become drawn out and difficult.' Ciano also informed the Bulgarians of his intentions implying that they should act, but King Boris was reluctant: 'Above all he fears the Turks.'[122]

The Bulgarians saw the Turkish threat as very real, and in their negotiations with the Germans constantly returned to the theme of 'danger of intervention by third parties' and '37 Turkish divisions in Thrace'. An exasperated Hitler told Foreign Minister Draganov on 23 November 1940 that the Turks would not move as they knew this would mean 'Constantinople would share the fate of Birmingham and Coventry . . .'[123] When Italy did attack Greece on 28 October the Turks informed Bulgaria that if she attacked Greece Turkey would declare war. Hugessen reported on 28 October that Saraçoğlu had informed the Greek Ambassador in Ankara that Greece could count on Turkey absolutely in the event of a Bulgarian attack. The Greek Ambassador's view was that if Turkey were to hold Thrace against Bulgaria, 'this is all that Greece requires or could expect'.[124] The Turks rightly calculated that by doing this they would pin down the Bulgarians, enabling Greece to concentrate on containing the Italian attack from Albania. 'The Turks did not share the prevalent opinion that Greek resistance was hopeless . . . Without a doubt Turkish policy contributed substantially to the success of the Greeks.'[125] Ahmet Ş. Esmer declared in *Ulus* on 30 October: 'Italy's attack on Greece did not come as a surprise after years of bullying. The Italians have in any case found that Greece is a much tougher adversary than they suspected. Italy will see that a country rising, united, to the defence of its independence, honour and integrity is capable of performing miracles.'[126]

In keeping with their belief that it was always necessary to make clear that Turkey would fight if she were attacked, the Turks deprived Italy of an ally, without actively involving themselves. The press directed the attack on Italy and supported Greece. F. R. Atay quoted Mussolini's assurances that he had no aggressive intentions against any country bordering Italy or her Empire. He emphasised that Greece had always pursued a friendly policy towards Italy: 'Those who invented a thousand reasons and excuses to call a sea bordered by many independent countries "our sea", should not judge as excessive the claim of a free people to call the land of their fathers "our land".'[127] Y. Nadi of *Cumhuriyet* wrote that Italy had only bound Greece closer to Britain, 'now Britain is in a position to make use of all the Greek territory and coastline to inflict heavy losses on Italy'.[128]

Churchill felt that help for Greece was crucial as it was likely to have an important effect on Turkish opinion. He cabled Wavell, Commander in Chief Middle East in Cairo on 26 November:

It might be that 'Compass' (Operation of aid to Greece), would in itself determine action of Yugoslavia and Turkey, and anyhow in event of success, we should be able to give Turkey far greater assurance of early support than it has been in our power to do so far. One may indeed see the possibility of centre of gravity in Middle East shifting suddenly from Egypt to the Balkans and from Cairo to Constantinople.[129]

But Wavell and the British General Staff did not see it that way, and in view of their impending offensive against Graziani were loath to part with troops or aircraft.[130] The military, unlike the Foreign Office, although admitting Turkish military weakness, felt an immediate Turkish entry into the war was necessary. This way, Greece could be reinforced without weakening Egypt. A Chiefs of Staff memorandum of 17 November stated: 'The balance of advantage is in favour of doing all that we can to bring Turkey in as a belligerent at once. Further we believe that the effect of Turkey's entry into the war at this stage following the recent successes against the Italian armed forces by both ourselves and the Greeks might have a decisive effect on Italian morale.'[131] The military felt that if Turkey were not obliged to commit herself openly, 'She might stall and find reasons for not standing by the Alliance at a later stage.'[132]

The Foreign Office however, who had come around to the Turkish point of view, now disagreed with the military. They had come to appreciate that 'Turkey will decide whether or not to [come in] simply on her own estimate of her own interests, and nothing we can say can affect this decision . . .'[133] Halifax told the Military Chiefs in the War Cabinet on 22 November that increased pressure on Turkey 'would only bring a demand for increased munitions which Britain was hard put to meet'.[134]

In the end it would seem that the Foreign Office view prevailed on Churchill also who came to realise that Turkey could not be pushed. It would also seem that he had come to appreciate the military difficulties involved in helping Greece. When Palairet sent one of his many urgent appeals for help on 30 October asking for 'immediate and visible support' such as RAF units flying low over Athens, the Prime Minister replied on 31 October that it was 'idle to ask for visible signs of support . . .' and instructed his Ambassador in Athens in strong terms that he 'should not encourage vain hopes when forces to execute them do not exist . . .'

Halifax added his own instructions: 'No pledges have been made except that we will do our best . . . Greeks should not be allowed to forget that our guarantee was given in conjunction with France and our whole position in the Middle East has been terribly injured by the French desertion.'[135] J. Koliopoulos contends that at this stage, 'Essentially the British considered Greece a lost cause . . .'[136] The Turks were confirmed in their conviction that prudence was the best policy by the symbolic nature of the support given to Greece. Although some Australian and New Zealand troops were hastily scraped together and the few RAF units sent certainly did help to stem the Italian advance, Britain always gave priority to Egypt and her vital communications with India.

Turkey was valuable for Britain precisely because of her great strategic importance along these communications. The British realised that Turkey would not allow herself to be pushed and did not want to risk alienating her by doing so. The Foreign Office summed up the position for Palairet:

Nothing we can do will persuade her [Turkey] to take up arms. Not much can be spared for Greece because of the needs of the British in Egypt. Meanwhile Turkey is the keystone of our policy in the Middle East and is of far greater relative importance than Greece. Greece can be lost and the war in the Middle East still won. To lose Turkey would gravely imperil the whole of our position in the Middle East . . .[137]

Although Turkey had won a temporary respite from British pressure there was little doubt that Britain still wanted to bring her into the war. Churchill suggested the following instructions to Hugessen on 26 November: 'We do not wish to leave you in any doubt of what our opinion and your instructions are. We want Turkey to come into the war as soon as possible. We are not pressing her to take any special steps to help the Greeks.' He underlined however, that if Germany moved through Bulgaria, with or without Bulgarian co-operation, 'it is vital Turkey should fight there and then. If she does not she will find herself absolutely alone . . .'[138]

Evidence which has since come to light vindicates the Turks in their cautious policy. Hitler's Chief of Staff Halder wrote in his diary on 26 October 1940: 'If anything conclusive is to be achieved, Bulgaria and Turkey have to be subdued, if necessary by force, especially in the case of the latter, to leave the way open through the Bosphorus to Syria.'[139] On 24 November he wrote, 'If Turkey does not keep quiet in the event of an attack against Greece, she must be thrown out of Europe.'[140]

As early as June 1940 an influential lobby had evolved in Hitler's camp including General Jodl of the OKW and Commander in Chief of the German Navy, Grand Admiral Raeder, which advocated an enlargement of the war on the periphery rather than a direct attack on Britain. They maintained that the first priority had to be the Eastern Mediterranean. Hitler himself seems to have endorsed a contingency plan at the beginning of November involving an invasion of Turkey as part of this 'peripheral strategy'.[141] On 4 November 1940 Hitler had decided that fighters and fighter-bombers should be sent to Romania in preparation for 'Marita' (operation against Greece). He had given orders that Bulgaria should be supported against Turkey with ten divisions.[142] Meanwhile, the Chiefs of Staff in London were deciding that Germany might well not want to 'provoke Turkey' and not move against her, and advocated her immediate entry even though they admitted she was open to 'practically unopposed air attack'.[143]

Hitler, however, was becoming increasingly preoccupied with the Soviet Union, particularly after his meeting with Molotov in November. Both Hitler and his Staff felt that operations against the Soviets or Turkey were mutually exclusive. Halder wrote in his diary on 24 November: 'We have to see clearly that the possibilities against Russia disappear if we decide for Turkey.' Hitler told him 'We can get at the Straits only after Russia has been beaten.' Halder concluded, 'we have come to the considered decision to avoid conflict with Turkey at all possible cost'. Most sources agree that operation 'Barbarossa' and an invasion of Turkey were mutually exclusive projects. Van Creveld states that the Germans were ready enough to 'sell' Turkey to the Soviets but during the talks with Molotov it became clear that Russia would not support German plans in south east Europe.[144] The Turks could hardly have failed to sense which way the wind was blowing, as the Soviets seemed particularly keen on *rapprochement* with them as the German menace loomed nearer, and von Papen returned from Berlin on 19 November to tell representatives of the Turkish press that 'it was of the utmost importance to know what Turkey's attitude would be if Russia decided to put into practice her plans in the Straits and the Persian Gulf'.[145]

As she found herself surrounded by Axis forces, Turkey realised that she stood alone. Bulgaria joined the Axis in March. Yugoslavia and Greece were overrun by the Germans in April, bringing Germany to Turkey's western borders. In the east Syria was held by Vichy and a pro-German revolt flared up in Iraq. The only non-Axis frontiers were with the Soviet Union and Iran, the former at best a dubious comfort, the latter the scene of an Anglo-Soviet invasion of seemingly ominous portent. Britain, the ally Turkey had set so much store by, was at bay. Hugessen wrote to London on 8 January 1941, 'The Turks' faith in ourselves and France, particularly France, was considerably shattered by our asking them to come into the war at once, when they *knew* France was on the edge of the Abyss.'[1] But the British were far from giving up on Turkey. Although Howard claims, 'it now seems clear that in the last analysis neither the United States, nor the United Kingdom, nor even the Soviet Union, actually desired Turkish entry into the shooting war or had any well developed plans therefore', most of the evidence contradicts this.[2] Indeed, Churchill considered Turkey primarily as a source of manpower. Trumbull Higgins describes Turkey in 1941 as 'a neutral state whose large and poorly equipped army would continue to attract Winston Churchill's encouraging smiles and ultimately futile favours for three full years to come'.[3]

On the other hand the Germans saw Turkey as a country that first had to be neutralised, and then gradually brought over to their side by conclusive success in the Russian campaign. Von Papen reported on 13 May 1941 that having broached the subject of a Turkish–German Treaty to Saraçoğlu, the conversation left him with the impression that 'we can definitely and also very quickly find a treaty instrument with Turkey preparing the transition of Turkey to our camp'.[4]

117

THE GREEK CAMPAIGN

Although Turkey had avoided being pressed into fighting the Italians in Greece, the signs of an impending German attack made Turkish intervention seem necessary for the British. Greek victories had also raised their hopes of successful resistance. Now Churchill was 'itching to mobilise the armies of Turkey and Yugoslavia, and with the aid of these small allies to open a new front in southeastern Europe . . . '[5] For Churchill, Turkey was 'as always the pivot of our Balkan strategy'.[6]

Therefore the British urged the Turks to take a strong stance towards German 'infiltration' of Bulgaria in preparation for an attack on Greece. By 'infiltration' the British meant the large numbers of German military personnel coming into Bulgaria in the guise of civilian technicians or tourists. By the end of January 1941 the British estimated that 4,000 *Luftwaffe* personnel were in Bulgaria.[7] On 19 January Hugessen asked Saraçoğlu if Turkey would consider a German attack on Greece through Bulgaria a *casus belli* for Turkey to take action. The Minister 'said *yes* quite definitely'.[8]

The British made an effort 'to make the Turks realize their danger'. As the *Luftwaffe* moved into Bulgaria, on 29 January Churchill wrote a personal letter to İnönü suggesting that Turkey immediately receive three fighter and seven bomber squadrons of the RAF. But İnönü answered that he would not allow the 'infiltration' of British units or make airfields available for their aircraft as this would mean the entry of Turkey into the war.[9] 'Sensibly the Ankara Government refused the British offers of a few RAF Squadrons from the already overstrained Middle East Command on the grounds that these units were too small to resist a German assault but were large enough to provoke such an attack.'[10] İnönü's private reaction was: 'I am not Enver Paşa, they cannot drag me into a war.'[11] Instead, Turkey signed a Non-Aggression Pact with Bulgaria on 17 February.

On his way to Turkey in February Eden met with the Chiefs of Staff in Cairo. Although Wavell felt that it was desirable for Yugoslavia and Turkey to form a 'common front' to defend Salonika he had serious doubts about Turkey's military capacity.

When Eden and Dill arrived in Turkey on 26 February, although superficially all was pomp and agreement, and the press spoke of 'honoured British guests', the Turks exercised a strong reserve which provoked Eden's suspicion. He referred to Menemencioğlu as a 'natural negative' and talked of the 'formidable team' of İnönü, Menemencioğlu and Saraçoğlu facing himself, Dill and Hugessen.[12] The foundation for the mutual distrust which was to pervade dealings between Eden and Menemencioğlu was laid during this visit. The press dealt cautiously with the talks themselves. F. R. Atay in the official *Ulus* stressed the defensive and non-provocatory nature of the Anglo-Turkish Treaty; 'this alliance was not concluded with aggressive intentions towards anyone and does not stem from any calculated profit motive . . . '[13]

Although the Turks agreed that all immediately available military help should go to Greece, all Eden could get out of them was a promise that they would fight if attacked and that they were ready to concert common action with Yugoslavia. 'No doubt the Turks were unimpressed by the force the British proposed to send [to Greece], much as they praised the decision in principle.'[14]

On 14 March Hugessen summed up the outcome of the visit and the Turkish attitude. He felt sure of Turkey's loyalty although he felt the Turks had 'been confirmed in their policy of extreme caution and hoped to get through without ever having to go to war . . . '[15] Hugessen recommended that Turkey's present weak attitude be overlooked and she be strengthened 'for an active policy as soon as possible'. The Foreign Office agreed but emphasised, 'In the long run of course, there is no alternative to the major policy of getting Turkey into the war as soon as circumstances permit.'[16]

Subsequent to the Eden–Dill mission Anglo-Turkish relations became more and more strained. According to Hugessen, 'The occupation of Bulgaria produced no reaction.'[17] On 1 March Hitler had written a personal letter to İnönü explaining that the German move in Bulgaria was in no way directed against Turkey but against the British in Greece, and that he had ordered his troops to keep well back from the frontier.[18]

When Eden met with Saraçoğlu in Cyprus on 14 March all he could get out of him was a vague promise to consult with Yugoslavia about a German threat to Salonika. But on 23 March the Turks broke off talks with the Yugoslavs on grounds of no confidence. This 'breach of the Cyprus promise' made the Foreign Office furious. O. Sargent of the Southern Department minuted: 'The Turks have succeeded in playing out a sorry farce . . . They will be prepared to do and accept anything in order not to be attacked . . . maybe even to the point of joining the Tripartite Pact . . . '[19]

The record shows that the first half of 1941 was a time when the

Turks kept everyone at arms length. İnönü in his answer to Hitler on 12 March stated: '[Turkey] cannot allow her sacred right to inviolability to be judged from the point of view of the victory of any foreign country . . . '[20] Also, the Soviet *démarche* of 25 March stating that Turkey could count on the understanding of the Soviet Union should she be obliged to go to war in self defence evoked no enthusiasm from the 'mistrustful and cautious Turks'.[21]

The German offensive in Greece and Yugoslavia starting on 6 April 1941, and the overrunning of Greece, seemed to confirm Turkey's worst fears. What was considered a poor showing by Britain reinforced the conviction that Turkey had been right not to allow herself to be prodded too far. The press gave vociferous support to the Greeks: 'The midget defeated the giant before our very eyes . . . Now the defeated giant is calling an even bigger giant to the rescue. Whatever destiny may bring, the Greek people have shown by their heroism and their miraculous resistance that they deserve independence . . . '[22]

But on the whole the press reflected falling morale. In early April it reported on the German entry into Salonika, and on the home front on facilities being provided by the government to evacuate the population of İstanbul to Anatolia. On 11 April *Ulus* reporting on the bombing of Belgrade declared: 'Belgrade is a mass of ruins and graveyards . . . '[23] There were also stirrings of anti-British feeling in the National Assembly where it was felt Britain had been pushing Turkey forward when she had shown herself unable to defend Greece.[24] The British defeat in Crete further accentuated this feeling: 'Military experts are talking of possibilities in Syria and Cyprus after Crete . . . '[25] Even Churchill mentioned the 'growing pessimism' in Turkey in a letter to Roosevelt on 3 May.[26] He noted however that little could be done except attempting to foster 'moral stiffening' on the part of the Turks.

TREATY WITH GERMANY

By late spring, the German position on the Balkans had become so strong that Turkey realised something more than 'moral stiffening' was needed if she were to survive. The Turkish government therefore agreed to begin negotiating with the Germans when von Papen proposed it at the beginning of May.[27] The same tough bargaining the Turks used against the British was now brought to play against the Germans.

Ribbentrop wanted a treaty allowing Germany unlimited transit facilities for troops and equipment. In return he suggested on 18 May that Turkey be promised frontier rectification near Edirne and possibly 'one or other island in the Aegean Sea'. It is worth noting that, as the British collapse in Greece approached, the British also suggested the Turks occupy the islands of Chios, Mytilene, and Samos. Saraçoğlu refused on the grounds that it might provoke war with Germany. The British were fully aware that such an occupation would also bring about disagreements between Greece and Turkey. On 2 March in his talks with the Greek Foreign Minister Koryzis, Eden had been told that the Greeks put great store on the use of the Greek Legion in any operation for the capture of the Dodecanese.[28]

In the course of the negotiations von Papen had to convince Ribbentrop that unlimited transit facilities were a vain dream, and pointed out to his Minister that the Turks refused any obligation aimed against Britain.[29] Indeed the Turks kept the Foreign Office informed of the negotiations and strove to convince them that the projected treaty was an emergency measure of mutual interest to Britain and Turkey as Turkey was 'from a geographical and strategical point of view completely isolated'.[30] Turkish resistance to arms transit exasperated Ribbentrop who felt that the Turks should know that Germany was in a position to 'blot out the Turkish state within a few weeks'.[31] The German Ambassador had to constantly tone down the temper of his senior and told him: 'it would be erroneous to assume that the German promise of this or that island or the English promise of the areas in northern Syria could influence the course which the Turkish Government is determined to pursue in the interests of its clean reputation . . . '[32]

The Turkish–German Treaty of Friendship and Non-Aggression was signed on 18 June 1941. On the eve of the German leap into the Soviet adventure it was essential that Germany neutralise Turkey. It deserves mention that Turkish military-strategic potential was impressed on both warring sides, but through different angles of the prism. Von Papen was made to realise that: 'The neutralization of the fifty Turkish divisions . . . is a military requirement which can for the present be achieved only in the diplomatic field . . . '[33] But as they impressed the Germans with their intention to resist, the Turks emphasised to the British their inability to offer much resistance. The Turkish Deputy Chief of Staff told the British Military Attaché on 22 May that: 'Turkey was a fortress and a reserve of manpower . . . [but]

it would be quite unsound for Turkey to come in now, as she would be overrun like Greece and Yugoslavia . . . '[34]

The Turkish press was made to work hard to create an auspicious atmosphere for the treaty. On 13 June the unsigned leader in *Ulus* stated: 'Germany holds Turkey in especially high esteem, much more than she does any other neutral country.' It was noticeable that Turkey was referred to as a 'neutral' whereas before the press had taken pains to underline Turkey's position as 'outside the war'.[35] After the actual signature the press gave the treaty a warm welcome and underlined that Turkish–German friendship was not a new thing. The official *Ulus* stated that the treaty had 'removed a few misunderstandings related to the goals of the New Order'.[36] Others emphasised that all Turkey's international commitments were of a defensive and precautionary nature: 'The first fact to be borne in mind is that: Turkey is not by way of this treaty, leaving one camp and joining the other . . . We are allied to Britain and friends with Germany.'[37] Indeed, the prevalent view had become that Turkey had moved towards full neutrality: 'The English treaty had now become a purely academic tie. It had only platonic significance . . . '[38]

In the overall view, however, these pronouncements must be taken once again as Turkey making the appropriate noises for the appropriate people at the appropriate time. After Britain had stabilised the situation in Syria and there were British forces within striking distance of Turkey, the Turkish Chief of Air Staff told the British Air Attaché on 24 July: 'The Turco-German Treaty meant nothing and that the English Treaty was the cornerstone of Turkey's foreign policy.'[39] Yet on 29 September, Menemencioğlu told von Papen about the British Treaty: 'Adherence to agreements that had been entered into was of vital importance to Turkey's prestige but that the treaty of alliance as such was no more than an ornament.'[40]

GERMANY ATTACKS THE SOVIET UNION

Although the British were 'momentarily panic stricken', they decided to accept the inevitable and not push Turkey into an even more difficult position by retributions.[41] Hugessen cabled the Foreign Office that it was primarily fear of German air power which had been instrumental in bringing about the treaty.[42] The might of the German air force, demonstrated with catastrophic effect in Greece, Yugoslavia and Crete had caused a 'deterioration in Turkish morale'. He added that they felt 'that their treaty with England, far from securing their interests has got them into difficulties . . . ' Hugessen, however, warned against driving the Turks nearer to Germany 'by rubbing salt into their albeit self-inflicted wound . . . '[43]

The German invasion of the Soviet Union itself caused Turkey to heave a sigh of relief. Hugessen reported on 23 June that Saraçoğlu was 'delighted over the Russo-German war'.[44] Papen cabled Berlin: 'Turkey is in transports of joy.'[45]

Cumhuriyet underlined the 'crusade-like' nature of this war by elaborating on the different nationalities taking part in the German assault.[46] F. R. Atay wrote on 23 June that the Soviets had brought this attack on themselves, and that the Turks were shocked by the revelation of Molotov's demands in Berlin in November 1940. He called the Russo-German war the 'major event of the century'.[47]

Following the German attack on the Soviet Union the Turks now began to fear that Britain would become too close to the Soviets for their liking. Hugessen cabled on 25 June that: 'There are signs that Turkey fears that we may engage ourselves too closely with Russia . . . '[48]

On 28 June, Y. Nadi wrote a leading article for *Cumhuriyet* entitled 'The Ironies of Politics', in which he outlined the western Allies' attitude to the Soviets from the time they had called her 'enemy No. 2', when she invaded Poland and the Baltic countries, to now offering her all the aid and assistance in their power. Nadi pointed out that the democracies were not prepared for war, and barely had enough to cover their own needs let alone help others: 'Help for the poor Norwegians against German aggressors, help for Holland and Belgium, help for Yugoslavia and Greece. We have seen what mediocre form this help has taken in relation to the great nations providing it . . . And now help for yesterday's "accomplice", "enemy No. 2" – Russia.'[49]

The British did not help themselves by statements like Churchill's speech on 22 June, when he said Russia had been hard done by in the First World War. The Turks pointed out that the Russians' major aim in that war had been the Straits.[50]

The Foreign Office belatedly realised the Prime Minister's gaffe and attempted to rectify the situation. Hugessen was instructed on 29 June to tell Saraçoğlu that suspicion over the Prime Minister's speech was completely without foundation. Britain was not upholding the Soviets but fighting Nazism.[51]

On 26 June Hugessen had reported that the Turks in general and Saraçoğlu in particular were, 'in a very touchy frame of mind'.[52] On 5 July the Ambassador urgently cabled his superiors, 'We should at once and without further delay say something to remove suspicions created by Prime Minister's reference to Russia.' The Foreign Office were extremely worried and discreet hints were put out in Churchill's direction urging him to moderate his language.[53] On 13 July the Ambassador reported that Marshal Fevzi Çakmak had told the Air Attaché that Turkey hoped Germany would exhaust her resources in Russia, as if she did not, Çakmak said: 'We realise that if Germany has a quick success over Russia we will be the next sheep for slaughter . . . '[54]

IRAQ AND SYRIA

In mid 1941 two related developments highlighted the delicacy of Turkey's position; the situation in Vichy-controlled Syria in June and July and the anti-British rebellion in Iraq in early April. If Turkey were attacked from the Balkans or Caucasus, Syria would be the vital connecting link with the British in Palestine. Similarly if Iraq were to fall to the Germans, Turkey would be surrounded and cut off from her supply route from Basra. Ensuring Turkish loyalty was an important factor in British reactions to these crises.

Eden emphasised to Churchill that in order for Turkey to 'hold fast' it was essential that she avoid encirclement by the Axis in Syria and Iraq. Britain, he said, had to 'deal at the earliest possible moment with the situation in these areas.[55] Speedy action was essential also for the Germans, who wanted to pass German troops and equipment through Turkey to Iraq. Ribbentrop told Papen on 19 May: 'If we want to help Iraq we must do it fast.'[56]

The Vichy French also further complicated the situation by asking permission to send war material through Turkey. Saraçoğlu refused on the grounds that he would be helping one of Turkey's allies against the other.[57] It is also ironic that when the Vichy French asked for permission for the transit of war material, Hugessen suggested on 24 May that Turkey stall, using as an excuse the fact that France had not fulfilled her obligation to deliver war material to Turkey.[58] This was precisely what the Turks would repeatedly tell the British!

Thus the Turks found themselves in a paradoxical situation. They had no wish to see Iraq occupied by Germany or blockaded by

Britain. Germany on the other hand was quick to approach them with offers of frontier rectification in Western Thrace and in the hinterland of Edirne, both territories ceded by Turkey in the First World War.[59] To get themselves out of this tight corner on 5 May they offered their services as mediators between Iraq and Britain. Although General Wavell was in favour of accepting Turkish mediation, Churchill 'eliminated once and for all any possibility of German intervention' by strong action. The Iraqi revolt was crushed on 30 May.[60] Thus although the Turks ended up allowing some war material to reach Iraq from the Axis in mid-May they stalled just long enough to enable the British to re-establish control.[61]

The situation in Syria was potentially more dangerous. A major Axis build-up on Turkey's southern frontier would mean she would be cut off geographically from the British. On 3 June Saraçoğlu told von Papen that for strategic reasons Turkey was considering occupying the Baghdad railway up to Aleppo. Ribbentrop refused to consider the suggestion. Meanwhile the Turkish military authorities told von Papen that Turkish troop concentrations along the Turkish–Syrian frontier in eastern Anatolia were directed not against the Axis but against the Soviets. Von Papen did not appear convinced. As in the Iraqi case, the Turks again offered to mediate between the Gaullist and Vichy forces: again the British refused.[62]

But there were indications of serious strain in Anglo-Turkish relations over this issue. P. Nichols of the Southern Department in the Foreign Office stressed the need to occupy Syria right up to the Turkish border 'to keep the Turks in line'.[63] The Turks on the other hand moved heavy troop concentrations to the frontier. Von Papen reported on 3 June, 'It was quite obvious here they were afraid of an English attack on Syria.'[64] The British repeatedly tried to get the Turks to make a written statement that they would not allow troop transit. The Turks repeatedly refused, as this would tie them down and do away with their bargaining flexibility, so vital in their relations with the Germans. As was seen in the German–Turkish treaty negotiations the Turks had no intention of allowing troop transit and were prepared to tell the British as much verbally.

On 30 June Hugessen reported that Menemencioğlu had told him that he was 'reluctant to get into anything savouring of another Treaty'.[65] When Hugessen inquired on 2 July whether Turkey would demobilise and allow the transit of German troops, Saraçoğlu reassured him and reminded him that German and Vichy requests had already been firmly refused. Hugessen had submitted a personal note and had been asked by Saraçoğlu to submit an official note. The Ambassador felt that this was a pretext enabling Saraçoğlu to respond that he could not reply to an official note. The Minister said such an exchange 'would amount to something in the form of a new treaty', and that he did not want to be accused of 'pactomania'. Saraçoğlu was also defensive about the German treaty, when Hugessen pressed him on continued German concessions he retorted that 'Turkey could fend for itself.'[66] In other words, the Turks resented being pressured by the British to do something they intended doing anyway.

THE ANGLO-SOVIET INVASION OF IRAN

The most ominous development from the Turkish point of view in 1941 was the British–Soviet invasion of Iran on 25 August. The intervention led the Turks to draw disturbing parallels. It was obviously a question of Iran simply being the only feasible supply route for British and American supplies to the Soviets. To the Turks, the British worry about German fifth column activities in Iran was nothing but a pretext to gain military control of the country.

Apart from the matter of the supply route another important aspect of the invasion for Britain was maintaining their hold over Turkey. Churchill wrote to Roosevelt on 1 September that the invasion also served the purpose of 'encouraging Turkey to stand as a solid block against German passage into Syria and Palestine'. According to the Prime Minister the invasion would be 'an enormous advantage if we can hold Turkey and sustain Russia'.[67]

The presence of German advisers in Iran was thus used chiefly as a pretext for invasion.[68] As early as 10 July General Wavell had cabled the Defence Committee: 'It is essential we should join hands with Russia through Iran, and if the present government is not willing to facilitate this it must be made to give way to one which will.'[69]

The British were under no illusions as to how the Turks would see the projected invasion. Hence they approached the United States government with a request that it inform Turkey that the United States approved of the Anglo-Russian action in Iran.[70] Kuniholm however has pointed out that the United States was none too much at ease with the project. Secretary of State Cordell Hull sought a formal Anglo-Soviet statement that Iran's territorial integrity would be respected.[71]

The British and Soviet Ambassadors then delivered notes to the Turkish government on 11 August promising to safeguard Turkish territorial integrity. Britain also took pains to avoid giving Turkey the impression that Iran was being presented with an Anglo-Soviet ultimatum. After the Anglo-Soviet reassurances with respect to Turkey, Eden was for pushing forward the invasion before the Turks found time to ask awkward questions. The intention was clearly to avoid giving the Turks the slightest suspicion that anything beyond the expulsion of undesirable Germans was considered: 'Another argument against any further delay was the attitude of the Turkish government which might at any moment result in our having to face a very awkward situation . . . '[72]

The joint invasion itself provoked widespread criticism in Turkey. Hugessen cabled on 23 August that he had heard Turkey was contemplating a lorry route through eastern Anatolia to support the Iranians: 'The Soviet Ambassador seemed to fear that Turkey would take hostile action if we made any move in Persia . . . I stated that I was aware that the Turkish government did not like what we were doing.'[73]

Press criticism was in fact vociferous. Yunus Nadi of *Cumhuriyet* likened the invasion to German aggression against neutral countries and stated: 'it has absolutely no basis in legality and is nothing but a straightforward act of aggression and invasion. The sad spectacle of British principles of fighting for freedom and independence being relegated to the domain of mythology is enough to upset world opinion . . .'[74]

Even more moderate papers like *Akşam* took a strong view. N. Sadak wrote on 26 August: 'Turkey cannot conceive any justification in the whole field of international political standards of behaviour for the invasion of an independent country . . . To find the least justification which would render the invasion of Iran necessary, leave alone right would be impossible . . . '[75] On 27 August, the anonymous leading article in *Cumhuriyet* proclaimed: 'The Anglo-Russian campaign in Iran has caused deep surprise in all quarters. This has been enhanced by the fact that Russia had joined in this move by Britain.'[76] On 28 August, N. Sadak wrote again in *Akşam*: 'The reason for this invasion is the opening of a freely accessible supply line to Russia before the winter campaign. The fault of Iran was not the welcoming of a few hundred Germans but the fact that she was in the way . . . '[77]

The general impression which emerged from the Turkish press was that Turkey was particularly worried that Britain should have invited the Soviet Union to participate in the invasion of an independent country. The outrage in the press was no doubt to some extent 'orchestrated' by the government. On 9 September Hugessen reported on a general coldness towards Britain and attributed it to 'the effect on the public mind of officially inspired press comments on our action in Persia'.[78] Of course Axis propaganda did not fail to make capital out of this situation and claimed that after Iran Turkey would be the next country to be confronted with Anglo-Soviet demands. Hugessen reported on 12 September, 'This particular whisper has not been altogether ineffective . . . '[79]

Soviet behaviour in their occupation zone also caused further worry. Although the official Soviet line was that the population had welcomed the Red Army, reports were soon filtering in of Soviet support for separatist activity in Azerbaijan.[80] On 29 September the British Chief of Imperial General Staff seemed actually surprised that: 'The Soviet government did not show interest that the Persian civil administration continued in being . . . '[81] To the Turks all these developments must have appeared as the height of predictability, and as once more vindicating their conviction that a strong stance towards all parties was indispensable. Iran had been weak and she had been devoured. No amount of British broadcasting of their intentions to safeguard her independence could change this.

CHROME AND PAN-TURANISM

These two issues were the object of much controversy in this period. The 'Chrome War' in which both Britain and Germany attempted to secure the monopoly of this strategic ore (vital to the construction of armour plating and high-grade steel) presented the Turkish decision-makers with many problems but also provided many opportunities to turn this rivalry to profit. In the early negotiations with Britain, Turkey had urged the former to contract over a long-term period; but the British would not go beyond a two-year commitment. They were now to regret this.

In September 1941 Turkey entered into negotiations with Germany. Menemencioğlu, Turkey's chief negotiator told the Germans that chrome would be forthcoming only in exchange for war material on a tit-for-tat basis. The chief German negotiator Clodius, was to write from Ankara on 9 September 1941: 'My first impression is that the Turkish attitude will be very stubborn in this question . . . '[82] Moreover the Turkish side told the Germans that they would refuse to breach their contract with Britain and that no deliveries could be made until 1943, as all production until then had been promised to Britain. Menemencioğlu repeatedly told the Germans that although Turkey could, if the Germans wished, play up the 'political and psychological importance' of the agreement '(Turkey) could not sacrifice its honour by breaking its word.'[83]

Menemencioğlu had two cards up his sleeve in these negotiations. One, he knew that Turkey was Germany's only feasible source of chromium ore. Two, he also knew that the Germans always made great political stock out of economic agreements. During the negotiations both cards were used to good effect. After the agreement was concluded in which Turkey contracted to begin deliveries in 1943 the First Secretary of the Ankara Embassy, Kroll, summed up the situation for Berlin on 13 October: 'In almost six years of working with the Turks I have found that they are skilful enough to find a loophole in any treaty instrument . . . '[84] The Secretary arrived at the conclusion that although for propaganda purposes the agreement should be played up, it was a failure in real terms, as the Turks had made no attempt to find such a loophole in their contract with Britain.

The agreement concluded that Turkey would sell Germany a maximum of 90,000 tons of chrome in 1943 and 45,000 tons in 1944 in return for substantial military equipment: 'As in the past, the Turks drove a hard bargain. They gave the Germans much less than they asked for; in return, they were promised essential materials which their allies found difficult, even impossible, to supply.' The Turks actually insisted that the amount of chrome in the arms they would receive from Germany would go a long way towards compensating for the chrome they sold to Germany.[85]

Even in this watered-down form the agreement caused resentment in Allied and pro-Allied circles. The United States was particularly critical in its attitude. Halifax cabled from Washington on 10 July that the State Department was of the view that: 'Actual deliveries of chrome must be the acid test of their policy . . . '[86] The British however, took a more realistic view. Eden told the War Cabinet on 9 October: 'This [the Turkish promise to deliver 90,000 tons in 1943] was not very satisfactory but things might have turned out much worse . . . '[87]

A potentially much more dangerous issue for Turkey was that of Pan-Turanism. The idea of uniting all Turkic peoples from the Volga to China had been a recurrent theme since the days of the Ottoman Empire.[88] As the German forces began conquering areas of the Soviet Union inhabited by Turkic peoples, the idea was born of using these as a bargaining counter against Turkey. If Turkey could be persuaded to profit directly or indirectly from this situation, the Germans hoped, she might be sufficiently tempted into moving towards them or even joining them in their campaign to crush the Soviet Union.

The official policy of the Turkish government was to deny all Pan-Turanian tendencies along with all irredentist claims. However, it could not remain indifferent to the fate of 40 million Turkic people in the event of a German victory over the Soviets, and realised the need to ensure an official contact with the Germans over this issue. Thus it maintained an official attitude of reserve while awaiting the outcome of the Nazi–Soviet struggle.[89] Although İnönü himself saw the danger and consistently applied the official line, the evidence shows that some very senior Turkish *cadres* felt that the opportunity should be exploited.

The British were keeping close tabs on Pan-Turanian activity in Turkey, and feared that when German forces entered the Caucasus these elements would become much more active and influential. In May and June 1941 in some British circles distrust of Turkey had reached serious proportions. Cavendish Bentinck of the Foreign Office minuted on 30 June:

Since the outbreak of the war the Turks have whittled away at their obligations to us and have acted contrary to the spirit of their treaty with us to such an extent that one cannot help feeling disgusted with them. However, I suppose that we must go on with the unequal task of trying to prevent them becoming active allies of the enemy. But I doubt whether this will be successful when the German forces are in the Caucasus . . . [90]

The Germans encouraged Pan-Turanian circles in Turkey and von Papen reported on 25 July that special interest was evinced over the fate of the Azerbaijan Turks. A committee of experts on Turanian affairs had been formed including Şükrü Yenibahçe, deputy for İstanbul, Nuri Paşa (Enver Paşa's brother and an officer in the Islamic Army which had entered Baku in 1918), Professor Zeki Velidi Togan, a well known Pan-Turanist historian, and Turkey's Ambassador to Kabul, Memduh Şevket Esendal.[91]

Although the government probably winked at the activities of this committee, it is unlikely to have had any official status. Given İnönü's background and experience with the Germans in the First World

War, it is unlikely that Nuri Paşa would have been given an official position. As to Togan, he had been exiled during Mustafa Kemal's lifetime for involvement in Turanian activity.[92] It would appear that the furthest the Turkish government would be prepared to go was to consider the creation of semi-independent Turkic states which would be under Turkey's political tutelage.[93]

From 15 October to 5 November 1941, two Turkish Generals, Ali Fuat Erden and Emir Erkilet, were invited by the German General Staff to tour the Eastern Front. The latter was Turkey's unofficial 'contact man' with the Turkic elements in the Soviet Union. Upon their return the two Generals attempted to convince İnönü, Saraçoğlu, and Chief of Staff Çakmak that the war on the Eastern Front had been won. They seem to have had considerable success with Saraçoğlu and Çakmak but 'İnönü did not appear at all convinced . . . '[94] İnönü's personal reserve in this issue was the overall determining factor: 'İnönü's resistance to adventurist or irredentist notions severely limited the influence of the Pan-Turanian movement at this time.'[95]

Unofficial contact was nonetheless maintained. Nuri Paşa and Zeki Velidi Togan visited Berlin in July and September respectively and they briefed the Turkish government about their visits.[96] However, the German officials he met were not too impressed with Nuri Paşa. Woerman of the *Wilhelmstrasse* assessed him as a man who ' . . . spent his youth under the spell of his brother Enver Paşa . . . His Pan-Turanian ideas have a certain romantic flavour . . . '[97] This German report dated 10 September underlined the divergent attitudes of Nuri Paşa and his government and concluded: 'All this speaks in favour of treating the Pan-Turanian ideas cautiously.'[98] Indeed the Turks' official stance of reserve achieved its purpose, Ribbentrop was to comment on 11 August that Germany had to 'promote and keep alive the hitherto somewhat dormant Turkish imperialist tendencies . . . '[99]

There are however indications that under the official mask of reserve senior Turkish statesmen did have some rather more 'forward' views. In a report dated 8 August 1942, von Papen stated he had spoken with Saraçoğlu who had said that as a Turk he was fully in favour of the collapse of the Soviet Union. Germany could ensure this only by killing half of the Russians, enabling the minorities to stand on their own feet and educating them as enemies of Slavism. In order to replace the Turkic intelligentsia liquidated by the Russians, promising youths should be educated in German and Turkish universities.

The Turkish Prime Minister concluded that the collapse of the Soviets should furnish the context for an Anglo-German peace agreement.[100]

Koçak's summary assessment of this issue is a valid one: 'The desire of the Turkish government was to keep the Pan-Turanian movement, which had sympathizers in government itself, under close observation and control. The main idea was to provide a contingency plan in the event of clear German victory. This is not out of keeping with Turkish foreign policy which typically sought to cover all options . . . '[101]

8 . 'ACTIVE NEUTRALITY': 1942

As war raged all over the world after the Japanese attack on Pearl Harbor and the German penetration deep into the Soviet Union, the Turks moved towards stricter neutrality and told both sides that this was also in keeping with their interests. Towards the end of the year, with the beginning of Allied ascendancy, they shifted their policy gradually more in favour of the Allies. But the essentials of Turkish foreign policy remained the same, merely the exterior manifestations changed to suit circumstances. F. R. Atay declared in *Ulus* on 3 January 1942:

We cannot predict whether this nation, who for centuries has never seen a generation be born and die in peace, will be able to survive this war unharmed and unbloodied . . . But this is our wish. We are after no territorial gain, only an act of force can bring us into the war. But we are not willing to sacrifice any of our honour, our rights or even one hand's breadth of our soil in order to have peace . . . The war has laid siege to countries such as ours and turned them into fortresses.[1]

COMPROMISE PEACE

Eden's Moscow visit in December 1941 had worried the Turks who feared some deal at their expense. To reassure them Eden declared before the House of Commons, on 8 January, that the references to Turkey had been in all respects friendly, and such as the Turkish government themselves would have been glad to hear. 'Turkey had nothing to fear from an Allied victory, its territorial integrity was in no way threatened by either Great Britain or the USSR and the Anglo-Soviet pledges that we gave to Turkey last autumn would be fully honoured.'[2]

No doubt such reassurances were welcome but they never fully satisfied the Turks. According to von Papen the British desire to

133

establish 'a new order in Europe' with Soviet assistance greatly disturbed the Turks. They had no wish to see Germany ruin the British Empire – but nor did they relish the prospect of too close co-operation between the Soviets and Britain. The ideal for them in von Papen's view was 'to find the possibility of a compromise'.[3] This theme of seeking an opening which would allow room for Turkish foreign policy needs in a compromise between the two sides was to be repeated throughout 1942. It had indeed been prevalent in Turkish thinking all along. On 8 April 1941 von Papen had reported to his Ministry that Menemencioğlu had told him, 'We have no use for either a total English or a total German victory, because for us the existence of a stabilized central Europe remains a basic prerequisite.'[4] Only with the adoption of the principle of 'Unconditional Surrender' in the Casablanca Conference would the idea fade out.

Meanwhile, the press welcomed Eden's reassurances and used this as an occasion to once more underline Turkey's position. Y. Nadi wrote in *Cumhuriyet* on 10 January: 'As honesty in politics is one of the foremost considerations of the Turkish Republic we naturally welcome this statement by the British Foreign Minister . . . We would like to think that even our northern neighbour Russia, has found new and sound reasons to support our honest policy . . .'[5]

The desire to avoid war appeared as paramount in the press during this period. The plight of Greece was used as a living example of what war could do: Yunus Nadi wrote of the hunger and suffering in Greece: 'We are now witnessing this tragedy in Greece because the great nations of the world choose to indulge in a contest of wills . . . This country was defeated while heroically defending itself against vastly superior forces, due to the insufficiency of the aid she received.'[6]

The reference to what was considered inadequate and tardy British aid unmistakably indicates that Turkey was making sure the same did not happen to her. As Allied support for the Soviets increased and the German offensive did not proceed as rapidly as expected, the Turks began to fear an all-powerful Soviet Union. As early as 4 January, the British Joint Intelligence Committee appreciation report stated that it was becoming accepted in Turkey that the first year of campaigning on the eastern front had been a failure. 'However, satisfaction at the weakening of Germany and her inability to furnish forces in new directions is tempered by a permanent fear of the ultimate emergence of a stronger Russia.'[7]

The Italian Ambassador De-Peppo was not far off a true appreciation of the situation when he said: 'The Turkish ideal is that the last German soldier should fall upon the last Russian corpse.' Ahmet Şükrü Esmer stated that it was hoped the Germans and Russians would wear each other out; 'We hoped they would both lose.'[8] But they did not want any part in it, and told the British time and again that they expected to be attacked in the spring of 1942, hoping by these means to convince them that it was essential that Turkey save her energy. They seemed to have convinced the British Ambassador. Hugessen wrote to the government of India that the Axis rumour that Turkey was about to go over to the Axis was entirely untrue: 'There has been no sign of any change in the Turkish policy which up to date has been conducted with great skill and which, based on the Anglo-Turkish Alliance and Non-Aggression Pact with Germany has as its primary object the avoidance of war in the absence of any direct attack from whatever quarter.'[9]

ARMS FROM GERMANY AND 'ACTIVE NEUTRALITY'

One of the most remarkable achievements of Turkish diplomacy in this period was that it managed to procure arms from both sides involved in the conflict. Not only did the Turks manage to avoid being attacked by Germany, they convinced the Germans that the interests of the Reich lay in arming them. On 9 February, Hugessen reported that Saraçoğlu had informed him that von Papen had sounded Menemencioğlu about the possibility of German arms deliveries to Turkey. G. R. Clutton of the Foreign Office Southern Department, summed up the Menemencioğlu–Papen interchange as an attempt by Papen to test Anglo-Turkish relations.

The Foreign Office noted however that this move was in accord with Menemencioğlu's determination, 'to keep Turkey neutral while striving to get the best benefits . . . Numan, the best bargainer the Turks ever had is reluctant to let slip by any chance of extra arms . . .'[10] The Turks were aided by Papen who claimed that he had lost faith in a German victory in Russia and believed that equipment for one or two armoured divisions would enable Turkey 'to pursue a much more independent policy between the two camps'.[11]

Accordingly, in the summer of 1942 Turkey was granted a loan of 100 million Reichmarks for arms shipments. The Foreign Office which had considered the possibility of such an agreement 'remote in the extreme' in February were taken by surprise.[12] Eden noted in a

War Cabinet memo on 20 July that none of the material the Germans were giving to Turkey could be supplied by Britain and the United States: 'If the Germans fulfil their promises to supply this equipment within six months they will be supplying Turkey in a sixth of the time with three times as much equipment as we have done. Present circumstances make it impossible for us to outbid this German offer ourselves and there seems little we can do . . .'[13]

It was at this point that the Turks began to openly speak of their policy of 'active neutrality'. This policy which was the brain-child of Menemencioğlu, meant that Turkey could not be satisfied by declaring herself neutral and awaiting events. She would try to influence world developments in her favour and acquire modern armaments. Turkey's later offers to mediate between the two sides stemmed from this policy. Saraçoğlu referred to this position in a speech to the Assembly on 6 August: 'Turkey does not pursue adventures beyond her frontiers, she has sought means of remaining outside the war and has found them in a conscious and active neutrality . . . Turkey could not have safeguarded her position by passive neutrality and cannot do so in future . . .'[14]

The Foreign Office were none too enamoured with this policy and G. L. Clutton was strident in his criticism:

An active neutral has a foot in both camps. It is permissible for him to have an alliance with one of the belligerents so long as he has a pact of friendship with the other. This policy enables the country to preserve its neutrality, but at the same time gives an opportunity for cashing in on the side of whichever belligerent wins the war. It also enables the neutral power to preserve its preference for one belligerent or the other. There is something Ghandi-esque and positively immoral in this policy, but it is, I fear, typically Turkish and its astuteness and cleverness cannot be denied.[15]

On the Axis side, Hitler told Mussolini on 29 April that 'Turkey was moving slowly but surely over to the Axis.'[16] Ribbentrop on the other hand told Ciano: 'Turkey nourishes fundamentally hostile sentiments towards us which she succeeds in hiding by the clever use of Oriental hypocrisy.'[17] Seen from the points of view of parties desiring to push Turkey into this or that line of action it was natural that a process of deliberate selection should have come into play regarding the utterances and actions of Turkish statesmen, which appeared contradictory to the outside eye. For the Turks, however, whose only aim was to ensure survival there was no contradiction.

The press also maintained a position of balance between the two sides while neither had a clear advantage. F. R. Atay wrote in *Ulus* that all effort was being made to keep Turkey out of entanglements: 'The world is in flames. Anyone who has not lost their mind will not think they can gain anything by joining the holocaust. The one wish of the countries not yet involved in the war is not to widen its spread, but to contain it and facilitate the making of peace . . . as soon as possible.'[18]

In reporting on the war, *Ulus* was careful to stress the victories and defeats of both sides. The paper noted on 17 February that Britain was 'suffering heavy blows' and claimed: 'The British public have become critical of the conduct of the war . . .'[19] But the same paper reported on 28 February that large numbers of Germans were in danger of being cut-off in southern Russia, and ran pictures of German motor lorries being pulled by horses.[20]

On 17 March İnönü made Turkey's position clear: 'We have taken all our precautions. Our decisions for the future are open and clear. We will strive to stay out of the war. We will order our business and if it proves impossible to avoid war we will do our duty honourably . . .'[21] The general tenor of Turkish declarations, therefore, became much more strictly neutralist.

THE SOVIET WORRY AND 'ACTIVE NEUTRALITY'

After the United States came into the war as a full belligerent and joined Britain in supporting the Soviets, the Turks came to fear Soviet preponderance in eastern Europe. This gave impetus to their efforts to secure a compromise peace between Britain and Germany in keeping with their policy of active neutrality. On 16 February von Papen noted that until the German attack on the Soviets Turkey had feared, 'above all a complete victory of the Axis . . . and the domination of Italy over the eastern Mediterranean . . .' But now he said, they feared that an American supported Soviet Union would 'dictate the laws of the new order in Europe.'[22]

On 4 March Menemencioğlu sounded Hugessen about the possibility of a negotiated settlement and offered to mediate. British defeats in the Far East, particularly the loss of Singapore took their toll on Turkish public opinion which began to fear that British weakness would cause them to make a separate peace with Germany at Turkey's expense. If such a possibility existed, the Turkish statesmen thought, they should wish to mould it to their interests. G. L. Clutton of the Foreign Office summed up the Turkish position: 'In the face of these dangers which in Turkish eyes mean they will be in the power of either Germany or Russia – there seems to be no solution except a compromise peace.'[23]

Hugessen felt that the Turks had been greatly disappointed by British performance, 'They are, as last year, wondering how they will get through till the autumn.'[24] The British however, stamped on this Turkish offer whenever it was made. Eden wrote to his Ambassador in Moscow, Sir Archibald Clark Kerr, that Menemencioğlu was given to uttering such sentiments from time to time, 'This Turkish dream which M. Saraçoğlu also shared would never be realized . . .'[25]

Von Papen encouraged the Turks in their efforts to secure a compromise peace.[26] But Eden repeatedly told Hugessen that all such talk was in vain and on 19 April he cabled to Ankara that von Papen was insincere and that he was flattering Saraçoğlu: 'The Turks . . . should be firmly discouraged from lending a ready ear to von Papen's suggestions.'[27] But talk of compromise peace continued in Ankara. On 30 April Hugessen reported, 'some circles [were] in possession of some peace terms which they are anxious to promote in order to prevent Turkey being drawn into war . . .' Hugessen emphatically told them, 'compromise peace *yok!*' (*No* compromise peace!)[28]

In keeping with their desire to see a compromise the Turks took extreme pains not to offend Germany. Hugessen reported on 22 April that Saraçoğlu had told him he would be prepared to do 'anything' for Britain but he had to be able to meet a German protest with a convincing answer: 'I replied that he seemed to be in the position of a small boy at school who has been forbidden to smoke, but would do so up the chimney on any possible occasion when there was no danger of discovery.'[29]

The Turks were worried about the possibility that either the Soviets or Britain would make a separate peace with Germany which would cut Turkey out. On 5 May Menemencioğlu told Hugessen that he had heard the Soviets were about to make a separate peace: 'His main theme was that it would be disastrous for Great Britain if Russia made peace with Germany, and that if peace were to be advantageous it should be Britain who made it first.'[30]

On 11 May Eden referred to rumours in several capitals about peace negotiations. He reiterated that instructions had been sent to all posts that these rumours should be completely ignored for fear of awakening Russian suspicions.[31]

Turkish suspicion of Russian intentions was also reflected in the

press. On the occasion of Molotov's visit to London and the agreement reached there on no separate peace and non-interference in the
affairs of European states after the war, F. R. Atay heaved a public
sigh of relief: 'There is no doubt that to know that the Soviet Union is
fighting only to save its own territory has been cause for real relief for
some nations of the democratic front.'[32]

The anniversary of the German–Turkish Treaty of Non-Aggression furnished another occasion for a statement of the Turkish position: 'The Germans who have no designs on Turkish territory have
seen the value of a neutral Turkey fully aware of the delicacy of her
geographical position and fully capable of defending it. Time and
events have also shown that this neutrality can only be of aid to our
ally, Britain . . .'[33]

Yet to the British observer it was very easy to doubt the sincerity of
Turkey's exclusive concern with her own safety. The Foreign Office
feared that during this period Turkey was in a period of transition
while she prepared to join the Axis. Hugessen reported on 29 August:
'Supply of war, industrial and railway material is bait for immediate
attraction. These developments suggest Turkey is insuring herself
with Germany . . . The Turks are a hard-headed race and are
doubtless trying to get as much as possible out of both sides.'[34] At this
stage Turkey felt she had to make it exceedingly clear that *all* attempts
to transgress on her neutrality would be resisted, by implication, even
a move on the part of Britain. G. L. Clutton commented on this
attitude: 'What we would really consider an impertinence would be a
Turkish excuse that they were accepting armaments from Germany
to protect themselves against us. Drawn to its logical conclusions this
is the Turkish argument . . .'[35] Indeed the Turks had seen Syria and
Iraq become an arena for the warring sides, and also the partition of
Iran into zones of influence. The British presence in Syria led them to
draw unpleasant parallels.

This is not to say that the Turks had gone over to the Axis.
Menemencioğlu, for one, genuinely feared that the British would lose
Egypt, and Turkey would be completely encircled. On 27 June Hugessen reported that Menemencioğlu had told him that the loss of
Egypt would mean the loss of Syria and then 'Turkey would be
completely cut-off.'[36] Other Turks made similar statements, on 14
July Sir Miles Lampton reported from Cairo that the Turkish Ambassador there had said, 'Egypt was Turkey's southern front . . .' and her
bulwark in resisting German pressure.[37]

The Foreign Office, however, were only too aware that only military results would hold the Turks. On 29 August Hugessen cabled: 'Unless the military situation improves we may rapidly approach an awkward crisis in relations between Turkey and Germany and Turkey and ourselves . . .'[38] On 18 September the Ambassador emphasised that: 'What is certain is that the Turks will not be moved from any quarter by appeals to sentiment or by blustering . . . but only by main force and interest.'[39]

TERRITORIAL ASPIRATIONS

The Turks' official line towards territorial claims was that they had none. Yet they did put out feelers towards both sides. The Foreign Office certainly did not believe Turkish claims of disinterested self-sufficiency. On 25 March the Chancery at Ankara reported, 'what is undoubtedly a fact is that the Axis have been offering neighbouring territories to Ankara . . .' The report stated the Germans had offered Turkey Aleppo and some of the Greek islands.[40] The evidence from the German side seems to justify their suspicions. Papen wrote to Ribbentrop on 14 July 1941 that in order for Turkey to join Germany her territorial aspirations in northern Syria had to be met.[41] First Secretary of the German Embassy, Kroll, believed that Turkey expected to be given northern Syria, Aleppo and Mosul.[42] It is interesting to recall at this point that the British had also considered suggesting that Turkey occupy Aleppo.[43] On 22 June, G. L. Clutton at the Foreign Office commented: 'Quite likely the Turks have territorial aspirations in the Aegean islands, but unless they play a more active part in the war, they are unlikely to see them realised.'[44] The implication here was very clear; the Turks might well receive consideration if they proved more co-operative.

On 9 September 1942 Clutton wrote a summary of 'Turkish territorial aspirations.' On the Pan-Turanian issue he said the Turks would be too wary of the Soviets to press forward claims in trans-Caucasia. 'It is doubtful even if Russia collapses whether they would accept a gift of Russian lands from Germany so long as they believed in eventual British victory . . .'[45] But the situation in Iran was different, 'it is very possible that at the end of the war we may see Turkish claims to a rectification of the Turco-Persian frontier . . .' In Bulgaria, Clutton expected Turkey to, 'put in a claim for frontier rectifications south of Burgas when Bulgaria's day of reckoning comes'. On the Dodecanese, Clutton's view was that 'The Turks undoubtedly expect to receive the major portion of the islands . . .' On Mosul: 'The Turks would undoubtedly like Mosul but this is a claim we are unlikely to hear anything about so long as the Turco-British connection exists . . .'[46] Clutton's memo concluded that none of these claims were practicable because of previous British commitments to other parties.

ALLIED ASCENDANCY

The successful British counter-offensive at El Alamein in October 1942 and the successful Soviet counter-offensive at Stalingrad in November brought increased pressure to bear on Turkey. Now more than ever Turkey became a potential tool for shortening the war. The Turks found themselves in a very tricky situation, as they could no longer claim that they were blocking the way to the Axis advance into the Middle East. The Axis were now retreating and a new formula had to be found to counter British pressure.

The Turkish reaction to this predicament was to stress that they were still radically short of all necessary war material and to insist that the Germans might want to lash out against England with a prestige victory, their contention being that Turkey was the ideal target for such an attack. The British on the other hand suspected that Turkey was seeking to be strong for a possible postwar confrontation with the Soviet Union. Foreign Minister Menemencioğlu told Hugessen on 9 October that Germany might well attack Turkey because of the aggressive 'mad dog' psychology of the Nazi leaders. The Foreign Office treated this view as 'so much nonsense'. Clutton commented: 'The Nazis never behave like that, the fact is the Turks are afraid of Russia.'[47]

Although the Turkish statesmen took care to stress the public official line, that they did not impute evil intentions to the Soviets, privately and unofficially they let their worry show. On 5 November P. Dixon of the Southern Department noted, 'We have abundant indirect confirmation about the extent to which Russia is in the forefront of Turkish calculations and fears.' Menemencioğlu, he said, had recently told Hugessen that Turkey suspected, 'that we and the Russians were deliberately keeping her short of arms.'[48] Ahmet Şükrü Esmer also told this author that the Turkish leadership suspected Britain was keeping arms deliveries low as a result of Russian pressure.[49]

However, Churchill in any event, wanted Turkey to be well equipped so that she could play the role he had set for her in his own mind: 'The President and I had long sought to open a new route to Russia and to strike at Germany's southern flank. Turkey was the key to all such plans.'[50] On 9 November he expounded on what would become an *idée fixe* to the American Ambassador to London, John G. Winant. Turkey, he said, with its forty-five divisions of 'superior fighting men' should be armed and equipped for a push into the Balkan peninsula.[51] On 18 November the Prime Minister wrote to the Chief of Staff Middle East: 'A supreme and prolonged effort must be made to bring Turkey into the war in Spring.'[52] The Foreign Office were aware that Allied ascendancy had complicated Turkey's policy. The position was assessed in a memo dated 19 November:

There is no doubt that Turkey's position has become more critical in these last few days from the military–political point of view . . . The Ankara Governments have always tried in these last years to maintain a perfect balance between the two sides, and it must be acknowledged that due to the traditional skill of Turkish diplomacy they have succeeded.[53]

Churchill's target date for the concentration of force in Turkey was April or May 1943. Turkey was to be offered an Anglo-Russo-American guarantee of territorial integrity, and all throughout the winter 'A ceaseless flow of weapons and equipment must go into Turkey.'[54]

As the fortunes of war swung against the Germans, and all the Allied leaders seemed to be in agreement that Turkey should be brought in, Turkey emphasised that Germany might well strike at the Straits for a 'prestige victory'. The second point of emphasis was that Britain should not trust the Soviets; Stalin only sided with Britain because he was in a fight to the death.[55]

The argument that the Turks were to press on Britain from this time on was that British interests demanded that she oppose Soviet expansion in the Middle East, and for this she would need Turkey. The Foreign Office on the other hand thought they had found a new card to play to 'achieve the task which the Prime Minister has set for us of bringing the Turks into the war in the Spring'.[56] This was the fear that unless Turkey did her bit she would be left alone to face the Soviets after the war. Sargent of the Southern Department felt Britain should, 'play [her] cards well and foster the Turkish fear with care, tact and patience . . .', in order to 'exercise in the coming months that gentle pressure the Prime Minister has called for in order to bring the

Turkish Government into the frame of mind we want it to be in next Spring'.[57]

Although most Anglo-American sources claim that Britain played down the Turkish fear of the Soviets, the evidence points in the other direction.[58] Eden and Hugessen both agreed to exploit Turkey's fears when they discussed this issue in London on 5 December.[59] On 21 December Clutton said he had agreed with Hugessen that, 'Turkey's anxieties regarding the possibility of some arrangement between this country and the Soviet Union for collaboration in the peace settlement were worth exploiting.'[60]

However, any such 'exploitation' could only be counter-productive, as one of the major factors feeding Turkey's determination to keep out was the spectre of 'liberation' by the Red Army.

9 . ON THE RAZOR'S EDGE: 1943

For Turkey 1943 represents the most critical year of the war. The Allies were now definitely in the ascendant and pressuring Turkey to implement her obligations. On the other hand the Axis were on the defensive but still within easy striking distance of Turkey's vulnerable vital areas.

For Churchill in particular, Turkish participation in a Balkan campaign became something of a 'pet plan' in the place of his old project of invading Norway: 'With Allied equipment, what the Prime Minister liked to consider forty five divisions of superior Turkish manpower should have a certain potential for distracting minor German forces from other regions of more immediate moment to Mr Churchill . . . Throughout 1943 he would not forget Turkey and her unemployed manpower.'[1] Until late in the year Turkey would therefore be seen as a potential source of fighting men. Only due to American and later Soviet reluctance, would Churchill shift his emphasis in favour of Turkey providing air base facilities. After the Adana meeting with Turkish leaders (30–31 January), on 2 February Churchill sent Roosevelt a copy of his 'Morning Thoughts' in which he spoke of Turkey coming into the war '[as] a full belligerent, and her Armies advancing into the Balkans side by side with the Russians on the one hand in the north and the British to the south'.[2] Nothing illustrates the Anglo-Turkish contradiction better than the copy of the same 'Morning Thoughts' given to the Turks which emphasised Turkey's role as a 'full partner at the peace conference' and the need for her to be 'strong to resist invasion'. Any active involvement was quite definitely played down.[3] In the Anglo-Turkish conundrum when the British spoke of wanting Turkey 'to be strong' they meant 'for war'. When the Turks spoke of their need to be strong they meant 'so that we can stay out'.

144

THE CASABLANCA CONFERENCE AND UNCONDITIONAL SURRENDER

We have seen how in the final months of 1942 Churchill became convinced that an escalation of the pressure on Turkey was essential. He now set out to sell this plan to the Americans who proved somewhat reluctant buyers. General Marshall, along with others in the American military establishment, were markedly reluctant about Turkish entry and feared that this would 'burn up our logistics right down the line'.[4] Nevertheless Roosevelt agreed on 18 January that Churchill should be 'allowed to play the Turkish hand'.[5] Also the adoption of the principle of unconditional surrender as forming the basis for any termination of hostilities with the Axis worried Turkey. To them this was a measure which would fanaticise Axis resistance and create a vacuum in Central Europe which only the Soviets would benefit from. For Turkey, Germany was an essential factor in central Europe.[6] We have seen in the previous chapter that compromise peace had been regarded by the Turkish leaders as an ideal solution for ending the war. The doctrine of unconditional surrender seemed to kill all their hopes.

THE ADANA CONFERENCE

Churchill had told Hopkins at Casablanca that in his coming meeting with İnönü in Adana he would tell the Turkish President: 'In the event of their remaining out, he would not undertake to control the Russians regarding the Dardanelles.'[7] He now arrived in Adana on 30 January to 'play his Turkish hand'. As aptly put by Kuniholm: 'Churchill – perhaps because of his experience with the Gallipoli campaign in World War I – believed himself an expert on Turkish psychology and policy; presumably, he intended to exercise that expertise in Adana.'[8] But he was to be no more successful in Adana than he had been in Gallipoli. The fundamental contradiction between British and Turkish approaches to the same problems reached its greatest extent at the Adana meeting. The Turkish side tried to convince the British that the Soviets would become a serious threat to Europe after the war, and emphasised their own vulnerability to German air attack. Prime Minister Saraçoğlu in particular was strident in his anti-Soviet views.[9] They also feared an Anglo-Soviet deal at their expense, their historical conditioning pointing to just such deals at the expense of Persia in 1907 and 1941, and against Turkey herself in 1915.[10]

Churchill therefore found himself obliged to reassure the Turks regarding present and future Anglo-Soviet intentions. To this end he wrote them his famous 'wooing letter' containing 'an offer of platonic marriage'.[11] The Turks however knew from their historical experience that any 'marriage' with a major power was always 'consummated'.

During the negotiations Churchill outlined his plan for reinforcing Turkey, code-named operation 'Hardihood'. Menemencioğlu recalls in his memoirs that in the course of a speech in grand Churchillian style he interrupted the Prime Minister and pointed out that granting air base facilities in the region of the Straits to a foreign power was against the Montreux Convention. Churchill was displeased at the interruption and looked at him as if to say, 'How can anyone be so lacking in political sense?' Menemencioğlu admits that the point he took up with Churchill was, 'a matter of the tenth importance' but records that, 'I did not want to indulge in politics at the expense of the Montreux Convention, even if it meant incalculable gain.'[12]

Nonetheless Churchill came away from the discussions satisfied and believing that, 'there is no doubt the Turks have come a long way towards us'.[13] The Turks for their part, looking at the meeting as a possible source of pressure requiring commitment, were convinced they had been successful in avoiding such commitment and relieved at the relative absence of pressure. Yet it would gradually become clear that at Adana the Turks and British were speaking at cross purposes: 'At Adana and in the months that followed the Turks and the British had not spoken the same language.'[14]

In the days immediately after the conference, however, there was a marked improvement in Anglo-Turkish relations as the Turks made a show of how 'understanding' their ally had been. The Foreign Office took Turkish flattery at face value, and P. Dixon of the Southern Department commented: 'I do not myself think it good tactics to show overwhelming gratitude to the Turks for their welcome change of heart. We can and should express pleasure while conveying the impression that we accept these tributes as our due.'[15]

The one concrete outcome of the Adana Conference was the 'Adana Lists' of military equipment embodying the lavish promises made by Churchill to deliver to Turkey war material, 'to the full capacity of Turkish railways . . . '[16] The Prime Minister could not have known that these lists designed to lure Turkey into the war would become a major device for keeping her out.

The press during this period was remarkable more for what it denied or left unsaid than what it actually printed. There were numerous ostentatious expressions of good faith. Hüseyin Cahit Yalçın of *Yeni Sabah* wrote: 'It is clear that the British Prime Minister has not come to our country to change Turkish policy or to apply pressure on Turkish diplomacy, as it has been reported in some countries.'[17] An unsigned leading article in *Cumhuriyet* countered Italian accusations that Churchill had come to Adana to, 'trick Turkey into joining the war on his side' by stating: 'A statesmen of Churchill's sagacity and intellect could not possibly be pursuing some half-baked dream.'[18] Yunus Nadi in the same paper claimed Turkish neutrality and 'stability' had been of service to both sides: 'Turkey has not wavered in her consistent policy during these four years of world crisis . . . Finally all sides have come to appreciate that . . . Turkey has rendered them a great service.'[19] Other writers stressed that at Adana postwar problems had been discussed for the first time and claimed that the conference had 'broadened the scope of the Anglo-Turkish Alliance'.[20]

However, the diametrically opposed positions of the Turks and the British, although ably camouflaged by the post-Adana rhetoric, were bound to come out into the open. It is only surprising that the seeds sown in Adana took a year to flower. On 14 February 1944 Ahmet Emin Yalman, the *doyen* of Turkish journalism, was to write a scathingly anti-British article called 'The Two Britons': 'The good Briton is the flower of mankind. He is always ready to see the two sides of any problem or dispute. But there is also the Bad Briton . . . He adopts all disguises, resorts to all intrigues . . . Nazism and Fascism have not invented anything new. They have merely become jealous of the English imperialist . . . ' Yalman then referred to the Adana lists and declared that 'none of the promised material' had arrived, whereas the 'Bad Briton' was now asking the Turks to, 'throw themselves into the fire'.[21] Although this was not an official pronouncement, given the degree of government control, Yalman could not have written such a strong article without official sanction.

MILITARY CONVERSATIONS

After the Adana conference Hugessen commented: 'It seemed understood between ourselves and the Turkish government that we could count on them if required, as soon as they were adequately equipped.'[22] As far as the Turks were concerned the British could count on no such thing. The Adana Lists became the focal point of the Anglo–Turkish contradiction. As put by Weisband, the Turks 'managed to change the issue from *what purpose this equipment* to *what amount of equipment.*'[23]

In April 1943 a British military mission arrived in Ankara to discuss 'Hardihood.' General Sir Henry Maitland Wilson headed the mission. Sir Henry was soon to note: 'Possibly with memories of General Liman Von Sanders and his mission to Turkey in 1913, missions were not welcome in Ankara.'[24] 'Hardihood' was a four-stage plan, starting with the provision of twenty-five RAF fighter squadrons, and ending with the arrival of two full armoured divisions.[25] Not even the first stage was completed. For the Turks realised that the completion of all the stages would mean their coming into the war. Thus started the process Weisband has called 'Operation Footdrag.'[26]

On 1 April the Ankara Embassy reported that the Turks were raising difficulties about the official status of the military mission and refused to discuss anything unless Service Attachés were present, 'any other mission would be regarded as private persons'.[27] The War Cabinet replied that fully fledged military talks had been agreed upon at Adana, it now seemed that 'the Turks have gone back on this'.[28] Maitland Wilson was to complain of 'tortuous and interminable negotiations' and noted that the Turkish military authorities seemed briefed not to enter into discussions of anything beyond defensive measures.[29]

Marshal Çakmak, Turkish Chief of Staff, who remembered only too well German high-handedness in the First World War, was anxious to avoid Turkish troops falling under foreign command, or permitting foreign forces to operate independently in Turkish territory.[30] The lack of technical skills was both a reality and a stalling tactic. Wilson urged Turkish commanders to teach their men mechanical skills but noted that this often meant that prospective tank crews 'had to be taught the workings of the internal combustion engine from page one of the book'.[31] But the fact was Turkish authorities did not want 'Hardihood' to succeed. Numerous bureaucratic barriers were put in the way of the speedy construction of airfields and

.at one point İnönü was actually warned by his staff that work on these installations was proceeding too rapidly.[32]

The Foreign Office became increasingly exasperated by Turkish behaviour at this time. When Saraçoğlu made a speech on the anniversary of the Turco-German Treaty in which he referred to Turkish success in keeping out of hostilities, G. L. Clutton found it, 'Objectionable and self-complacent bunk . . .' and added, 'but the time is surely coming when the Turks will be taught the lesson which exists in the Christian Bible and doubtless in the Kuran – that you cannot serve two masters'.[33] On 19 June Hugessen reported, 'I have pretty well given these people up . . . They simply will not listen to what they do not want to hear.'[34] Eden actually felt 'that a review of our policy to Turkey was due'.[35] On 26 June Menemencioğlu told Hugessen that he was extremely sensitive to 'groups of three powers working in Turkey'. The Ambassador felt the Minister of Foreign Affairs was of the opinion that the British were forcing the pace and not leaving 'Turkey to choose her own time to come in as she claimed had been agreed at Adana'.[36] The polite mask of Adana had been stripped away.

The Turkish press emphasised that Germany was still strong and could easily crush Turkey.[37] Yunus Nadi of *Cumhuriyet* stated that Turkey would fight only if attacked, this attitude was perfectly in keeping with Turkey's 'alliances and sympathies' which 'Churchill had understood and accepted . . . in Adana.'[38] It is worth noting that the Foreign Office files contain an admission dated 31 August 1943 that even if Turkey did not provide troops and only allowed use of her territory for air operations, 'either way the German attitude would be the same. German forces were very close to Turkey on the Dodecanese islands and Bulgarian border. Germans could attack and destroy vulnerable towns like İstanbul and İzmir.'[39]

THE FALL OF ITALY AND CATASTROPHE ON RHODES

Thus, both the British and the Turks knew that Germany was still strong enough to effect crippling damage on Turkey. Yet even so the British insistently told the Turks otherwise.

When Mussolini fell from power, on 25 July 1943, Churchill saw his chance to increase his pressure on Turkey.[40] But the Turkish reaction to the fall of Italy was noticeably low key. It was an indication of the

shifting emphasis of Turkish policy that the collapse of the power
which had been the major factor in their concluding the 1939 Treaty,
did not evoke a more vivid response. The British Embassy in Ankara
reported on 13 September, 'The Italian events might just as well have
happened in another world.'[41]

The key for Churchill's Turkish plans was Rhodes, along with the
other islands in the Aegean. These he believed could be snapped up
fairly quickly and would be valuable as a bargaining lever on Turkey.
The speedy capture of the key island, Rhodes, just off the Turkish
coast, 'might be decisive on Turkey . . . '[42] While in Washington and
apparently without informing Roosevelt (who had not been in favour
of diverting landing craft for Churchill's venture) the Prime Minister
wired General Wilson, 'This is the time to play high. Improvise and
dare.'[43]

But the British plan which relied on the co-operation of the Italian
garrison in Rhodes failed miserably. By 13 September Rhodes was
entirely in German hands. Churchill, however, refused to give up and
ordered landing parties onto the other islands, hoping ironically to
'reduce the island [Rhodes] by the methods adopted by the Turks in
1522 . . . '[44] But Süleyman the Magnificent did not have to contend
with paratroopers and Stuka bombers. Hitler too, saw the islands in
terms of their possible bearing on Turkey's attitude, and diverted
valuable forces to hold them. One by one, the weak invading forces of
the British capitulated.

As far as Turkey was concerned, the intense bombardment of
targets just off their shores demonstrated what the Germans could as
easily do to İzmir or İstanbul, despite Churchill's assurances at
Adana. Churchill himself noted: 'Turkey, witnessing the extraordi-
nary inertia of the Allies near her shores, became much less forthcoming and denied us her airfields.'[45] What the Prime Minister could
not have known was that the Rhodes fiasco simply furnished a splendid excuse for a predetermined line of action.

The Foreign Office noted on 5 October that although the Turks
had been very helpful during the British fight to hold the islands, the
loss of Kos and Leros would have an adverse effect on them. 'But it
can hardly be encouraging for the Turks to take another step along
the path of co-operation, to realise that their first step was quite
needless because we were unable to hold Kos . . . '[46] The British
Consulate in İzmir reported on 12 October that their informant had
been to Bodrum (the small Turkish town right opposite Kos) and:

Here the population had a clear notion of the course of events. They reported that the occupation had been a half-hearted affair, badly conceived and prepared. We had carried it out with the assistance of the local population and anti-fascists. But as soon as the Germans got the upper hand in Rhodes and sent dive bombers over, the Italians reverted to fascism, and the British with their local supporters now not numbering more than a couple of hundred had to take to the hills. The arrival of the British fugitives in bad order in Bodrum was additional evidence of the German success and gave rise to much gloomy comment. The German re-occupation has greatly disturbed public opinion and it is felt that British prestige calls for a prompt clean-up of the islands.[47]

The Foreign Office had no illusions about the failure in the Dodecanese. G. L. Clutton wrote on 20 October, 'My personal view is that we have no chance whatever of getting anything serious from the Turks until we have got the Dodecanese . . . In fact we missed the bus when we allowed 30,000 Italians on Rhodes to capitulate to 7,000 Germans.'[48]

The Turkish press was very definite on that point. The clear contradiction between Churchill's assurances and the way things turned out in Rhodes found its echo in the press as Anglo-Turkish relations cooled. Yalman responded to the urgings of 'The Bad Briton': 'Just give us bases. [Says the Bad Briton.] The Germans? . . . We know how few aircraft they have in the Balkans. What? They attacked us during the Rhodes campaign in waves of hundreds of aircraft? So why remind us of that? . . . '[49] Other articles vehemently denied that the fall of any island could influence Turkish policy. 'Turkey cannot be influenced by the capture or loss of Leros.'[50]

But the British failure in close proximity to Turkish shores gave Turkey a chance to invest in British goodwill. Although she did not allow use of her territory to provide air cover, supplies were delivered to the beleaguered British forces and Turkish fishing boats and light craft helped evacuate units of the Royal West Kent, Irish Fusilier and other regiments.[51] The Foreign Office reported on 20 October that ammunition, petrol and military supplies had been transported on Turkish railways.[52] The same light craft evacuated Brigadier Baird, Colonel Tzigantes (commander of the Greek Sacred Squadron), General Soldarelli (the Italian commander), the Greek Archbishop and hundreds of civilians from Samos on 18–19 November 1943.[53]

Foreign Minister Menemencioğlu personally directed all Turkish co-operation in the islands: 'The fact that . . . Menemencioğlu was personally in charge of these operations further strengthens the evidence that he was neither particularly a foe of Britain or a friend to the Germans.'[34]

The Foreign Ministers Conference in Moscow bringing together Eden, Hull, and Molotov on 19 October marks the beginning of Soviet pressure on Turkey. As the fortunes of war began to favour Soviet arms there had been increasing comment in the official Soviet press that Turkish neutrality favoured Germany.[35] Against this background at the first session of the Conference Molotov presented his proposals to shorten the war. These were the cross-channel invasion and bringing in Turkey. This seemed to give Churchill's pet plan a new lease on life, and he now saw another opportunity for 'opening up the Dardanelles and Bosphorus'.[36]

At this stage the British had to tread carefully. Although overjoyed at the Soviet support for his policies, Churchill did not want to alienate the Americans, who he knew were not keen on a Balkan Campaign.[37] Therefore Eden tried to make it look as though they were being swayed to the Soviet view: 'If however our Soviet friends thought we ought to press Turkey, we should be glad to consider the matter.'[38] Although he dutifully recounted the official line of misgivings over Turkish entry Eden said, 'It was not a point of view which was held very strongly.' As to the overall Anglo-Soviet position on the issue, 'there was no disagreement between them as to the desirability of bringing Turkey into the war.'[39]

Thus the British brought their policy into agreement with the Soviets. Churchill's thinking seems to have evolved along the following lines. If Turkey came in as a result of contractual agreements with Britain alone she would demand the material promised to her but which was now in short supply. But, if Turkey 'came in of her own accord', in other words as a result of Anglo–Soviet–American pressure, or possibly as a result of German attack, the same advantages would be reaped without the attendant sacrifices.[60] Accordingly, on 28 October Eden told the conference that he proposed to study the Soviet proposal and to examine whether, 'by any means [we can] bring sufficient pressure to bear on Turkey to force her to enter the war, without placing ourselves in the position of having to discharge a commitment which is beyond our power at the present time'.[61] The Turkish statesmen, Menemencioğlu in particular, were soon to get the impression that Britain wanted to push them into the war whether they were prepared or not.[62]

The American reaction was lukewarm. Hull, when approached by Molotov on this issue said, 'he preferred not to speak on military matters'.[63] Hull then referred the question to Roosevelt 'Roosevelt's reply to Hull reflecting this note of caution was negative.'[64] Molotov however kept up the pressure and implied that the success or failure of the conference hinged on the Turkish issue. If agreement was not reached he said, Turkish entry might turn into 'a sore that might fester once the good effects of the Conference had worn off . . . '[65]

In response to American insistence that no forces be diverted to Turkey from the Italian and European theatres, on 2 November Eden told Harriman, the American Ambassador to Moscow, that Britain had 'no intention of sending Turkey any additional assistance beyond the arms now being supplied and a small fighter force they expected to move from the Middle East'.[66] Eden, therefore, intended forcing Turkey into the fire without giving her anything like the support she had been promised. The final outcome of the conference was a joint protocol agreed on 2 November whereby Turkey would be asked to come in 'before the end of 1943' and before that immediately provide air bases. In the final instance, 'Roosevelt also acquiesced (4 November) subject to the proviso that no resources be committed to the Eastern Mediterranean.'[67]

The reaction of the Turkish press to the conference was a mixture of ostentatious trust, suspicion, and wary reserve as to its conclusions. On 21 October F. R. Atay wrote in the official *Ulus*: 'The Soviets have always said that they equate the establishment of a just and secure peace with their security. Soviet policy has not shown signs of expansionism and irredentism. Even the arrangements she made with Germany can be seen as security precautions against a Germany expanding towards her frontiers.'[68] Compared to the strident tones of Turkish journalism *vis-à-vis* the Soviets in the previous stages of the war, the same columnists now seemed to be actually seeking excuses for past Soviet behaviour. The notoriously anti-Soviet Hüseyin Cahit Yalçın was to write on 22 October: 'It would be irrational to think that our Soviet neighbours with whom we have had friendly relations for so long would have anything but friendly intentions towards Turkey.'[69] Although leading writers declared that they did not suspect Britain or the United States of any deals made with the Soviets at Turkey's expense they were anything but at ease. Despite Roosevelt's public reassurances of faith in the Soviets' role in the post-war world the conclusion of the conference left them wondering: 'What did the Conference accomplish? Only Mr Roosevelt's trust (in post-war collaboration) has been reinforced . . . Translated into military terms, this is like proclaiming that important advances have been made when one or two kilometres of ground have been gained . . . '[70]

THE EDEN–MENEMENCIOĞLU MEETING

It was against this background of innuendo and distrust that Menemencioğlu met with Eden in Cairo on 5–7 November. The situation was not helped by the fact that the two men disliked each other. Eden quite simply thought that Menemencioğlu was pro-Axis, and Menemencioğlu saw Eden as a 'theatrical man' who was 'full of himself'.[71] Menemencioğlu claims in his memoirs that he found a surprise awaiting him at Cairo: 'Mr Eden told me that Mr Churchill wanted Turkey to declare war on Germany within a month at the latest.'[72] The Minister stated that Eden was guided by considerations of Russian loyalty: 'Mr Eden has brought back a deplorable impression from Moscow . . . The brutal insistence of the Russians had led him to fear that they would abandon the struggle against Germany . . . ' Therefore, 'Turkey was the only suitable offering to appease the Gods . . . '[73] The British and American record however, conflicts with this account and states that Eden spoke primarily of air bases and assured Menemencioğlu, 'there was no intention to press Turkey to go to war on an all-out basis'.[74]

Menemencioğlu saw no difference in the two courses of action and pressed Eden with questions which were, by his own admission, 'very indiscreet'. He harried Eden over Soviet intentions, asking pointedly about Iran and Poland.[75] In short, Menemencioğlu felt that Eden was acting as a mouthpiece of the Soviets: 'I was soon convinced that it was at Russian instigation that Mr Eden was pressing for the precipitate entry of Turkey into the war . . . '[76] Indeed, Eden could only have strengthened this conviction when he threatened Menemencioğlu by pointing to 'the unenviable position in which Turkey would find itself *vis-à-vis* the Russians in the event it declined to meet the British wishes'.[77]

It was a clumsy move and proved completely counter-productive. Menemencioğlu flatly stated that the proposed RAF squadrons would only draw German wrath without providing adequate support, and refused to accept them.[78] After a particularly tough session Eden cabled Churchill: 'My persuasions were the less effective as both the Foreign Minister and Açıkalın [The Secretary General] seemed to be particularly deaf . . . when I appealed to the younger official he too seemed to have difficulty in hearing what I said. No one can be so deaf as a Turk who does not want to be persuaded.'[79]

When Eden, attempting to end the meeting on a friendly note, asked if Menemencioğlu had any message for Churchill, the latter replied: 'Please ask Mr Winston Churchill to remember Adana, and re-read the document he gave us one morning. I am sure he will understand.'[80] This was a clear reference to Churchill's 'Morning Thoughts' in which he had played down any active involvement on Turkey's part and stressed that he would not force Turkey.

THE AFTERMATH OF THE EDEN–MENEMENCIOGU MEETING

The Eden–Menemencioğlu meeting marks a watershed in Anglo-Turkish relations. It led to the declaration on 17 November, which Turkey accepted in principle, that she would come into the war. The Turks therefore shifted their ground from the specific to the general. Although they refused bases they insisted on talking quite definitely about full Turkish participation. This way they hoped to resist British prodding by repeating that an 'overall plan' was needed. An 'overall plan' which needed discussion meant time gained. They also knew that the Americans were against a Balkan campaign and that the Soviets were becoming increasingly suspicious of British intentions in the Balkans. It was clear that Churchill would have to go the way of his allies. Thus by demonstrating apparent goodwill by insisting on inclusion in a long-term campaign they knew to be unlikely the Turks insured themselves against short-term demands which might involve them in the war.

Menemencioğlu was well aware of Soviet–American reluctance as to Churchill's Balkan option: 'Mr Churchill's idea of a Balkan action did not have Mr Roosevelt's ear.'[81] Yet Eden had written to Churchill: 'What the Turks are after is some statement from us about our future Balkan strategy and the part they can play in it. I doubt whether we can give them much comfort on this score.'[82] Soon after he returned from Cairo, Menemencioğlu saw the American Ambassador in Ankara, Steinhardt, and made a plea against British efforts to push Turkey into the war. Steinhardt reported that Turkey preferred to discuss full entry rather than a mere granting of bases. Menemencio-ğlu had emphasised that Eden was being unreasonable in asking for Turkey's involvement, 'without at least a partial disclosure of Allied military plans in respect to the Near East and the Balkans.'[83]

During Menemencioğlu's Cairo visit and after, the press insistently denied that Turkey was yielding to pressure in one sense or another. A. E. Yalman was to reassure public opinion that: 'All decisions taken during the Cairo talks and after will be based entirely on consider-ations of our own interests, and not external pressures or wishes . . . '[84] Turkish columnists wrote polemical articles answering Reuter's reports that Turkey was about to furnish air bases and depart from neutrality: 'But as Turkey has no ambitions outside her borders and her national cause is only the safeguarding of her integrity, it is difficult to find reasons which would make us follow such a course . . . '[85]

Nadir Nadi criticised foreign journalists for irresponsible guess-work: 'Since 1939 whenever a Turkish statesman has met any official of a friendly or allied country the world press has abounded with articles promoting half-baked ideas . . . '[86] Thus, although the papers spoke of 'journalists' their language suggests a clear warning to British statesmen. A leading Turkish columnist and foreign policy expert, A. Ş. Esmer told the author that it was suspected in some quarters that Britain might be intending to face Turkey with a *fait accompli* by giving her just enough aircraft to provoke German attack.[87] This way, although Turkish official channels adopted a much more reserved tone towards the British, the papers were allowed to hint that Turkey would not be bullied into any decision not her own.

THE TEHRAN CONFERENCE

However, to secure American and Soviet aid in pressing Turkey to take just such a decision was Churchill's primary aim at Tehran. In Hopkins' words: 'He [Churchill] reverted to the desirability of getting Turkey into the war, as he did over and over again with a persistence that was both admirable and monotonous.'[88] Although Molotov had been the prime mover in Moscow in forcing Turkish entry, at Tehran the Soviets were now remarkably reluctant. This *volte-face* is difficult to explain, except if seen in context with Turkey's repeated 'sincere' pleas for an 'overall plan' in the Balkans which the Soviets were anything but keen on. As Kuniholm has pointed out: 'Turkish diplomacy, by insisting on military cooperation in the Balkans, circumvented Soviet machinations: the use of Allied troops would have conflicted with Soviet ambitions in the area.' It is interesting that Kuniholm's explanation also tallies with Turkish sources. Erkin states that the Soviets were hoping to separate Turkey from Britain and thus ensure their domination over her in the postwar world. Similarly, Aydemir points out that the Soviets did not want a strong Turkey on their doorstep.[89]

At the first Plenary Meeting of the conference on 28 November, Churchill concentrated on Stalin and actively tried to fan back into flame Soviet determination on Turkish entry. But Stalin refused to be drawn and went on to criticise the dispersal of forces in Italy, Turkey etc. and inquired whether it would not be better to concentrate on 'Overlord.'[90] Stalin further insisted that he did not think it would be possible to bring Turkey in as the Turkish attitude so far had been reluctant and their attitude negative. Here Churchill interjected, 'then in his opinion the Turks were crazy'. Stalin replied: 'there were some people who apparently preferred to remain crazy'.[91] The British Prime Minister who only seven months previously had gone on record as stating in the Commons: 'Turkey is our Ally. Turkey is our friend . . . ' and calling Turkey, 'a solid barrier against aggression from all directions' now concurred with Turkey's most likely postwar enemy that the Turks were 'crazy'.[92]

Roosevelt, always hesitant about bringing Turkey in, was swayed to the view of his military advisers who feared that an Aegean or Balkan campaign would detract from 'Overlord.' Thus, although he agreed to meet with İnönü and 'do everything possible to persuade him to enter the war . . . ' Roosevelt's view was, 'if he were in the Turkish President's place he would demand such a price in planes, tanks and equipment that to grant the request would indefinitely postpone "Overlord"'.[93]

Faced with American–Soviet opposition over his favourite idea, Churchill now hit upon the surprising tactic of whetting Soviet postwar appetites *vis-à-vis* Turkey. On 29 November Churchill told Stalin that a failure to respond to a three-power invitation would lead the

Fig. 6 The Cairo Summit. (*Courtesy of Cumhuriyet*)

British government to tell the Turks that this 'would have very serious political and territorial consequences for Turkey particularly in regard to the future status of the Straits . . . '[94]

When the Soviet delegation showed signs of wariness at this sudden generosity, Eden asked Molotov on 30 November why they had been so much more enthusiastic in Moscow over Turkish entry. Molotov answered that the Turkish attitude after the Eden–Menemencioğlu meeting had damped their enthusiasm.[95] The Turks would also have regarded with horror the spectacle of Churchill giving helpful advice to the Soviets on the weakness of the Turkish armed forces. When Stalin asked Churchill 'what the Turkish Army lacked in the way of armaments', Churchill generously supplied information about the sad state of the Turkish forces which he said were lacking in anti-tank and anti-aircraft weaponry with very few serviceable aircraft.[96] The Prime Minister volunteered to lay before İnönü: 'the ugly case which would result from the failure of Turkey to accept the invitation to join the war, and the unappetising picture of what help could be afforded her if she did'.[97]

By 1 December, however, the Soviet delegation seemed to be rising to the bait, as Molotov asked Churchill what he had meant by his statement about the Straits. Churchill replied that, 'he personally favoured a change in the regime of the Straits if Turkey proved obdurate . . . ' [98] Churchill's attitude doubtless worked to encourage the Soviets in their later demands on Turkey. It is interesting to note that the very same Prime Minister who on 1 December announced that he would 'wash his hands of Turkey' and not guarantee the safety of the Straits if she did not behave, had said of Turkey on 11 February of the same year: 'We wish her [Turkey] well, and we wish to see her territory, rights and interests effectively preserved.'[99]

THE CAIRO SUMMIT

The Turks had looked upon the Tehran Conference with some fore-boding as they feared the Soviets and British would convince the Americans that Turkey should fight unprepared. They approached the Cairo summit in the same spirit.

The interesting factor before the summit was that the British seemed to consider İnönü as pro-war but held back by a reluctant government and public opinion. As early as 31 October the Foreign Office picked on İnönü's National Day speech to indicate that Turkey was getting ready to take a more active part. A Foreign Office translation gave one passage as mentioning:

The honour and the prestige of the heroic and industrious Turkish people whose sole concern is to reconstruct the motherland and to contribute to the advancement of the family of people which are free and independent. We do not shirk from great sacrifices, and this truth will be further enhanced in a future fraught with uncertainties.[100]

G. L. Clutton of the Foreign Office seized upon the section mentioning 'sacrifices', as meaning that Turkey was shifting her attitude: 'All press messages from Angora hail this speech as a definite indication that Turkey is now about to take a more active part in the war.'[101]

It is a measure of the British misunderstanding of Turkey's position that they took a speech, which specifically referred to Turkey's 'sole concern' as being 'reconstruction', to indicate that Turkey was moving towards war. It is a measure of the same lack of comprehension that they took 'sacrifice' to mean sacrifice in furtherance of *their* interests. On 3 December Hugessen cabled the Foreign Office:

İsmet personally is our chief hope of belligerency and everything now depends on tactics employed with him. He is taking some risk in coming to Cairo and it is surprising that he has been able to carry a reluctant Parliament with him even to the point now reached . . . It is all a matter of timing and pushing but not rushing the President. Certainly he is willing and I think he could bring the country along in a short time.[102]

The Ambassador also said that there was considerable opposition to belligerency, particularly among an 'influential group of Deputies and Editors' which he felt might even threaten the position of the President. He advised the Foreign Office not to do anything which might threaten the position of the President.

Against all the evidence of his subsequent performance in Cairo this assessment of İnönü suggests that the President was deliberately exaggerating the opposition, in order to prompt the British into affording him the leeway he needed. Menemencioğlu used the same tactics in claiming that he had converted a whole Assembly of Deputies to his point of view, causing Clutton to comment that this statement should be taken 'with a pinch of salt'.[103] Also, in view of the grip İnönü had on his government and the press it was unlikely that a group of 'Deputies and Editors' could have shaken him. There was indeed heated debate in the Council of Ministers as to how İnönü should respond to the invitation to go to Cairo, but the outcome was that İnönü accepted, 'On condition that as between equals he is being invited to a free discussion and is not merely to be informed of decisions already arrived at in Tehran concerning Turkey.'[104] This reply bears the stamp of İnönü's historical conditioning. Too many Turkish delegations in the past had been 'summoned' to hear the great powers pronounce on their fate.

The provision of two aircraft, one American, the other British, one piloted by the President's son and one by the Prime Minister's son, led Menemencioğlu to suspect a degree of 'competition' between the two Allies. He noted the same competition to get at the Turkish delegation after the latter had arrived at Cairo on 4 December.[105] The Turkish delegation was to make good use of this.

The other thing Menemencioğlu noted was the conspicuous absence of the Russian delegation which could not be fortuitous at a meeting at this level: 'I suspected from then on that the Russians were keeping themselves behind a curtain which was not yet iron . . . '[106] These were in fact suspicions that Menemencioğlu had brought forward from his meeting with Eden. At one point during the proceedings he overheard Eden whisper to Roosevelt who seemed to be wavering: 'But Mr President, you are forgetting our commitments to the Russians.' It all seemed to fit together in Menemencioğlu's reasoning. The Soviets were pressing for a second front which the Americans could not yet provide, 'and the entry of Turkey into the war was to be their compensation'.[107]

The Cairo Summit represents the high point of pressure on Turkey. From the very outset Churchill played on Turkey's sensitivity regarding the Soviets, and warned İnönü that Turkey would find herself isolated after the war.[108] İnönü, in reply, pointed out time and again that the real danger to Turkey was that she should become involved in the war without proper preparation. Turkey was a loyal ally but she was totally unprepared. 'Turkey had mobilised everything she had, even material dating from the Middle Ages.'[109] İnönü proposed a two-stage plan: (a) a stage of preparation; (b) a stage of co-operation. 'What would suit Turkey best would be that she should fight side by side with British and American contingents on her own part of the world.'[110]

During the second Tripartite Meeting on 5 December İnönü's stalling tactics became clearly discernible. He refused to consider set dates for the various 'stages' in the British plan to incorporate Turkey and pointed out that the deliveries of the Adana Lists were already in arrears. When Churchill told him that the Turks had been slow in taking delivery of aircraft and learning how to use them, İnönü retorted that these were outmoded Hurricane fighters and insisted on more modern models.[111] When Churchill pointed out that the Portuguese had given the Allies air bases and the Germans did not bomb them, Menemencioğlu immediately pointed out that the Germans could not bomb the Azores where the bases were. A particularly thorny issue was the infiltration of British personnel in civilian disguise into Turkey for the preparation of airfields. Menemencioğlu had particularly strong feelings about this: 'All this was to take place right under the Germans' noses and one could not imagine that they would have allowed it without reacting vigorously.'[112] It is worth noting that Hopkins applied considerable pressure of his own over the issue of war material, stating that if Turkey did not come in the material would be sent elsewhere and admitting, 'We wanted Turkey in the war even if she could not have all she wanted.'[113]

Churchill stressed that 15 February 1944 was the 'critical and serious moment' after which he would declare his Turkish policy a failure.[114] To İnönü this meant he had to hold out past that point at all costs. He clutched at straws, claiming that a new class of conscripts was yet to be called up, or that the period of mud had not yet begun in Thrace (mud would serve to slow down any motorised attack).

Although most of the evidence seems to indicate that Roosevelt was not in favour of bringing Turkey in, it should be noted that another possibility exists. Roosevelt was not against Turkey fighting, as long as he did not have to supply material that would otherwise have gone towards the preparations for 'Overlord.' If Churchill managed to sway him by insisting that very little material would be needed, Turkey's entry could be seen as a very useful diversion for German forces that might otherwise have been used against 'Overlord.' Kuniholm points out that: 'One source observes that in 1943 the Turkish threat to the Nazi position in the Balkans kept 26 German divisions immobilized on the Bulgarian frontier.'[115] Roosevelt had after all contemplated operations in the upper Adriatic by reinforcing the Partisans under Tito. Sherwood records that Hopkins was 'surprised' at the Tehran Conference by Roosevelt's mention of an operation pushing into Romania from Yugoslavia linking up with the Red Army descending from Odessa.[116]

On 6 December Roosevelt saw İnönü alone before the conference adjourned. He did this at Hopkins' prompting, the latter having urged him to ask İnönü to come in by 15 February.[117] Although no record is to be found in the USFR series, a Cabinet Minister of the İnönü administration has stated İnönü told his Cabinet that

Roosevelt pressed him to come in if Turkey did not want to find herself alone after the war.[118]

In sum, all the Cairo Conference succeeded in doing was to postpone the definite date of Turkish entry. This date, the Turks hoped, would never arrive as, 'Without any greater commitment than 17 squadrons, which hardly constituted an adequate defense and certainly was not the collaborative plan the Turks required, the British wanted Turkey to assume an extremely vulnerable posture.' Although the Turks admitted in principle that they were going to come in, they reserved the right to decide whether or not they would allow 'fly-in of Allied air forces' by 15 February.[119] Eden felt there had been precious little gain. At the airfield, İnönü embraced Churchill in a gesture of farewell. Eden noted in his memoirs: 'This attention delighted the Prime Minister who said as we drove back to Cairo: "Did you see, İsmet kissed me." My reply, perhaps rather ingracious, was that as this seemed to be the only gain from fifteen hours of hard argument, it was not much to be pleased with.'[120]

THE AFTERMATH OF THE CAIRO SUMMIT

The Germans were kept informed by the Turks as to the proceedings of the conference and its aftermath. No doubt their ability to read the Turkish diplomatic cipher allowed them tremendous advantage.[121] Also, von Papen was able to double check on Menemencioğlu's information through his agent 'Cicero' planted on Hugessen.[122] The German Ambassador made it clear after the Turkish delegation returned that even one Allied aircraft on Turkish soil meant war with Germany. On 18 December Menemencioğlu was to assure Papen that Turkey would remain neutral. Measures had been taken against any *fait-accompli*, Turkish forces had strict orders to fire on any uninvited aircraft, and preparations had been made to destroy all air installations in case of a forced Allied 'fly-in'. British military personnel already in the country were being watched day and night.[123]

Immediately upon his return İnönü held a Cabinet meeting where he informed his Ministers of decisions taken at Cairo. The Turkish Chief of Staff, Marshal Çakmak, was then asked to give his appraisal of the state of readiness of the Turkish forces. The Marshal painted a dark picture. Only one-third of Turkish aircraft were operational. They had some anti-aircraft equipment but none of the crews knew how to use them. The German air force based on the islands and in

Bulgaria was easily capable of wiping out İstanbul, İzmir, all major railway connections to Ankara, and all industrial areas within twenty-four hours. İnönü thanked Çakmak and told those present that his views completely coincided with the Marshal's: Turkey had to be kept out.[124] Accordingly, on 12 December Turkey gave the Allies her official answer. Turkey could not accept 'fly-in' by 15 February, as the material condition of the Turkish forces was not up to meeting German attack. Turkey insisted on military preparations and a general plan of operations in the Balkans.[125]

As always the press closely followed the official line. Yalçın in *Tanin* underlined that although Turkey was loyal to her obligations, their fulfilment, 'depends on talks between the two allies and the fulfilment of certain conditions'.[126] Nadir Nadi, although applauding the conference as an example of frank discussion, concluded that indispensable military supplies were still lacking.[127] Significantly, Asım Us of *Vakit* recalled that İnönü had also been the chief negotiator of the Lausanne Treaty in 1923: 'İsmet İnönü has completed the great service he rendered to the Turkish nation as the chief negotiator of the Lausanne talks after the War of Liberation, by his success in the Cairo talks as the Turkish President.'[128] From the British standpoint this comparison with Lausanne could hardly have been welcomed.

Indeed, in the last days of 1943, the Anglo-Turkish contradiction began to find reflection in the increasingly rancorous tone adopted by both sides. The British became quite adamant in their insistence on what G. L. Clutton openly called, 'The next steps in dragging Turkey into the war . . . '[129] The Turks on the other hand, dug in and refused to be intimidated, realising that if they held now, by Churchill's own admission at Cairo, Turkish entry at a later date would have no value.

On 12 December Hugessen reported that Menemencioğlu had asked for 126 Spitfire fighters, 500 Sherman tanks and some 66,800 tons of petrol. These demands he said were far in excess of the 58,000 ton British ceiling for military supplies to Turkey: 'I left the Minister in no doubt as to the deplorable effect of these demands, and said that whereas I had hitherto been ready to believe in Turkish sincerity even I was now seriously shaken . . . '[130] On the same day the Ambassador reported further that Menemencioğlu had been very bitter in his insistence that 'Turkey was being sacrificed to a bargain with Russia . . . Turkey was being pressed to enter the war in consequence of this bargain regardless of sacrifices this would entail.'[131]

The Foreign Office retorted on 13 December that the Turkish reply was 'an outrageous affair'. Clutton emphasised that Turkish railways could not possibly carry the equipment demanded, and if it were true that Turkey had only two days' supply of petrol and bread, 'the whole Turkish government including Numan Menemencioğlu should resign as being totally incompetent'.[132] Yet Hugessen replied that he had got no more joy from other Turkish officials; 'I was unable to induce the Secretary General to budge one inch.'[133]

Still, pressure from London mounted. On 13 December Churchill telegraphed to Eden that Hugessen should be instructed to 'put the screw on hard' at Ankara. The Ambassador was to tell the Turks that if satisfactory results were not forthcoming in the projected Anglo-Turkish military co-ordination talks, Britain would not support Turkey *vis-à-vis* the Soviets after the war: 'The Turks must be made to see that with the development of aerial warfare the Dardanelles no longer held a crucial importance and that they were not indispensable.'[134]

Gambling that short-term unpopularity would give way before Britain's long-term needs of security for her Empire, the Turks dug in their heels.

10 . THE TURKISH GAMBIT: 1944

The contradiction which had been inherent in Anglo-Turkish relations since 1939 only flared-up publicly in 1944. The relations of the two allies hit an all-time low with bitter language being used on both sides. However, for the Turkish statesmen, guided by their historical conditioning, the Anglo-Soviet partnership was an unnatural one. Hugessen's assessment of Menemencioğlu's view was that the latter, 'seems to have taken it for granted that the war once over, the old jealousies would revive . . .' making Turkey indispensable as a barrier against the Soviet Union.[1] In Menemencioğlu's own words: 'We knew that sooner or later our trusting relationship would be restored and that this bad mood would pass . . .'[2] On the other hand, although he appreciated the value of Turkey's location for British interests, İnönü could not allow himself to drift too far from his ally as the Soviets were growing daily more powerful. He therefore set in motion a series of moves designed to win his way back into favour.

THE LINNEL MISSION

In keeping with the arrangements made in Cairo, a British military mission arrived in Ankara in early January headed by Air Marshal Linnel. Linnel soon reported that the Turks were not going to give up their claim to any of the material asked for in December 1943.[3] The talks were to take on a bitter tone and Hugessen reported that Menemencioğlu was obsessed with the idea of an 'unholy compact' between Britain and the Soviet Union.[4] In his private papers Menemencioğlu has indicated that during the course of the negotiations he noticed that most of the proposed British installations were in the south of Turkey. This led him to wonder whether the British were deliberately leaving the north to the Soviets: 'Why was the North being left empty? Empty in provision for what? I was tormented by

166

these questions . . .'[5] In his view British policy was dangerously misguided as it was ruled by short-term considerations. Also, if Turkey allowed British bases on her territory this might set a precedent enabling the Soviets to ask for the same privileges.[6]

The Turkish attitude thoroughly exasperated Churchill who proposed on 19 January that unless İnönü allowed 'fly-in' by 15 February the alliance should be pronounced null and void. The Foreign Office however, restrained him and Eden pointed out that a Soviet-dominated or unfriendly Turkey would not be in keeping with Britain's long-term interests: 'Before we go to extremes, we should be certain that our immediate military needs justified action contrary to our long-term political (and military) interests.'[7] This was to be the first of several occasions on which the Foreign Office restrained Churchill. They were also aided by the Joint Chiefs of Staff who still wanted to keep Turkey in hand as a potential source of danger for Germany.[8] Churchill therefore settled for a 'policy of aloofness' as the Linnel Mission abruptly left Ankara on 4 February and Hugessen was instructed to 'put up his shutters and lie low'.[9]

The policy of aloofness came almost as relief to the Turks as it had the effect of postponing any definite action on their part. Indeed the Ankara Embassy reported on 21 February that Menemencioğlu was encouraged to the point of telling Axis representatives in Ankara that, as long as he was at the Turkish Foreign Ministry, Turkey would not abandon neutrality.[10] In fact Menemencioğlu was rapidly becoming the focus of all British reproach. On 10 February S. Bennet reported from Ankara that it was felt that Menemencioğlu had given the Axis extensive information about Turco-British military talks.[11]

Turkish public opinion reacted to the departure of the British mission with a mixture of self-righteous indignation and somewhat nervous self-justification. N. Sadak in *Akşam* wrote: 'We liken this dispute with the British to the situation in the days before the French Armistice when the British asked us to come into the war only to admit later that they had been over hasty, and that we were right to stay put . . . We will be proven right once again.'[12] Peyami Sefa in *Tasvir-i Efkâr* referred to *The Times* comment that unless Turkey helped rid Europe of Nazism she would be left out after the war: 'In the Anglo-Turkish Treaty document, there is no clause on "freeing Europe from Nazism". We have never promised to any nation that we would enter into any ideologically based war . . .'[13] Nadir Nadi of *Cumhuriyet* inquired whether there had been a change in British policy, concluding: 'Saying that if Turkey does not do this or that she will be alone in the world, or that she has only so much time, and other pronouncements wavering between threat and ultimatum can only have an adverse effect on Turkey.'[14] N. Sadak attacked *The Times* for hinting that Turkey should do the best she could with the arms she had: 'If arms are not needed as *The Times* suggests, why was the condition of arms supply put in the Treaty? . . . It is horrifying even to contemplate what would have happened if we had thrown ourselves into the fire (when France collapsed), counting on our allies . . .'[15]

THE CHROME ISSUE

The first opportunity for Turkey to win its way back into favour with the Allies came over the chrome issue. The Allies felt that the export of this strategic ore to Germany was a serious breach of faith. During January and February 1944 the Turks had actually increased their chrome shipments to Germany from 13,564 tons in 1943 to 56,649 tons. But this was still well below the 90,000 tons suggested in the Clodius agreement.[16] In March 1944 the British and Americans considered applying blockade measures on Turkey and stopping their pre-emptive buying.[17]

Chrome had also become an extremely sensitive issue as the Allies had noticed that other neutrals seemed to be taking their cue from Turkey over the question of strategic exports. On 18 March Hugessen reported that the Spanish had made attempts in Turkey to gather all information possible on Turkish chrome shipments to Germany including quantities and methods of shipment. The Spanish Minister concerned had told Menemencioğlu that, 'the idea was to take a leaf out of the Turkish book and get a share in the pickings by making a deal with the Germans over Spanish wolfram'. The Foreign Office conceded that the Spanish had a case as Turkey as an ally had been allowed to send strategic ore to Germany. They noted that the Portuguese had also made similar inquiries at Ankara.[18]

Therefore, the Allies decided to put an end to this obvious discrepancy and on 19 April Hugessen and the American Ambassador, Steinhardt, confronted Menemencioğlu with notes of protest against chrome shipments to Germany. Menemencioğlu, who also seemed to have thawed out considerably, told Steinhardt that he wished the Allies would 'relieve him from this dilemma by destroying the means of transportation between Turkey and Germany'.[19] On 20 April the

Turkish Foreign Minister announced that all chrome exports to Germany would cease. He further made it quite clear that the cessation of chrome deliveries was intended as a gesture towards Britain. On 20 April he told the General Assembly: 'As the foundation of our foreign policy is the treaty of alliance with Britain which you approved in 1939, and have supported since then, we are not neutral. In that case we must examine the notes presented by the Allies, not as a neutral but as an ally.'[20] Menemencioğlu did however take pains to point out that Turkey had not been guilty of unethical behaviour as she had first offered her chrome to Britain on a long-term basis but they had refused.[21]

The press was also quick to defend the official line and emphasised that trade was a necessary life-line of the country. N. Sadak commented in *Akşam*: 'The question to be borne in mind when asking for sacrifices . . . is the following: does a neutral country sell certain goods deliberately to help the enemy, or in order to procure for itself vital economic necessities?'[22] However, a dramatic change came over Sadak after the government's decision was announced: 'It is clearly discernible from Menemencioğlu's words that Turkey has not considered the Allies' note from the point of view of a selfish neutral country, but from the point of view of a country eager to fulfil its obligations towards its alliance partner.'[23] Also, Nadir Nadi in *Cumhuriyet* and F. R. Atay in the official *Ulus* underlined that Turkey was not acting as a neutral power but as an ally.[24]

PASSAGE OF AXIS SHIPPING THROUGH THE STRAITS

This obvious shift in favour of the Allies was to be further accentuated over the issue of Axis shipping. According to the Montreux Convention of 1936, when Turkey is not a belligerent in time of war, merchant ships of all flags have liberty of passage through the Straits. In wartime, if Turkey is non-belligerent the Straits are closed to warships of all countries. The convention describes war vessels according to tonnage, speed, equipment and function.[25] But there is a grey area covering auxiliary craft which was further complicated during the war as most merchant vessels of belligerents were armed for defence purposes. The matter had in fact become something of a running sore in Anglo-Turkish relations throughout the war with Churchill repeatedly putting pressure on Turkey to interpret the Montreux Convention in a manner blatantly favouring Britain. Although the

Foreign Office told him that it was most unlikely that Turkey would 'tear up' the Montreux Convention for their convenience, 'This was a hard fact which Churchill, then and later found . . . difficult to accept.'[26]

Barker notes that Turkish policy was a constant handicap for Britain's economic warfare in the Balkans. In June and July 1940 as German armies occupied Romania, Romanian barges and tugs which had been chartered by the British to prevent their carrying Romanian oil, escaped to Turkey but were immobilised by Turkey's strict interpretation of neutrality. Also in 1941 the Vichy government instituted a *démarche* in Turkish courts to gain possession of former French craft in Turkish ports. In fact, when an invasion of Turkey seemed imminent in 1941, the British made plans to sink all of these vessels. But the Turks avoided handing over the vessels to the Axis by prolonged stalling tactics in the courts.

It is interesting that Foreign Office records show similar stalling tactics were applied to the British who complained in August 1943: 'We bring successful action in the Courts but when it comes to executing the judgements we find that every obstacle is put in our way . . .'[27] Yet Turkey attempted to maintain a balance, and in early May 1944 two Romanian liners which were going to be used to evacuate German troops from Sevastopol were not allowed to leave İstanbul harbour.[28]

What brought matters to a head was Turkey allowing passage to three *Kriegstransport* and three EMS class vessels, both sets of craft being assessed as auxiliaries. On 3 June 1944 Hugessen filed a strong protest with Menemencioğlu claiming that, 'Everything was done to facilitate their passage according to a timetable desired by the Germans.'[29] However, Menemencioğlu adhered strictly to the letter of the Montreux Convention and argued that Turkey had to decide on whether a ship was a warship on the evidence at the time of passage through their controls. What purpose she served after she had cleared the Straits was beyond Turkey's jurisdiction.[30] This caused an uproar in Britain, with Eden accusing Menemencioğlu of 'inadequate and hurried inspection' and of lending himself to a 'palpable manoeuvre'.[31] Yet the British case was considerably weakened by the fact that they had violated Turkish neutrality with tacit Turkish approval during the Aegean Campaigns of 1943.[32]

Menemencioğlu proposed settling the issue by referring the matter to an independent Swiss jurist. Both the Germans and the British rejected this solution as too lengthy. Indeed it was rapidly becoming clear that the British wanted to make this a test case of the Turkish attitude. On 8 June Hugessen told Saraçoğlu that the situation was becoming untenable as 'one day Turkey seemed to favour us and the next the Germans'. He also put the matter to İnönü who agreed to be co-operative subject to assurances that relations would return to the previous basis of the alliance.[33] The Turks therefore insisted on a thorough search of the *Kassel* which revealed that she was heavily armed.[34]

It thus became obvious to İnönü that the cause of *rapprochement* with Britain required a public sacrifice. Menemencioğlu was the obvious choice. Throughout the war his vigorous efforts at maintaining Turkish independence and freedom of action had earned him the label of 'Pro-Axis', and he was regarded as, 'the Minister largely responsible for the Turkish refusal to enter the war on the side of the Allies'.[35]

On the occasion of his resignation on 15 June the Foreign Office gave vent to its feelings: 'There is evidence I am sure from 1940 that Numan, then Secretary General, was widely considered to be in German pay and completely in the German pocket.'[36] G. L. Clutton commented on 17 June that the news of Menemencioğlu's resignation arrived, 'When we were considering whether or not we should not make the attempt to get rid of Numan by direct action.'[37] İnönü also made sure that Hugessen got the full details of the Cabinet meeting at which Menemencioğlu's resignation was concluded.[38]

The press also stressed the change in emphasis of Turkish policy by openly stating that Menemencioğlu had been out of step with the new orientation. On 17 July an unsigned editorial in *Yeni Sabah* stated: 'Foreign Minister Menemencioğlu's recent policies have not met with the approval of the Cabinet . . . The government cannot tolerate the tipping of the scales in Germany's favour for any reason or in any form . . .'[39] H. C. Yalçın of *Tanin* stated that Menemencioğlu's 'specialised training' had made him unable to be flexible in times of changing fortunes of war: 'The Turkish Republic, at this most critical time has once more demonstrated its ability to take sudden and radical decisions. This has led it to make a sharp change in the course of its foreign policy. We must see Numan Menemencioğlu's resignation in this light.'[40] Leading columnists constantly underlined that this was a new tack for Turkish foreign policy. Compared with possible stock excuses for a resignation like 'reasons of health', the government (i.e. İnönü) made sure that the press gave the right message to the proper quarters.

Menemencioğlu's major worry in his handling of the Straits issue was that favouritism shown towards one party might set a precedent for demands from another. He wrote in his private papers: 'We were not a belligerent and our alliance with Britain by itself was not a reason for an arbitrary application of our contractual agreements . . .' It has been seen how he had stressed the issue during the Adana Conference in 1943. He emphasised that Turkey could have infringed on her neutrality on almost any other issue but: 'For the Straits we did not have this latitude . . . Those whom we might favour as allies, might one day be the very ones to use this argument against us and accuse us of having, at one moment in time, made the treaty-law of Montreux an instrument of our national policy . . .' Any sign of weakness on this issue would have given 'those who were only waiting for one lapse on our part . . .' the excuse to claim that Turkey was too weak to defend an international waterway.[41] The events of 1945 were to show how right he was.

The British were not slow to register the change in Turkey's attitude. On 6 May Eden circulated a memorandum to the War Cabinet noting the 'sudden readiness of the Turkish government to co-operate' at the expense of their relations with Germany.[42] Another memo dated the same day said the Turkish leaders had become frightened of the position of isolation they were seemingly drifting into, and were now beginning to think 'that they have not after all been so clever as they thought they were'.[43]

THE BREAK WITH GERMANY

With Menemencioğlu out of the way, the British moved towards securing Turkey's break from Germany. However, Menemencioğlu's resignation changed little in the fundamentals of Turkish policy which was based on the triple assurance of American reluctance to get involved in the Balkans, the Soviet reluctance to see an Allied campaign there, and the British reluctance to supply them with more arms. Thus when Hugessen confronted the Turks on 13 June with a demand that they break off diplomatic relations with Germany, Turkey was more determined than ever to conserve her strength. Both the United States and the Soviet Union lent only lukewarm support to the British move.[44]

The Turkish government broadly followed the tactics set by Menemencioğlu, even after his fall. They insisted that a declaration of war or a mere break in relations was not enough, and that Turkey was willing, indeed eager, to come into the war as a full ally. But in order for this to happen she must be supported militarily and assigned a specific role in a 'general plan'. When on 30 June Hugessen renewed pressure on Turkey to break with Germany, Saraçoğlu came back to the 'general plan' motif. Hugessen then confirmed Turkish doubts about a potential Balkan campaign by telling him that he knew of no British plans for the area. Saraçoğlu could then afford to suggest that Turkey give an ultimatum to Bulgaria and join with Russian troops in sweeping the Germans out.[45]

The Foreign Office and Churchill, on the other hand, almost wanted a diplomatic break rather than a full declaration of war because, as Eden told the Cabinet on 7 July, 'it would have the same moral effect on Germany without long discussions about war material'. Such a move the Foreign Secretary hinted, might even provoke the Germans into an act of vengeance which would directly involve Turkey in the war.[46] Eden's cynicism was matched by Churchill's who on 12 July sent a message to Stalin stating that the break in relations would be a step towards war as Turkey would be involved in a 'vengeance' attack from the air.[47] The Soviets, however, still showed reluctance claiming that a break-off of relations was a half-measure not in keeping with recent Allied military success.[48] The United States also made its reluctance to a Balkan campaign officially known to the Turks on 20 July by telling them that although the United States favoured full Turkish belligerency they were 'definitely opposed to the diversion of resources from the approved operations in Italy and the western Mediterranean'.[49]

The insistence on a general plan was reflected in the press. Yalçın of *Tanin* asked: 'Have the authorized representatives of our allies ever spoken of a plan, of a specific duty? How can a nation declare war without knowing what it is to do, without knowing where, against whom and as part of what general plan it is to fight?'[50]

When Turkey did break off diplomatic relations with Germany on 2 August the Soviet attitude was reserved. There were open attacks in *Pravda* and *Izvestia* referring to the Turkish move as a half-measure, saying Turkish entry would serve no useful purpose, and that it was no longer desired by the Soviet Union.

THE END OF PAN-TURANISM

The desire to improve relations with the Soviet Union was a major factor in the clamp-down on Pan-Turanian activity from the spring of 1944 onwards. The gradual recovery of the Crimea in April and May

1944 by the Red Army led Turkish statesmen to make the Pan-Turanian issue a gesture of goodwill towards the Soviet neighbour.[51] On 9 May 1944, F. R. Atay was to write in *Ulus*: 'Racism and Turanism are against the principles of the Constitution. A Racist or Turanist cannot be a member of the Republican Peoples' Party. Racists and Turanists are a threat to our national unity and Turkey's security . . .'[52]

The trial of Nihal Adsız, a prominent Turanist, on 3 May 1944 led to protests and disturbances which were put down by security forces. Soon after Adsız' final trial on 9 May he was convicted and sentenced to ten years' imprisonment but the sentence was commuted. On this occasion the official press organ was even more unequivocal. Atay declared that 'fascists' had 'exploited' Turkish nationalism and condemned the 'Turanist organization': 'This organization is after . . . the creation of a fascist dictatorship and lives on dreams of expansionism . . . It aims to spread its tentacles everywhere just like the Romanian Iron Guard . . .'[53]

İsmet İnönü in his annual address to Turkish youth openly declared: 'We are Turkish Nationalists but we are also the enemy of the precepts of racism in our country . . . The Turanian idea is a harmful and sick development of recent times . . .'[54] İnönü's speech was circulated by order to primary and secondary schools as well as *lycées*. All schools had to write reports for the Ministry of Education covering the activities they organised in keeping with the principles and directives in the speech.

On 7 September the İstanbul Martial Law Court began its proceedings against twenty-three prominent Turanists.[55] Koçak emphasises that the events were deliberately exaggerated as a gesture to the Soviets and press releases as well as İnönü's public statements were aimed at the same quarter.[56]

THE TURKISH GAMBIT

Throughout the war İnönü and the formulators of Turkish foreign policy had been pursuing a calculated gamble. This gamble was based on one of the most basic foundations of Turkish foreign policy – Turkey's vital strategic location. It was hoped that any short-term falling out with Britain would be remedied after the war when the British would realise that Turkish goodwill was a geopolitical necessity for their Empire.

There is evidence indicating that even at the nadir of Anglo-Turkish relations Turkish calculations had begun to be proved correct. On 4 April Eden presented a memorandum to the War Cabinet evaluating Turkish goodwill from a strategic viewpoint: 'Great Britain's position in the Mediterranean, Persian Gulf and Iraq would benefit if she could count on a friendly Turkey in sympathy for the general policy of Britain in the Middle East . . .'[57]

In another memorandum prepared for the Cabinet in June 1944 Eden insisted that Turkish friendship was indispensable to Britain in her efforts to prevent the spread of Soviet influence in the Balkans. Indeed Britain should give up her policy of forcing Turkey into the war if Turkey's collaboration in this sphere was to be secured.[58] However, as has been seen above, both Eden and Churchill had pushed for Turkey's break of diplomatic relations with Germany, hoping this would provoke a German 'vengeance' attack which would land Turkey in the war 'voluntarily'.[59] The reason for the apparent contradiction in these two positions can only be speculated upon. It remains possible that both Eden and Churchill were calculating that a Turkey dependent on Britain as a result of such an attack would be doubly reliant on British aid, and were attempting to convince their Soviet allies who had become suspiciously reluctant about Turkish entry.

Certainly by mid-August suspicion of Soviet intentions had clearly begun to plague the Foreign Office. On 21 August Sargent informed Clark Kerr, Britain's Ambassador in Moscow, that the Soviets were using the Turkish question as a 'stalking horse' for the pursuit of their long-term objectives in the Balkans.[60] Thus, as the Soviet armies descended upon the Balkans, British policy became increasingly difficult. On the one hand Turkey had to be secured for future strategic considerations, yet all care had to be taken to avoid offending their present ally, the Soviet Union. This was precisely the gist of the summary instructions given to the new Ambassador to Ankara, Sir M. Peterson, in late September. As Turkey's treaty with Britain would be equally binding in the case of German, or Soviet, aggression a way had to be found for Britain to maintain the alliance, but to allow the treaty to lapse. Peterson was told that British long-term interest in Turkey was unaffected by Turkish behaviour in the past, while the recent increase of Soviet influence in the Balkans made her continued friendship desirable. But how was this to be done without offending the Soviets? The instructions emphasised that no new agreements were to be concluded with Turkey until the post-war conditions became clear.[61]

As Churchill prepared to leave for Moscow in October 1944, the Turks once again hovered between hope that their gambit would pay off and apprehension that Britain would make concessions at their expense.

Although the Foreign Office had decided that in view of post-war needs it was inopportune to force Turkey, there was apparently disagreement with Churchill on this score. On his way to Moscow, the Prime Minister proposed that he meet with President İnönü and make one last attempt at persuading him. A detailed Foreign Office memo strenuously advised against this, noting that the Red Army had now occupied Bulgaria and that Turkey would be better off keeping a low profile rather than provoking Soviet reaction by spectacular attempts at rehabilitation. Churchill gave up the idea.[62]

The Foreign Office fully expected the Soviets to make demands for the revision of the Montreux Convention. A memo prepared for Eden's use in Moscow, stressed that although some revision might be unavoidable it was certainly not desirable. Britain's position in southeast Europe was very weak and she needed to make the most of the Turkish alliance. The memo also referred to the 'age long British opposition to Russian ambitions regarding the Straits . . .'[63]

At Moscow the divergence of views between the Foreign Office and Churchill became much more apparent. It was in Moscow that the Turks nearly lost their gambit of banking on their indispensability to Britain, as Churchill came very near to giving the game away. The chickens the Prime Minister had let loose in Tehran came home to roost in Moscow, as Stalin brought up the matter of the Straits on 9 October, stating that the British Prime Minister had been sympathetic to Soviet views in Tehran. Churchill then proceeded to say that Britain could have no objection to free passage through the Straits for Soviet warships and that Britain had no connection with Turkey except the Montreux Convention which was now 'inadmissible' and 'obsolete'.[64] This sort of pronouncement led a despairing Eden to make frantic efforts to curb the Prime Minister's language: 'The Prime Minister said much, but he would have said a great deal more but for my appeals and injunctions . . .'[65]

On 10 October Eden confronted Churchill with the Foreign Office view and underlined Turkey's importance to Britain's long-term objectives. He pointed out that it had been a mistake to ask the Soviets to present their demands, and advised the Prime Minister against any further discussion. Churchill deferred to this view but pointed out that any assurance given to Turkey was 'more than voided' by her refusal to give any help in January 1944.[66]

As the Turkish leaders anxiously awaited the conclusion of the Moscow talks they could not have known that their gambit had already been successful. Although in his telegram of 20 June 1944 Hugessen had criticised Menemencioğlu for his 'narrow' views and his 'apparent inability to forecast the shape of the postwar world and to realise the immense revolution in international relations which must follow the end of the war . . .', his superiors were clearly sceptical about such a 'revolution'.[67] Even as Hugessen wrote these words, Eden and the Foreign Office were making plans precisely along the lines of Menemencioğlu's thinking. Yet Churchill had been all too ready to whet Russian ambitions on the Straits at Tehran and Moscow. Now Turkey had to prepare to deal with the results of his mistakes.

11 . THE SOVIET DEMANDS: 1945

When the Yalta Conference was convened in early February 1945, the
Turks were still living under the shadow of their 'cooling-off' with the
British in the previous year.[1] Professor A. Ş. Esmer has noted that,
'the possibility of Churchill's making concessions to the Russians . . .
caused great worry as Churchill was angry at Turkey'.[2]

But since his October 1944 visit to Moscow the Foreign Office had
prevailed on the British Prime Minister to take into account the
long-term importance of Turkey for Britain. In Yalta he was much
more defensive of the Turkish position. When on 8 February Stalin
brought up Turkey as an example of the sort of country that had
'wavered and speculated on being on the winning side . . .' Churchill
replied that the Turkish attitude had been 'friendly and helpful
although she had not taken on the chance provided a year ago to enter
the war.'[3] On 10 February Stalin brought up the Montreux Convention, pointing out just as Churchill had done the previous year, that it
was 'outmoded' and ought to be revised. Both Britain and the United
States agreed in principle.

It is difficult to understand what prompted Churchill to comment
at this point that in 1915, 'he had tried very hard to get through the
Dardanelles, and then the Russian Government had made available
an armed force to help but it did not succeed'. Stalin equally anachro-
nistically replied that Churchill in 1915 'had been in too much of a
hurry in withdrawing his troops since the Germans and Turks were
on the verge of surrender'.[4]

On 20 February Sir M. Peterson informed the Turkish Foreign
Minister Hasan Saka of the Yalta decision on the 1 March deadline
for a Turkish declaration of war on the Axis, if she was to be invited to

178

the United Nations Conference. Accordingly on 23 February 1945 Turkey declared war on Germany and Japan. As the Soviet armies were within 50 kilometres of Berlin and the Anglo-American forces were nearing Cologne at this date the Turkish declaration of war was clearly symbolic.[5]

After the declaration of war the Turkish press took pains to point out that Turkey had been invited to join the United Nations as a loyal ally. H. C. Yalçın of *Tanin* justified the Turkish position and made an indirect reference to the Turco-German Friendship Treaty of 1941: 'While Turkey was doing her duty, she did not neglect political manoeuvres and precautionary measures. She could not forget that to act blindly would have no effect other than that of endangering the [Allied] cause.'[6] An unsigned editorial in *Yeni Sabah* compared the wartime policies of the European neutrals: Sweden, Spain, Switzerland and Turkey, commenting that Turkey had never been a strict neutral and 'had long since taken her place on the democratic front'.[7] Even Nadir Nadi who had acquired a reputation as the most 'pro-Axis' of Turkish columnists was to write: 'We always saw the fate of civilisation and mankind as hinging on allied victory . . .'[8] A few days after Turkey's declaration of war, Yalçın reminded the Allies of services rendered: 'Like our Russian friends we also appeared [at one time] to be on friendly terms with the Germans. But we barred the way to the Near East, Iraq, and Africa. We protected the Caucasus and the Black Sea coast.'[9] As accusations against Turkey mounted in the Soviet press, Sadak of *Akşam* was to ask: 'Is Turkey to be blamed for carrying out her duties as an ally without being a burden to anyone, without being invaded and destroyed?'[10]

THE SOVIET NOTES OF 19 MARCH AND 7 JUNE

In early March 1945 the Soviet media had mounted a virulently anti-Turkish campaign and in the same month the Soviet government announced that it would not renew the Turco-Soviet Friendship Pact of 1925. This was a long expected move and the Turkish statesmen sensed that in a one-to-one renegotiation over a future treaty Turkey would appear to be one of the countries in the Soviet sphere of influence.[11]

Soon after he returned from the San Francisco Conference on 7 June Molotov confronted the Turkish Ambassador to Moscow, Selim Sarper, with the 'price' for Soviet friendship. First, Turkey had to agree to a frontier rectification along her eastern border involving the 'retrocession' of the provinces of Kars and Ardahan which Molotov maintained had been ceded to Turkey at a time of weakness. Second, Turkey was too weak to defend the Straits by herself and must grant the Soviets bases in this area for their joint defence. Together with this Turkey must agree to a revision of the Montreux Convention giving the Soviet Union greater control of the Straits. Menemencioğlu's nightmare had come true.

The Turks noted that the Soviet demands were well timed. American and Soviet troops were embracing on the Elbe and the Soviets were the heroes of Stalingrad. Turkey by contrast was cast in the role of a selfish country imputing evil intentions to the Russian heroes.[12]

THE WAR OF NERVES

Stalin had insisted during the Potsdam Conference that Turkey must grant bases to Soviet forces in the vicinity of the Straits. When Churchill attempted to stem the flood he had started in 1944 and declared that Turkey would never accept such conditions, Stalin countered that she had before, in 1805 and 1833, accepted very similar treaty clauses.[13] Menemencioğlu's lively sense of historical precedent was thus more than vindicated.

Indeed since March the Soviets had been carrying out an intense war of nerves on Turkey. Ominous troop concentrations and movements were undertaken in Bulgaria and the Caucasus. Professors claiming to be Armenian and Georgian put forward 'learned works' which claimed Kars and Ardahan were part of ancient Armenia while sections of the Turkish Black Sea coast as far as Trabzon were part of Georgia.[14] On 25 September the British Embassy in Moscow reported that there was 'evidence of the preparation of public opinion, and more particularly of the Red Army for trouble with Turkey . . .'[15] The Chancery at Moscow further noted on 23 October that troop buildups were continuing, 'and the talk of Kars and Ardahan being Armenian was continually cropping up in conversation all over Transcaucasia where there was an attitude of expectancy about it.'[16] Throughout the autumn of 1945 British military missions in Bulgaria and Romania reported on the concentration of tanks and heavy artillery that was moving into Bulgaria.[17] The War Office informed the Paris Military Attaché on 26 October: 'Russia probably has 130,000 good quality troops in Bulgaria . . .'[18]

After the Soviet demands of 7 June became known the press responded with a campaign of concerted outrage. H. C. Yalçın was allowed
to drop all reserve as he attacked the Soviets as 'Red Fascism,' and
proclaimed, 'Turkey will not leave her Western Allies and become
part of an Eastern–Asiatic Red Dictatorship . . .'[19] C. Oral wrote in
Bugün that the Soviet Union had been one of the host countries at San
Francisco and was now making demands on Turkey which were
clearly against everything the United Nations Charter stood for.[20]

There is evidence indicating that the British were becoming increasingly wary of Soviet intentions. They were also sceptical about
the claims of 'Soviet Armenia' in Turkey. On 25 August the Ankara
Embassy described the Soviet claim that the treaty of 1921 was made
under duress as 'without foundation'. The initiative, it underlined,
had come from the Soviet side. Ethnological grounds for the claims
were also no good: 'Before 1914 Armenians in Kars were at best a
minority. Kars and Ani have not been Armenian cities since the early
Middle Ages, and even at that time historical and archeological
evidence indicates that they represented a mixed culture, as much
Turco-Arab as Armenian.'[21]

When Ernest Bevin visited Moscow and spoke with Stalin on 21
December he told the Soviet leader that Britain was anxious about the
Soviet attitude towards Turkey:

Stalin said there were two questions. Firstly the Straits which the Turks could
close at will. Secondly there were the provinces in Turkey inhabited by
Georgians and Armenians where the old frontier must be restored. But all
talk of war against Turkey was rubbish. When I asked him how the matter
would be settled, Stalin said by negotiation with Turkey and the Allies. On
my asking him exactly what the Soviet Union wanted Stalin said they wished
to regain the frontier which existed before the treaty of 1921. I pointed out
that Russia had not been in possession of these provinces for long; Stalin
admitted this but said the population was largely Georgian and Armenian
and had always been so. As regards the Straits Stalin said his claim for a base
still stood. The Soviet Government did not claim the right to close the Straits
themselves but they did not wish Turkey to be able to do so either . . .[22]

Although the British fully saw the need to support Turkey, Foreign
Office documentation shows that there was considerable confusion
about what could actually be done. The discussion centred around
the question of whether or not the treaty of 1939 with Turkey was
legally binding against the Soviet Union. It was agreed that the treaty
was still valid, but a number of reasons were put forward to show how
Britain could justify escaping her obligations. It could be pointed out

that circumstances had changed and that the treaty was incompatible with the situation created by the enforcement of the United Nations Charter.[23]

THE TURKISH CASE

On 1 November İnönü made a speech before the Assembly, giving a step-by-step justification of Turkish attitudes during the 1939–45 period. In 1939, he said, Turkey was the only nation among its peers to openly side with Britain and France. In 1940, when Britain had fought alone Turkey had openly declared that Turkish sympathies were with Britain. But, 'The outbreak of war between our two allies dictated that we maintain a strict neutrality.' In 1941 surrounded by Axis forces, Turkey had barred the way to the Middle East with only its own men and resources. The President then went on to respond to specific criticisms of the Turkish position:

I would now like to respond to the criticisms levelled at Turkey beginning at the end of 1943 and show here in your presence the injustice of the allegations against us. We were criticised for having concluded a treaty of Non-Aggression with the Germans. But with what right could anyone expect us to do anything else at the time when the Germans were at the gates of İstanbul, Britain feared invasion of the British Isles, Russia had a Non-Aggression Pact with Germany, and America was not in the war.[24]

İnönü said the Turkish position was quite acceptable to the Allies then, and only now after 'the dark days were over', she was being criticised. Turkey was being accused of maintaining large forces in the Black Sea and Caucasus regions: 'we told the Soviets that we were concentrating troops in Hopa and Trabzon to forestall an attempt by the Germans to strike at the Caucasus from the rear'. Turkey had been accused of being late in her declaration of war; she had not declared war before, when the Allies were winning because, 'We had not wanted to declare war after the days of glory – seemingly to claim a share of the booty.' Turkey was also being accused of not having declared war immediately after the break in diplomatic relations in 1944; 'The position agreed in writing between the British and us was the following: the rupture of relations would be a first step leading to effective belligerency.'

İnönü also reiterated that the accusation that Turkey had not allowed ships to go through the Straits bearing supplies to the Soviet

Union, was not correct. He said the reason for this was not Turkish restrictions but the fact that the Axis controlled the Aegean shipping lanes. 'It has been proven during the Second World War that the Straits were in safe hands and open to the free passage of ships of all nations . . .' Also when the British had protested about the nature of certain shipping, 'our investigations and categorical action took only a week'. The President of the Republic concluded by saying: 'If the adoption of humanitarian values as a basis for the World of the future is not an empty promise we believe that Turkey will be recognised as a useful element in the new world peace. We declare openly that we have no debts to pay in land or the rights of Turks.'[25] It was an important statement of Turkish foreign policy during the Second World War by the major author of that policy. The replies to specific criticisms were obviously intended primarily for Soviet ears, although İnönü directed his arguments proving loyalty mainly at the British and Americans.

CONCLUSION

In early 1944 Hugessen asked Menemencioğlu where Turkey stood in relation to the war. The Minister replied with a legendary Nasrettin Hoca story:

One day there occurred a death in the Hoca's village. When the friends of the deceased asked the Hoca where they should take up position while the coffin was being carried to the graveyard he replied: It does not matter where you are as long as you are not in it.[1]

From 1939 to 1945 Turkey came under direct pressure from at least three major powers. Britain, Germany and the Soviet Union all brought strong pressure to bear on Turkey to pursue a policy in keeping with their interests. Not only did Turkey avoid involvement but she was able to influence both warring camps in her favour: 'Turkey succeeded in staying out of the war and beyond that made each belligerent power block pay a high price for Turkey's continued resistance to the demands of others. Small power diplomacy in the midst of a world conflict could hope to achieve no greater success.'[2]

Turkish leaders such as İnönü and Menemencioğlu were able to accomplish this because they practised realistic power politics. They knew only too well that the strategic location of their small state could as easily lead to its downfall as to its salvation, as the example of Iran amply demonstrated in 1941.[3] They knew also that militarily or economically Turkey was no match for either of the two camps, and that the precious little reconstruction which had been completed in the Atatürk era could be nullified as the result of one ill-considered move. Yet this did not lead them to follow a policy of yielding to pressure as was practised in other neutral countries. Instead they declared to all and sundry that Turkey would defend herself to the end if she were attacked. Their achievement was that they managed to convince all sides that they meant it, and would not take refuge behind piecemeal concessions as was done by some small states.

184

It must be recognised that much of the diplomatic expertise shown by Turkish leaders at this time was a result of their Ottoman background. The struggle to maintain the Ottoman Empire when all real Ottoman power had disappeared bred a particular type of diplomat: 'From their long and humiliating years of trying to shore up a dying Empire the Turks had learned to be unsentimental and pragmatic in their approach to politics.'[4] But precisely those humiliations of the Ottoman era made the diplomats of the new Turkey all the more determined to avoid their repetition, and their realism and pragmatism were directed towards that aim: 'If one compares the policy pursued by Sultanic Turkey (which plunged her into war in 1914) with Turkish diplomacy during World War II the superiority of the latter over the former becomes evident. Whereas the earlier policy was hesitating, haphazard, and even irrational, the later diplomacy was characterised by singleness of purpose, cold calculation and farsightedness.'[5] In his answer to charges by German newspapers that Turkey was 'forgiving' the authors of the Sèvres Treaty, A. Ş. Esmer put his finger on the central reality of Turkish policy: 'Were we to remain eternally enemies with those who tried to get us to sign the Sèvres Treaty? In international relations there are no eternal friendships and eternal enmities, there is only the matter of eternal interest . . .'[6]

In safeguarding their interests the Turks showed considerable diplomatic skill and resourcefulness. Also one must recognise that Turkish foreign policy formulation at this time was very farsighted and most of the Turkish leaders' predictions regarding the post-war world were accurate.[7]

Most of the criticism of Turkish policy during this period assumes a 'moral' tone. Turkey is accused of having behaved selfishly in sparing herself the destruction and suffering which was the lot of so many countries. Seen from a non-Turkish vantage point this view is understandable but unjustified. As Kuniholm has pointed out:

But if one assesses Turkish problems from the point of view of Turkish national interests one can readily see that such condemnation is unwarranted. Britain and France, after all, handed Czechoslovakia over to Hitler. Russia and Germany contemplated a division of interests in the Near East at Turkey's expense. Both Britain and Russia contemplated pushing Turkey into the war . . . If one remembers these things, it is less easy to take a position on what principles other than self-interest Turkey should have followed.[8]

For Churchill, Turkey was a country which was 'both necessary to, and expendable in Britain's scheme of empire'.[9] And as such he was prepared to make concessions to the Soviets particularly regarding the Straits, and had to be reminded of Turkey's vital position as regards Britain's long-term interests. For the British Prime Minister, Turkey was a card to be played at the right moment. There was very little morality in this position: 'Churchill [was] convinced that it was the right and even the duty of the great powers to sacrifice small neutrals for the sake of victory over Nazism.'[10]

Accordingly, the Turks paid lip service to the British cause but still fended off any move to involve them actively in it. One way of doing this was to argue that Turkish entry would in fact be *against* British interest. Thus British officials were told that Turkey had to be pre-served as a 'reserve of manpower' blocking the way to the Middle East, and warned against 'wasting Turkey'.[11] Although the British never voluntarily acceded to the view that Turkey should stay out, they found themselves unable to do much about it.

Similarly the Germans were told that Turkish non-involvement was in *their* interests as a neutral Turkey 'protected Germany's right flank against Russia', and enabled her to concentrate her forces.[12] Again, when the Soviets accused Turkey in 1945 of having massed troops on the Turkish–Soviet border in 1941 and of having secured the German flank, the Turks were able to argue that Turkey's stead-fast position had protected the Soviet Union from a German pincer movement through Anatolia and the Caucasus. H. C. Yalçın of *Tanin* actually proclaimed that Turkey had, 'taken a leaf out of the Russian book' and, 'pretended to be friends with Germany', while she, 'blocked the way to the Middle East, Iraq and Africa, and protected the Caucasus and Black Sea Coast'.[13] Therefore, in all three cases the Turks followed the most plausible line of argument.

Turkey managed to exert her influence successfully on the major powers of the Second World War to reduce the probability of her becoming involved in the war. The influence she exerted was out of proportion with her status as a poor and underdeveloped country. This was largely due to the intelligent way she made use of her unique geographical position. This position could just as easily have become a trap which would have led Turkey to destruction. Instead through able leadership Turkey managed to survive because of her geographi-cal location.

Hostilities having broken out, Turkey still hoped that she could forge a link between Britain and the Soviets and enlist the Soviet Union in the British–French–Turkish combination. Friendship with the Soviets had been the mainstay of her foreign policy until then. The first unexpected development was the Nazi–Soviet Pact. The second was the collapse of France in June 1940; many in Turkey began to feel that she had insured herself with the weak side once again. As Greece went under and the whole of Europe came under Nazi domination, while invasion plans were being made for Britain, Turkey had to find ways of ensuring her survival. The insurance policy taken out with the British seemed to be rapidly becoming a liability. The obvious way to counter this threat was to re-insure, and this is what Turkey did with Germany on 18 June 1941, when she signed the Non-Aggression Pact. But as German victories turned to defeats, the pressure from her British ally which had never let up, gained renewed fervour. In 1943 and 1944 Turkey realised she could not maintain her freedom of action without making some tactical readjustments. Accordingly, after the Eden–Menemencioğlu meeting in November 1943 she conceded that in principle she agreed to join the war. But she had no intention of doing so. Menemencioğlu had correctly perceived during his talks with Eden, that British pressure was drawing its renewed strength from Soviet insistence that Turkey be brought in.

Military inadequacy was now pushed forward as a legitimate way of gaining precious time. İnönü knew that if he managed to last out the critical period, when Turkish entry was of maximum utility to the Allies, the worst of the pressure would be lifted. So now the Turkish side fell back on their last line of defence; pleas for involvement in a 'general plan' of campaign in the Balkans, a development they knew to be highly unlikely as it was viewed with disfavour by both the Americans and the Soviets. By now Turkey's old role as western-sponsored barrier to 'Soviet Intentions' in the Middle East had once more become a functional factor in British and American calculations. İnönü and the Turkish foreign policy leadership had relied on just this factor as crucial in outweighing any short-term falling out with the British over wartime differences.

Turkish tactics in this period can be likened to defence works around a citadel. The outer wall of neutrality was breached when the Turks admitted in principle that they would come into the war. They then retrenched behind the inner wall of arguments of military inadequacy. When it seemed as though the inner wall in turn was about to give way under Allied insistence, they retired to the bastion of 'sincere' pleas for a joint campaign in the Balkans alongside the Allies, knowing that neither the United States nor the Soviets was prepared to countenance such a plan. By these successive tactical retreats they were just able to outlast the critical period when the importance of their entry was paramount for the Allies.

APPENDIX

Treaty of Mutual Assistance between His Majesty in respect of the United Kingdom, the President of the French Republic and the President of the Turkish Republic.

The President of the French Republic, His Majesty The King of Great Britain, Ireland and the British Dominions beyond the Seas, Emperor of India (in respect of the United Kingdom of Great Britain and Northern Ireland), and the President of the Turkish Republic:

Desiring to conclude a treaty of a reciprocal character in the interests of their national security, and to provide for mutual assistance in resistance to aggression,

Have appointed as their Plenipotentiaries, namely:

The President of the French Republic:

    M. René Massigli, Ambassador Extraordinary and Plenipotentiary, Commander of the Legion of Honour;

His Majesty The King of Great Britain, Ireland and the British Dominions beyond the Seas, Emperor of India (for the United Kingdom of Great Britain and Northern Ireland):

    Sir Hughe Montgomery Knatchbull-Hugessen, K.C.M.G., Ambassador Extraordinary and Plenipotentiary;

    The President of the Turkish Republic:

    Dr. Refik Saydam, President of the Council, Minister for Foreign Affairs *ad int.*, Deputy for İstanbul;

Who, having communicated their full powers, found in good and due form, have agreed as follows:—

Article 1.

In the event of Turkey being involved in hostilities with a European Power in consequence of aggression by that Power against Turkey, France and the United Kingdom will co-operate effectively with Turkey and will lend her all aid and assistance in their power.

Article 2.

(1) In the event of an act of aggression by a European Power leading to war in the Mediterranean area in which France and the United Kingdom are

involved, Turkey will collaborate effectively with France and the United Kingdom and will lend them all aid and assistance in her power.

(2) In the event of an act of aggression by a European Power leading to war in the Mediterranean area in which Turkey is involved, France and the United Kingdom will collaborate effectively with Turkey and will lend her all aid and assistance in their power.

Article 3.

So long as the guarantees given by France and the United Kingdom to Greece and Roumania by their respective Declarations of the 13th April, 1939, remain in force, Turkey will co-operate effectively with France and the United Kingdom and will lend them all aid and assistance in her power, in the event of France and the United Kingdom being engaged in hostilities in virtue of either of the said guarantees.

Article 4.

In the event of France and the United Kingdom being involved in hostilities with a European Power in consequence of aggression committed by that Power against either of those States without the provisions of Articles 2 or 3 being applicable, the High Contracting Parties will immediately consult together.

It is nevertheless agreed that in such an eventuality Turkey will observe at least a benevolent neutrality towards France and the United Kingdom.

Article 5.

Without prejudice to the provisions of Article 3 above, in the event of either –
(1) aggression by a European Power against another European State which the Government of one of the High Contracting Parties had, with the approval of that State, undertaken to assist in maintaining its independence or neutrality against such aggression, or
(2) aggression by a European Power which, while directed against another European State, constituted, in the opinion of the Government of one of the High Contracting Parties, a menace to its own security,
the High Contracting Parties will immediately consult together with a view to such common action as might be considered effective.

Article 6.

The present Treaty is not directed against any country, but is designed to assure France, the United Kingdom and Turkey of mutual aid and assistance in resistance to aggression should the necessity arise.

Article 7.

The provisions of the present Treaty are equally binding as bilateral obligations between Turkey and each of the two other High Contracting Parties.

Article 8.

If the High Contracting Parties are engaged in hostilities in consequence of the operation of the present Treaty, they will not conclude an armistice or peace except by common agreement.

The present Treaty shall be ratified and the instruments of ratification shall be deposited simultaneously at Angora as soon as possible. It shall enter into force on the date of this deposit.

The present Treaty is concluded for a period of fifteen years. If none of the High Contracting Parties has notified the two others of its intention to terminate it six months before the expiration of the said period, the Treaty will be renewed by tacit consent for a further period of five years, and so on.

In witness whereof the undersigned have signed the present Treaty and have thereto affixed their seals.

Done at Angora, in triplicate, the 19th October, 1939.

      (L.S.)   R. MASSIGLI.
      (L.S.)   H. M. KNATCHBULL-HUGESSEN.
      (L.S.)   Dr R. SAYDAM.

PROTOCOL No. 1.

The undersigned Plenipotentiaries state that their respective Governments agree that the Treaty of to-day's date shall be put into force from the moment of its signature.

The present Protocol shall be considered as an integral part of the Treaty concluded to-day between France, the United Kingdom and Turkey.

Done at Angora, in triplicate, the 19th October, 1939.

    R. MASSIGLI.
    H. M. KNATCHBULL-HUGESSEN.
    Dr R. SAYDAM.

PROTOCOL No. 2.

At the moment of signature of the Treaty between France, the United Kingdom and Turkey, the undersigned Plenipotentiaries, duly authorised to this effect, have agreed as follows:—

The obligations undertaken by Turkey in virtue of the above-mentioned Treaty cannot compel that country to take action having as its effect, or involving as its consequence, entry into armed conflict with the Soviet Union.

The present Protocol shall be considered as an integral part of the Treaty concluded to-day between France, the United Kingdom and Turkey.

Done at Angora, in triplicate, the 19th October, 1939.

    R. MASSIGLI.
    H. M. KNATCHBULL-HUGESSEN.
    Dr R. SAYDAM.

NOTES

Introduction

1 Winston Churchill, *The Grand Alliance*, p. 484.
2 Şevket Süreyya Aydemir, *İkinci Adam* (The Second Man), vol. 2, p. 84.
3 Ibid., p. 87, Mustafa Kemal was referring to the Mondros Armistice of 1918.
4 FO. 371/E2170/135/44.
5 Ibid.
6 Hans Morgenthau, *Politics Among Nations*, p. 112. Morgenthau classes geography as 'the most stable factor' in his discussion of 'Elements of National Power.'
7 Metin Tamkoç, *The Warrior Diplomats*, p. 72: 'the more cohesive and centralised an international structure, the less latitude of choice remains for weaker states'.
8 Ibid., p. 300.
9 W. H. Medlicott, *Economic Blockade*, vol. 1, p. 269.
10 Ibid.
11 Aydemir, *İkinci Adam*, vol. 2, p. 109.
12 Edward Weisband, *Turkish Foreign Policy 1943–1945*, p. 52. Weisband is basing his argument on the captured files of the German Foreign Ministry. Therapia, 13 July 1943, *Captured Files*, German Embassy in Ankara, National Archives, Washington D.C., Micro copy, Serial T-120, Roll 2618, Frames E 364726/2, E 364726/5.
13 Ibid., p. 51.
14 *Documents on German Foreign Policy*, Series D, vol. xii, no. 231, p. 411; hereafter referred to as DGFP.
15 Morgenthau, 'Elements of National Power', in *Politics Among Nations*, p. 140.
16 Ibid., p. 141.
17 Ibid., p. 128.
18 Tamkoç, *The Warrior Diplomats*, p. 106.
19 Ibid., p. 106, *gâvur* means infidel or unbeliever.
20 Weisband, *Turkish Foreign Policy*, p. 3.
21 Elizabeth Monroe, *The Mediterranean in Politics*, p. 180. In this work Italy is seen primarily strategically and Monroe compares the British and Italian presence in the Mediterranean basin.

22 Ibid., p. 181.
23 Luigi Villari, *The Expansion of Italy* (London, 1930), p. 230.
24 In reply to my application for access to the archives of the Turkish Foreign Ministry, I received the following letter from the Archives Department dated 19 October 1977 and numbered 111.995.1161: 'According to the present regulations our archives dating from 1914 onwards are closed to research, consequently your request cannot be granted.'
25 Numan Menemencioğlu's memoirs, 'Les Détroits vus de la Mediterranée: aperçus, études, souvenirs' (unpublished), record his experiences at the Foreign Ministry. Hereafter referred to as 'The Menemencioğlu Text'.
26 Türkiye Cumhuriyeti Başbakanlık, Basın ve Yayın Umum Müdürlüğü (Office of the Prime Minister of the Turkish Republic. General Directorate of Press and Publications). *Son Değişikliklere Göre Matbuat Kanunu* (The Press Law comprising Recent Alterations). Ankara 1946. Basın ve Yayın Umum Müdürlüğü Yayınları No. 15, pp. 446–64; Section 11, Article 34, para. A (p. 455).
27 Cemil Koçak, 'İkinci Dünya Savaşı ve Türk Basını' ('The Turkish Press in the Second World War'), *Tarih ve Toplum*, No. 35, November 1986, pp. 29–33.
28 Ibid., pp. 30–31.
29 Royal Institute of International Affairs, *Review of the Foreign Press*, Series B, European Neutrals and the Near East. (Allied Governments, European Neutrals – Smaller European Enemies and the Near East.) Balliol College, Oxford, Nos. 1–291, 4 October 1939–27 June 1943; after 30 June 1943 Foreign Office Research Dept., Series N (The Near and Middle East), London, HMSO. After 1943 the publication was prepared by Research and Intelligence Department of the Foreign Office; hereafter referred to as Review.
30 Füruzan Hüsrev Tokin, *Basın Ansiklopedisi* (Press Encyclopedia) pp. 13–14.
31 Ibid., p. 45.
32 Nadir Nadi, *Perde Aralığından* (Through a Crack in the Curtain), pp. 89–94.
33 *Basın Ansiklopedisi*, p. 114.
34 Ibid., pp. 114–15.
35 Review No. 93, 10 July 1941 (8–14 May 1941), p. 269.
36 Review No. 50, 10 October 1940 (15–30 July 1940), p. 11.
37 Review No. 109, 31 October 1941 (21 August–3 September 1941).
38 During a personal interview on 29 October 1977, Ahmet Şükrü Esmer told the author that İnönü once criticised him for referring to the Chancellor of the German Reich curtly as 'Hitler' and suggested he refer to him as 'Herr Hitler' or 'Chancellor'.
39 Koçak, 'İkinci Dünya Savaşı ve Türk Basını', pp. 29–30. The Republican Peoples' Party, the 'Cumhuriyet Halk Partisi' or 'Cumhuriyet Halk Fırkası' will be referred to henceforward as CHP or CHF.
40 Review No. 18, 2 February 1940 (12–22 January 1940), p. 15.

41 Review No. 4 (6–14 October 1939), p. 47.
42 N. Sadak, *Akşam*, 11 December 1943.
43 *Yeni Sabah*, 18 June 1944 and 17 July 1944.

1 The economic background

1 Z. Y. Hershlag, 'Economic Development of Republican Turkey', in *Introduction to the Modern Economic History of the Middle East*, p. 171.
2 Salahi Ramsden Sonyel, *Turkish Diplomacy 1918–1923*, p. 208.
3 Robinson, *The First Turkish Republic*, p. 116.
4 Sonyel, *Turkish Diplomacy*, p. 200.
5 Şefik Bilkur, *National Income of Turkey*, National Statistics Office 1949.
6 Hershlag, *Introduction*, p. 165.
7 Ibid.
8 Aydemir, *İkinci Adam*, vol. 1, pp. 339–40.
9 Sonyel, *Turkish Diplomacy*, p. 203; see below, chapter 3.
10 Hershlag, *Introduction*, p. 167.
11 Robinson, *The First Turkish Republic*, p. 107.
12 Hershlag, *Introduction*, p. 168.
13 Ludmila Zhivkova, *Anglo-Turkish Relations 1933–1939*, p. 4.
14 Hershlag, *Introduction*, p. 167.
15 Ibid., p. 165.
16 Villari, *The Expansion of Italy*, p. 230.
17 Hershlag, *Introduction*, p. 167.
18 Ibid., p. 169.
19 Ibid.
20 Enver Z. Karal, *Türkiye Cumhuriyeti Tarihi 1923–1950* (History of the Turkish Republic 1923–1950) (İstanbul, 1954), p. 182.
21 İsmail Cem, *Türkiye'de Geri Kalmışlığın Tarihi* (The History of Underdevelopment in Turkey), p. 296.
22 Doğan Avcıoğlu, *Türkiye'nin Düzeni* (The Turkish Order), vol. 1, p. 165.
23 Cem, *Türkiye'de Geri Kalmışlığın Tarihi*, p. 300.
24 Ibid., p. 306.
25 Robinson, *The First Turkish Republic*, p. 105.
26 Hershlag, *Introduction*, p. 177.
27 Ibid.
28 Ibid., p. 178.
29 Ibid., p. 179. Hershlag refers to İnönü's article in *Kadro* of October 1933.
30 Ibid., p. 180.
31 P. P. Graves, *Briton and Turk*, p. 218.
32 Hershlag, *Introduction*, p. 185.
33 Ibid. £T = Turkish Pounds.
34 In 1923 less than 1,000 km of good roads and 8,300 km of broken surface roads existed. The State Steamship Company combined with the one private firm only had a total gross tonnage of 34.902 tns.; *Bayındırlık Dergisi*, Bayındırlık Bakanlığı, December 1948 (Public Works Journal, Ministry of Public Works).
35 *İstatistik Yıllığı 1942–1945*, p. 296.

36 Robinson, *The First Turkish Republic*, p. 115.
37 Hershlag, *Introduction*, p. 189.
38 Cem, *Türkiye'de Geri Kalmışlığın Tarihi*, p. 307; Aydemir, *İkinci Adam*, vol. 2, p. 60. *Vakıf* were Islamic religious endowments which were sometimes used to secure private wealth against confiscation.
39 Cem, *Türkiye'de Geri Kalmışlığın Tarihi*, p. 308.
40 Hershlag, *Introduction*, p. 172. The *aşar* was the Ottoman agricultural tax calculated on the basis of a tenth of the produce.
41 Ibid.
42 Ibid., p. 173.
43 Ibid., p. 174.
44 Ibid.
45 Aydemir, *İkinci Adam*, vol. 2, p. 62. Samsun is a rice producing area on Turkey's Black Sea coast.
46 Hershlag, *Introduction*, p. 190.
47 Ç. Keyder and Ş. Pamuk, '1945 Çiftçiyi Topraklandırma Kanunu Üzerine Tezler' (Some views on the 1945 Land Reform Act), *Yapıt*. December–January 1984–85, pp. 52–63.
48 Cemil Koçak, *Türkiye'de Milli Şef Dönemi (1938–1945)* (The Period of the National Chief in Turkey), Yurt Yayınları (Ankara 1986), pp. 356–67.
49 Aydemir, *İkinci Adam*, vol. 2, p. 206.
50 Medlicott, *Economic Blockade*, vol. 1, p. 269.
51 Zhivkova, *Anglo-Turkish Relations*, p. 73.
52 DGFP, D, vol. v, no. 545.
53 Barbara Ward, *Turkey*, p. 91.
54 Medlicott, *Economic Blockade*, vol. 1, pp. 270–1.
55 Ward, *Turkey*, p. 92.
56 Yuluğ Tekin Kurat, 'İkinci Dünya Savaşında Türk Alman Ticareti' (Turkish-German Trade in the Second World War), *Belleten*, vol. 25, no. 97–100, pp. 96–100.
57 Hjalmar Schacht, *Account Settled*, p. 81.
58 A. Davos, '*Faşist Almanya'nın Türkiye'ye Yayılışı*' (The Expansion of Fascist Germany into Turkey), T.K.P. Yayınları 1977, p. 22.
59 Aydemir, *İkinci Adam*, vol. 2, p. 68.
60 Zhivkova, *Anglo-Turkish Relations*, p. 62; DGFP, D, vol. v, no. 546.
61 DGFP, D, vol. v, no. 549.
62 Medlicott, *Economic Blockade*, vol. 1, pp. 29, 271.
63 Ward, *Turkey*, p. 94.
64 Medlicott, *Economic Blockade*, vol. 1, p. 273.
65 Ibid.
66 Ibid., p. 274.
67 Ibid.
68 Ibid., p. 275.
69 Medlicott, *Economic Blockade*, vol. 2, p. 604.
70 FO. 371/R4935/378/44.
71 Hershlag, *Introduction*, p. 183.
72 FO. 371/R4482/378/44.
73 FO. 371/R4935/378/44.

74 FO. 371/R1212/7/44.
75 FO. 371/R5810/7/44.
76 FO. 371/R12707/55/44.

2 Military inadequacy

1 Ward, *Turkey*, pp. 90–3.
2 William L. Langer and Everett S. Gleason, *The Undeclared War*, p. 801.
3 Şevket Süreyya Aydemir, *İkinci Adam*, vol. 2, p. 206.
4 See above, p. 14.
5 Frederick W. Frey, *The Turkish Political Elite*, p. 234.
6 FO. 371/E2214/2214/44. (This document is in the 1938 volume in the Foreign Office catalogue – under 'Turkey'.)
7 Ibid.
8 Ibid.
9 Aydemir, *İkinci Adam*, vol. 2, p. 134.
10 'Turkey, Rampart in the Middle East', *An Cosantoir*, vol. 12, no. 7, p. 315.
11 Ibid.
12 S. R. Rund, 'The Army of the Crescent and Star', *Infantry Journal*, vol. 60, p. 2.
13 *An Cosantoir*.
14 Ibid.
15 FO. 371/R1618/24/44: After the Adana Conference in February 1943, the Allies stepped up their supplies to Turkey. At the Cairo Conference in December 1943 General Wilson told Hopkins and Menemencioğlu that since Adana Turkey had been supplied with 350 tanks, 48 self-propelled guns, 200 mortars, 50 anti-tank guns, 300 medium and field guns, 99,000 hand guns of various makes and about 1 million anti-tank mines: see Foreign Relations of the United States (hereafter USFR), *Conferences at Cairo and Tehran*, Hopkins–Eden–Menemencioğlu meeting, December 5 1943, p. 279.
16 FO. 371/E2214/2214/44. Annual Report 1937.
17 FO. 371/E7020/91/44.
18 Ernest Phillips, *Hitler's Last Hope*, p. 54.
19 FO. 371/E2214/2214/44. Annual Report 1937.
20 Ibid.
21 Ibid.
22 FO. 371/E403/135/44.
23 FO. 371/E1218/188/44; Zhivkova, *Anglo-Turkish Relations*, p. 62.
24 FO. 371/E3254/188/44.
25 FO. 371/E3403/188/44.
26 FO. 371/E4406/188/44.
27 FO. 371/E7363/373/44.
28 Mete Tunçay, 'İkinci Dünya Savaşının Başlarında (1939–1941) Türk Ordusu' (The Turkish Army at the beginning of the Second World War, 1939–1941), *Tarih ve Toplum*. No. 35, November 1986, p. 34.
29 Ibid., pp. 35, 38, 39.
30 Koçak, *Türkiye'de Milli Şef Dönemi*, pp. 421, 422.

31 Ibid.
32 Tunçay: 'İkinci Dünya Savaşının Başlarında', pp. 36–7.
33 Aydemir, *İkinci Adam*, p. 130: Aydemir was the Chairman of the Ministry of Industry's Industrial Inspection Commission and was at the same time Deputy Director of National Supply. In the course of his duties he visited many of the state factories and was responsible for such things as flour supply to the army. He says lack of organisation was the rule rather than the exception.
34 Ibid., pp. 134–5.
35 Ibid., p. 135.
36 Koçak, *Türkiye'de Milli Şef Dönemi*, p. 421.
37 Ward, *Turkey*, pp. 86–90.

3 Process of government and the foreign policy leadership

1 Bahri Savcı, 'Modernleşmede Devlet Başkanımızın rolü', *Prof. Dr. Yavuz Abadan'a Armağan* ('The role of our Head of State in Turkish modernisation', *Memorial Issue for Professor Dr Yavuz Abadan*), SBFY, (Publication of the Political Sciences Faculty of Ankara University), No. 280, 1969.
2 Metin Tamkoç, *The Warrior Diplomats*, p. 109.
3 Frey, *The Turkish Political Elite*, p. 303.
4 Ibid., p. 157.
5 Ibid., p. 6.
6 Ibid., p. 8.
7 Tahsin Bekir Balta, *Türkiye'de Yürütme Kudreti* (Executive Authority in Turkey), Publication of the Political Sciences Faculty of Ankara University, no. 114–96, Ankara 1960, pp. 13–15.
8 Frey, *The Turkish Political Elite*, p. 13.
9 Mete Tunçay, *Tek Parti Yönetiminin Kurulması (1923–1931)*, pp. 329, 383.
10 Feyyaz Toker, 'Ali Rıza Türel'in Cevapları' (The Replies of Ali Rıza Türel), *Cumhuriyet*, 7 December 1959.
11 Frey, *The Turkish Political Elite*, p. 166.
12 Ibid.
13 Ibid., p. 43.
14 Ibid., p. 30; Frey quotes Donald Webster, *The Turkey of Atatürk*, The American Academy of Political and Social Science, 1939, p. 287.
15 Ibid., p. 69.
16 Ibid., p. 11.
17 C. H. Dodd, *Politics and Government in Turkey*, p. 23.
18 Aydemir, *İkinci Adam*, vol. 2, p. 24.
19 Ibid., p. 22.
20 Ibid.
21 Koçak, *Türkiye'de Milli Şef Dönemi*, p. 56.
22 FO. 371/E547/132/44.
23 Ibid.
24 FO. 371/E7377/69/44.
25 DGFP, D, vol. XIII, no. 236, p. 370.

26 FO. 371/E547/132/44.
27 Aydemir, *İkinci Adam*, vol. 2, p. 26.
28 Tamkoç, *The Warrior Diplomats*, p. 33.
29 Aydemir, *İkinci Adam*, vol. 2, p. 38.
30 Koçak, *Türkiye'de Milli Şef Dönemi*, p. 67.
31 Frey, *The Turkish Political Elite*, p. 35.
32 Tamkoç, *The Warrior Diplomats*, p. 33.
33 E. Weisband, *Turkish Foreign Policy 1943–1945*, p. 34.
34 Aydemir, *İkinci Adam*, vol. 2, p. 154.
35 Weisband, *Turkish Foreign Policy*, p. 35.
36 Ibid., p. 36.
37 Ibid.
38 Aydemir, *İkinci Adam*, vol. 2, p. 157.
39 Weisband, *Turkish Foreign Policy*, p. 38.
40 Interview with Suat Hayri Ürgüplü, 1 November 1977. Ürgüplü served as Minister of Customs and State Monopolies during the war years.
41 Weisband, *Turkish Foreign Policy*, p. 37.
42 Feridun Cemal Erkin, *Les Relations Turco-Soviétiques et la question des Détroits*, pp. 322–41. Saraçoğlu was serving as Prime Minister at the time.
43 Tamkoç, *The Warrior Diplomats*, p. 225.
44 Nihal Kara, 'Türkiye'de Çok Partili Sisteme Geçiş Kararının Nedenleri' (Reasons for the Transition to Multi-Party Politics in Turkey), *Yapıt*, No. 8, December–January 1984–85, pp. 64–75.
45 Interview with Suat Hayri Ürgüplü 1 November 1977.
46 Weisband, *Turkish Foreign Policy*, p. 46; Menemencioğlu served as Secretary General, and Foreign Minister.
47 René Massigli, *La Turquie devant la guerre*, p. 282.
48 Conversation with Mrs Nermin Streater in London, 9 June 1977. Mrs Streater is Menemencioğlu's niece and was in close contact with him in these years. Her father was Muvaffak Menemencioğlu, the older brother of Numan Menemencioğlu and the director of the *Anadolu Ajansı*, the Turkish official news agency.
49 Weisband, *Turkish Foreign Policy*, p. 49.
50 DGFP, D, vol. xii, nos. 231 and 295.
51 The Menemencioğlu Text, p. 267.
52 Weisband, *Turkish Foreign Policy*, p. 50.
53 Ibid.
54 Frey, *The Turkish Political Elite*, p. 265.
55 Weisband, *Turkish Foreign Policy*, p. 51.
56 Ibid., pp. 51, 176.
57 Ibid., p. 50.
58 Conversation with Mrs Streater, 9 June 1977; Interview with Suat Hayri Ürgüplü; 1 November 1977; Interview with Ahmet Şükrü Esmer, 29 October 1977. Both of these men said Menemencioğlu's primary aim was to keep Turkey out of the war.
59 Weisband, *Turkish Foreign Policy*, p. 52.
60 DGFP, D., vol. xiii, No. 231, p. 411.

61 Tamkoç, *The Warrior Diplomats*, p. 215.
62 Massigli, *La Turquie devant la guerre*, p. 32.
63 DGFP, D, vol. xii, No. 231, p. 409.
64 Ibid., p. 410.
65 Ibid., pp. 410–11.
66 Ibid.
67 Ibid.
68 Weisband, *Turkish Foreign Policy*, p. 53.
69 Türkkaya Ataöv, *Turkish Foreign Policy 1939–1945*, p. 9.
70 Menemencioğlu Text, p. 194.
71 Weisband, *Turkish Foreign Policy*, p. 51. Hugessen replaced Loraine as British Ambassador to Ankara in February 1939.
72 FO. 371/R10541/789/44, p. 3.
73 Ibid., p. 2.
74 Ibid., p. 3.
75 Massigli, *La Turquie devant la guerre*, p. 33.
76 Weisband, *Turkish Foreign Policy*, p. 54.
77 Ibid., p. 62.
78 Ibid.
79 Ibid., p. 64.
80 Martin L. Van Creveld, *Hitler's Strategy 1940–1941: The Balkan Clue*, pp. 139–76.
81 Tamkoç, *The Warrior Diplomats*, p. 304.

4 The historical conditioning of a generation

1 Suat Hayri Ürgüplü. Personal interview, 1 November 1977. The Minister was also a typical member of the elite in as much as he came from an Ottoman background, his father having been a leading figure in the *Ulema*, the Ottoman learned religious class.
2 Aydemir, *İkinci Adam*, vol. 1, p. 43.
3 Weisband, *Turkish Foreign Policy, 1943–1945*, p. 65.
4 Aydemir, *İkinci Adam*, vol. 1, p. 44.
5 B. Lewis, *The Emergence of Modern Turkey*, p. 214.
6 G. L. Lewis, *Turkey*, p. 56.
7 Professor Hikmet Bayur, *Atatürk, Hayatı ve Eserleri* (Atatürk: His Life and Achievements), Aydin Kitabevi, Ankara 1962, p. 59.
8 İsmet İnönü, *Hatıralar* (Memoirs), vol. 1, Ankara 1985, pp. 153–5. This volume consists of a series of interviews taped by the journalist Sabahaddin Selek and later published. They go up to the end of the War of Liberation. The later years have yet to appear.
9 Aydemir, *İkinci Adam*, vol. 1, p. 83.
10 Koçak, *Türkiye'de Milli Şef Dönemi*, p. 190.
11 Ulrich Trumpener, *Germany and the Ottoman Empire 1914–18*, p. 94. Trumpener maintains that the view that Germany pushed the Ottoman Empire into the war is a misconception. He states that although military advisers were present, all key positions were held by Turks closely supervised by Enver Paşa, pp. 62–108.

12 Ibid., p. 87.
13 Aydemir, *İkinci Adam*, vol. 1, p. 87.
14 D. Irving and D. C. Watt, *Breach of Security*, pp. 17, 123; see also D. Kahn, *The Codebreakers*.
15 Franz Von Papen, *Memoirs*, p. 68.
16 Ibid., p. 74.
17 Ibid., p. 72, Ali Fuat (Cebesoy).
18 Arif Hikmet Koyunoğlu, 'Koyunoğlu'nun Anıları' (Koyunoğlu's Memoirs) *Tarih ve Toplum*, no. 36, December 1986, pp. 36–7.
19 Şefik Okday, *Son Sadrazam Ahmet Tevfik Paşa* (My grandfather the last Grand Vezir Ahmet Tevfik Pasa) (Bateş Bayilik, İstanbul, 1986), p. 123. Tevfik Paşa represented the İstanbul government (i.e. the Sultan) in the 1921 London Conference at which both the İstanbul and Ankara governments were represented. He has gone down in the annals of Turkish history as a much respected figure for having deferred to the Ankara delegation and told Lloyd George that it was they who truly represented the Turkish people.
20 H. Howard, *The Partition of Turkey*, p. 114. The Independence Tribunals were bodies designed to further social control and were set up as a result of the Emergency Laws of 1925 after the Kurdish Revolt. It is indicative here that pro-German leanings are being used as past evidence of an attitude contrary to the interests of the state.
21 Personal interview with Suat Hayri Ürgüplü, 1 November 1977.
22 In a personal interview with A. Ş. Esmer; İstanbul, 29 October 1977.
23 A. Akşin, *Atatürk'ün Dış Politika İlkeleri ve Diplomasisi* (Atatürk's Foreign Policy Principles and Diplomacy), Part 2, İnkilap ve Aka Kitabevi, İstanbul 1966. p. 4. However it should be made clear that not all of the Turkish elite came away from the First World War as anti-German. Recep Peker and Hüsrev Gerede for instance, came to be known as pro-German and anti-Russian. İnönü made use of them in this capacity, using Peker's authoritarian leanings to his advantage and keeping Gerede in Berlin as Ambassador during the days of German ascendancy. It is significant that they were both removed from the scene when Germany began to lose the war.
24 R. H. Davison, 'Turkish Diplomacy from Mudros to Lausanne', in Felix Gilbert and Gordon Craig (eds.), *The Diplomats*, p. 173.
25 *Olaylarla Türk Dış Politikası* (Turkish Foreign Policy by events), Professor Dr Mehmet Gönlübol, and Doç. Dr Cem Sar, p. 19. (Hereafter referred to as *Olaylarla*).
26 Davison, 'Turkish Diplomacy', p. 174.
27 R. Robinson, *The First Turkish Republic*, p. 36.
28 Ibid.
29 D. Warder, *The Chanak Affair*, p. 77.
30 Ibid., p. 68; see also Harry N. Howard, *The Partition of Turkey, 1918–1923*, pp. 181–213.
31 B. Lewis, *The Emergence of Modern Turkey*, p. 241.
32 R. H. Davison, 'Lausanne Thirty Years After', *Middle East Journal*, Summer 1953, vol. 7, 1953.

33 *Olaylarla*, p. 13.
34 R. B. Mowat, *A History of European Diplomacy 1914–1925*, p. 288.
35 *Olaylarla*, pp. 18, 19; R. H. Davison, in *The Diplomats*, p. 181; Sonyel, *Turkish Diplomacy*, pp. 65, 103.
36 Documents in British Foreign Policy. (Hereafter referred to as DBFP) 1919–1939, series 1, vol. XIII, pp. 184–9.
37 Sonyel, *Turkish Diplomacy*, p. 103.
38 Howard, *The Partition of Turkey*, p. 260.
39 R. H. Davison, in *The Diplomats*, p. 193.
40 Mowat, *European Diplomacy*, p. 295.
41 Walder, *The Chanak Affair*, p. 82.
42 F. R. Atay, *Kurtuluş* (Liberation) p. 6. Enver, Cemal and Talat Paşas were the ruling triumvirate of the Ottoman state during the First World War.
43 *Nutuk: A speech delivered by Gazi M. Kemal Atatürk*.
44 *Olaylarla*, p. 54; Mowat, *European Diplomacy*, p. 298.
45 Lord Kinross, *Atatürk, The Rebirth of a Nation*, p. 354.
46 Ibid., p. 358.
47 R. H. Davison, in *The Diplomats*, p. 205.
48 Aydemir, *İkinci Adam*, vol. 1, p. 236.
49 Walder, *The Chanak Affair*, p. 278.
50 Kinross, *Atatürk*, p. 358. Mosul was an area that was in the National Pact, but was ceded to Britain in 1926.
51 Ibid., p. 358.
52 Sonyel, *Turkish Diplomacy*, p. 209.
53 Ibid., p. 225.

5 Turkey at the outbreak of war

1 Zhivkova, *Anglo-Turkish Relations 1933–1939*, pp. 5, 6, 7, also document in Appendix, pp. 119–20 of the same work.
2 FO. 371/E640/135/44.
3 Zekeriya Sertel, *Tan*, 10 March 1939.
4 Kemal Karpat, *Turkey's Foreign Policy in Transition 1950–1974*, p. 3. Indeed after the conclusion of the Montreux Convention, Turkey proposed to the Soviets an agreement not to allow the warships of aggressor powers hostile to the Soviet Union to pass through the Straits. The Foreign Office took a very serious view of this. They told the Turkish Ambassador to London on 14 October 1936, that this would 'amount to something very like a Russo-Turkish alliance'. The Foreign Office were worried that now that the Straits were being remilitarised this situation could be dangerous for them: they said on 1 October 1936, 'If this agreement goes through, Russian influence will again become paramount at Angora and our own diminish proportionately.' The Admiralty made it known on 23 October, that they felt this development could gravely endanger the British strategic position in the Mediterranean, and recommended most strongly that 'every endeavour should be made to prevent Turkey entering into an arrangement with Russia on the lines

envisaged . . .' These views were made known to Menemencioğlu who emphasised, on 25 October, that it was important to give Russia a 'soft answer' because 'Turkey wished to do nothing that might cool friendship with Russia which was the cornerstone of Turkish policy.' See FO. 371/E6231/E6467/E6499/E7711/E6707/E6712/5280/44.

5 Zhivkova, *Anglo-Turkish Relations*, p. xi.
6 Karpat, *Turkey's Foreign Policy*, p. 76.
7 Ibid.
8 FO. 371/R2214/2214/44. Annual report, 1937. The turn of phrase belongs to the British Ambassador.
9 T. Ataöv, *Turkish Foreign Policy 1939–1945*, p. 11.
10 FO. 371/R2688/661/67.
11 FO. 371/R2688/R2679/661/67.
12 D. Irving (ed.), *Breach of Security*, pp. 26–7.
13 DGFP, D., vol. vi, no. 413.
14 Dr Ahmet Şükrü Esmer and Oral Sander, *Olaylarla*, p. 150.
15 Feridun Cemal Erkin, *Les Relations Turco-Soviétiques*, p. 154.
16 Zhivkova, *Anglo-Turkish Relations*, p. 98.
17 DBFP, 3, vol. v, no. 378, 379.
18 Irving (ed.), *Breach of Security*, pp. 60–1; It is worth noting that the Germans closely monitored Anglo-Turkish negotiations leading up to the Declaration and the Treaty thanks to the efforts of the *Forschungsamt*.
19 G. Gafencu, *The Last Days of Europe*, p. 131.
20 Zhivkova, *Anglo-Turkish Relations*, p. 107. Britain had given guarantees to Greece and Romania that she would come to their aid if they were attacked.
21 Ibid., p. 92.
22 FO. 371/E4151/143/44. The Saadabad Pact was concluded in 1936 between Turkey, Iran and Iraq.
23 Ibid.
24 Ibid.
25 Ibid.
26 Ibid. The Dodecanese Islands, Italian islands off the Turkish coast, had been heavily fortified by Mussolini.
27 Ibid.
28 Falih Rıfkı Atay, *Ulus*, 25 August 1939.
29 Asım Us, *Vakit*, 25 August 1939.
30 Zekeriya Sertel, *Tan*, 25 August 1939.
31 Yunus Nadi, *Cumhuriyet*, 25 August 1939.
32 Ibid., 31 August 1939.
33 *Olaylarla*, p. 151.
34 DGFP, D, vol. vii, no. 266, pp. 281–82; *Nazi–Soviet Relations*, 1948, p. 81.
35 Ibid., 5 September 1939, p. 87.
36 Ibid., p. 88.
37 Ibid., 17 September 1939, p. 97.
38 FO. 371/E6044/9/44.
39 FO. 371/E6061/9/44.
40 Zhivkova, *Anglo-Turkish Relations*, p. 109.

41 FO. 371/R6759/661/67.
42 FO. 371/R6794/661/67.
43 DBFP, 3, vol. vii, no. 635.
44 FO. 371/E5932/7213/44. In January 1939 Turkey had signed a Credit Agreement with Germany which granted her a credit of 150 million Reichmarks.
45 FO. 371/R6757/135/44.
46 FO. 371/R6797/661/67.
47 FO. 371/R6872/661/67.
48 FO. 371/R6873/661/67.
49 FO. 371/R6757/R6784/135/44.
50 FO. 371/R7146/2613/67.
51 Ibid.
52 FO. 371/R6855/661/67.
53 FO. 371/R7063/661/67. The fact that the Turks pushed so hard for this gold loan was a measure of their economic weakness.
54 FO. 371/R7517/661/67.
55 CAB. 65/I WM 2 (39) 1.
56 CAB. 65/I WM 3 (39) 2, 5 (39) 2. German evaluation of decoded Turkish messages between Ankara and Moscow indicate that they too were well aware of the 'Dardanelles precedent' in British thinking. See Irving (ed.), *Breach of Security*, pp. 58, 59.
57 CAB. 65/I WM 19 (39) 13.
58 FO. 371/R8250/7378/44.
59 Ibid., Menemencioğlu, as Secretary General of the Foreign Ministry was chief negotiator.
60 Ibid.
61 CAB. 65/I WM 24 (39) 14.
62 FO. 371/R7820/661/67.
63 FO. 371/R8144/661/67.
64 FO. 371/R8117/661/67.
65 FO. 371/R8317/661/67. The Turks tried hard to create an auspicious atmosphere for the visit. The Istanbul newspaper *Vakit* emphasised that Saraçoğlu was going to Moscow to discuss 'ways of increasing the ties of friendship and peace' which united the two countries. 'The Turkish–Soviet friendship, which is indeed ordained by nature, will bear further fruit during this visit . . .' Sadi Ertem, *Vakit*, 23 September 1939.
66 Erkin, *Les Relations Turco-Soviétiques*, pp. 158, 159.
67 FO. 371/R8603/2613/67.
68 *Olaylarla*, p. 141.
69 DGFP, D, vol. viii, no. 175, p. 183; *Nazi–Soviet Relations*, p. 110.
70 DGFP, D, vol. viii, no. 211, p. 236; *Nazi–Soviet Relations*, p. 117.
71 Erkin, *Les Relations Turco-Soviétiques*, p. 162.
72 DGFP, D, vol. viii, no. 175, p. 183; *Nazi–Soviet Relations*, p. 110.
73 Erkin, *Les Relations Turco-Soviétiques*, p. 164. The treaty of Hünkâr İskelesi, 1833, gave Russia the right to participate in the defence of the Straits.
74 FO. 371/R8563/661/67.

75 Erkin, *Les Relations Turco-Soviétiques*, p. 167.
76 DGFP, D, vol. VIII, No. 219, p. 244; *Nazi–Soviet Relations*, p. 120.
77 FO. 371/R8954/328/37.
78 Yunus Nadi, *Cumhuriyet*, 19 October 1939.
79 Zhivkova, *Anglo-Turkish Relations*, p. 114, see above, note 4.
80 Treaty of Mutual Assistance between His Majesty in respect of the United Kingdom, the President of the French Republic and the President of the Turkish Republic, Ankara (19 October 1939), Cmd. 6155 (Treaty series No. 4, House of Commons Sessional Papers), vol. XII (1940). See Appendix.
81 Abidin Daver, *Cumhuriyet*, 4 September 1939.
82 F. R. Atay, *Ulus*, 2 September 1939.
83 Sadi Ertem, *Vakit*, 2 September 1939.
84 Asım Us, *Vakit*, 2 September 1939.
85 H. Ocaklıoğlu, *Yeni Asır*, 2 September 1939.
86 Etem İzzet Benice, *Son Telgraf*, 4 September 1939.
87 N. Sadak, *Akşam*, 10 September 1939.
88 F. R. Atay, *Ulus*, 18 October 1939.
89 H. C. Yalçın, *Yeni Sabah*, 19 October 1939.
90 R. Emeç, *Son Posta*, 21 October 1939.

6 The year of surprises: 1940

1 T. Ataöv, *Turkish Foreign Policy, 1939–1945*, p. 66.
2 FO. 371/E4151/143/44.
3 J. R. M. Butler, *Grand Strategy*, vol. 2, p. 70.
4 Faik Ahmet Barutçu, *Siyasi Anılar*, p. 36; Barutçu was Deputy from Trabzon during the war years and was reputed to be close to İnönü. He was involved closely with the events of the time. He went on to hold prominent positions in the C.H.P., and became its speaker when it was in opposition during Celal Bayar Presidency.
5 DGPF, D, vol. VIII, p. 931. This treaty the Ambassador said, would cover parts not conflicting with Anglo-Turkish obligations.
6 FO. 371/R3390/R3391/316/44.
7 A. J. Klinghoffer, *The Soviet Union and International Oil Politics*, p. 40.
8 R. Massigli, *La Turquie devant la guerre*, p. 381.
9 FO. 371/C5988/9/17.
10 Elizabeth Barker, *British Politicy in South East Europe in the Second World War*, p. 23.
11 FO. 371/C5988/9/17.
12 Massigli, *La Turquie devant la guerre*, p. 385.
13 Van Creveld, *Hitler's Strategy*, pp. 211, 212 note 36.
14 FO. 371/N3698/40/38.
15 Ibid.
16 FO. 371/C5988/9/17.
17 FO. 371/R4666/5/67.
18 F. Armaoğlu, *İkinci Dünya Harbinde Türkiye* (Turkey in the Second World War), Siyasal Bilgiler Fakültesi Dergisi, vol. 13, 1958, p. 199.

19 Barutçu, *Siyasi Anılar*, p. 54.
20 Aydemir, *İkinci Adam*, vol. 2, p. 159. These two battle cruisers were pursued by the Royal Navy and allowed to pass through the Dardanelles Straits by the Turks. On 10 August 1914 the ships were transferred to the Ottoman Navy by a fictitious sale. On 28 October the Ottoman squadron including these ships now renamed *Yavuz* and *Hamidiye* bombarded Russian Black Sea ports thereby involving the Ottoman Empire in the First World War. See W. Trumpener, *Germany and the Ottoman Empire 1914–1918*, pp. 25–31.
21 DGFP, D, vol. x, no. 198, p. 258; Massigli, *La Turquie devant la guerre*, pp. 465–9; von Papen, *Memoirs*, p. 463; Van Creveld, *Hitler's Strategy*, p. 76.
22 DGFP, D, vol. ix, no. 10.
23 Langer and Gleason, *The Undeclared War*, p. 115.
24 DGFP, D, vol. x, no. 272, p. 393.
25 FO. 371/N6243/30/38/R8117/242/44.
26 FO. 371/N6243/30/38.
27 FO. 371/R8116/203/44.
28 Y. Nadi, *Cumhuriyet*, 14 November 1940.
29 *Nazi–Soviet Relations*, pp. 244–6.
30 Ibid., p. 259.
31 Ibid., p. 274. Operation 'Barbarossa' was the code name for the invasion of the Soviet Union.
32 Barutçu, *Siyasi Anılar*, p. 40; Van Creveld, *Hitler's Strategy*, p. 82.
33 *Olaylarla*, p. 157.
34 Barutçu, *Siyasi Anılar*, p. 71.
35 Koçak, *Türkiye'de Milli Şef Dönemi*, pp. 129–34.
36 Barutçu, *Siyasi Anılar*, pp. 79, 80.
37 Ibid.
38 Ibid., p. 83.
39 Ibid., p. 104.
40 Y. Nadi, *Cumhuriyet*, 23 June 1940.
41 A. Ş. Esmer, *Ulus*, 22 June 1940.
42 E. Velid, *Tasvir-i Efkâr*, 22 June 1940.
43 E. Velid, *Tasvir*, 23 June 1940.
44 Conversation with A. Ş. Esmer, 29 October 1977.
45 Conversation with Suat Hayri Ürgüplü, 29 October 1977.
46 R. Massigli, *La Turquie devant la guerre*, p. 432.
47 Barutçu, *Siyasi Anılar*, pp. 106, 107, 127.
48 Ibid., p. 75. Rauf Orbay had been one of the leaders of the Turkish War of Liberation and was a leading member of the Kemalist clique. He was condemned in 1926 for plotting against Mustafa Kemal and banished for ten years. It is interesting that Rauf Orbay was sent to England as Ambassador in 1942, because he was considered pro-British, which seems to be in contradiction with his attitude above.
49 FO. 371/R6464/542/44. Presumably Saraçoğlu saw an invasion of Britain as imminent.
50 FO. 371/R6510/316/44.
51 FO. 371/R6510/316/44

52 Ibid.
53 FO. 371/R6641/316/44.
54 Ibid.
55 Ibid.
56 Ibid.
57 Selim Sebit, *Tasvir-i Efkâr*, 18 July 1940.
58 Barutçu, *Siyasi Anılar*, p. 109; Yahya Kemal was quoting from Yenişe-hirli Avni (1826–1833).
59 See Chapter 5, p. 88 and note 80.
60 *Olaylarla*, p. 57; Armaoğlu, *İkinci Dünya Harbinde Türkiye*, p. 150; H. Howard, *Turkey, the Straits and US Policy*, p. 164.
61 Barutçu, *Siyasi Anılar*, pp. 90–1. The intellectual heritage of the First World War is clearly observable in this instance.
62 FO. 371/R6459/542/44, tel. no. 541.
63 Ibid., tel. no. 548. DIPP.
64 Ibid.
65 Ibid., tel. no. 563.
66 Ibid., tel. no. 588 DIPP.
67 Ibid., tel. no. 455 DIPP.
68 Massigli, *La Turquie devant la guerre*, p. 443; CAB. 65.7/169(40)7.
69 FO. 371/R6269/58/22.
70 Ibid.
71 FO. 371/R6510/316/44.
72 Ibid.
73 Ibid.
74 DGFP, D, vol. x, no. 424, p. 25.
75 FO. 371/R6510/316/44, tel no. 482, DIPP.
76 Ibid., tel. 618.
77 *Olaylarla*, p. 160.
78 Barutçu, *Siyasi Anılar*, pp. 116–17.
79 Ibid., p. 100.
80 Ibid., pp. 90–1.
81 CAB 65/7 161(40) 7; The Turks had made known to the British their intention of applying Protocol 2 well before the actual official declaration of non-belligerency on 26 June.
82 CAB. 65/7. 166(40) 7.
83 CAB. 65/7. 167(40) 9.
84 FO. 371/R6608/316/44.
85 N. Sadak, *Akşam*, 17 June 1940.
86 FO. 371/R7555/316/44.
87 N. Sadak, *Akşam*, 21 October 1939.
88 Ibid., 16 July 1940.
89 Y. Nadi, *Cumhuriyet*, 21 June 1940.
90 F. R. Atay, *Ulus*, 16 June 1940.
91 DGFP, D, vol. ix, No. 434, p. 568.
92 Koçak, *Türkiye'de Milli Şef Dönemi*, p. 131.
93 DGFP, D, vol. ix, No. 308.
94 FO. 371/R6762/318/44.

95 FO. 371/E4151/143/44. See above, p. 76.
96 FO. 371/R6762/318/44.
97 FO. 371/R6821/542/44.
98 FO. 371/R6510/316/44. See above pp. 102–5.
99 FO. 371/R7274/764/19.
100 Ibid.
101 FO. 371/R6269/58/22.
102 FO. 371/R7487/764/19.
103 Barker, *British Policy in South-East Europe*, p. 112.
104 FO. 371/R6261/58/22.
105 FO. 371/R6269/58/22.
106 FO. 371/R7058/764/19.
107 FO. 371/R7211/764/19.
108 FO. 371/R7274/764/19, tel. no. 1077.
109 FO. 371/R7274/764/19.
110 FO. 371/R7555/316/44.
111 FO. 371/R7254/764/19.
112 FO. 371/R7400/764/19.
113 Koliopoulos, *Greece and the British Connection*, p. 140.
114 FO. 371/R7430/764/19.
115 FO. 371/R7464/764/19.
116 FO. 371/R7529/764/19.
117 FO. 371/R7912/316/44; C. M. Woodhouse declares in his review of Koliopoulos' book, *Greece and the British Connection* that Koliopoulos is mistaken in claiming that Turkey did not implement her treaty obligations. He says, 'surely there were no such obligations at that date (1940)'. He is mistaken in this view, there were explicit obligations at this time; see C. M. Woodhouse, 'The Intermittent King', *Times Literary Supplement*, 28 July 1978, pp. 860–1, and British and Foreign State Papers, Cmd. 6165 (19 Oct. 1939), House of Commons Sessional Papers, vol. XIII (1940).
118 Faik Fenik, *Ulus*, 8 October 1940.
119 F. R. Atay, *Ulus*, 12 October 1940.
120 A. Ş. Esmer, *Ulus*, 15 October 1940.
121 Count Galeazzo, *The Ciano Diaries 1939–1943*, Malcolm Muggeridge (ed.), p. 299; Pietro Badoglio, *Italy in the Second World War*, describes Ciano as the 'evil genius' behind the Greek campaign, p. 25.
122 *Ciano Diaries*, pp. 360, 299.
123 Van Creveld, *Hitler's Strategy*, pp. 73, 75, 111.
124 FO. 371/R8069/764/19.
125 Langer and Gleason, *Undeclared War*, p. 115.
126 A. Ş. Esmer, *Ulus*, 30 October 1940.
127 F. R. Atay, ibid.
128 Y. Nadi, *Cumhuriyet*, 14 November 1940.
129 Winston Churchill, *History of the Second World War*, vol. 2, *Their Finest Hour*, Cassel and Co., London, 1949, p. 483.
130 Wiskemann, *Undeclared War*, p. 115.
131 FO. 371/R8586/316/44.

132 CAB. 65/10. 294(40)3.
133 FO. 371/R8586/316/44.
134 CAB. 65/10. 294(40)3.
135 FO. 371/R8114/764/19.
136 Koliopoulos, *Greece and the British Connection*, p. 14.
137 FO. 371/8114/764/19; see also Barker, *British Policy in South-East Europe*, pp. 100–1.
138 Churchill, *Their Finest Hour*, p. 484.
139 Generaloberst Halder, *Kriegstagebuch*, vol. 2, p. 151.
140 Ibid., p. 191.
141 Van Creveld, *Hitler's Strategy*, p. 58.
142 Wiskemann, *Undeclared War*, p. 109.
143 FO. 371/R8586/316/44.
144 Van Creveld, *Hitler's Strategy*, pp. 75–7, 82, 83; Halder, *Kriegstagebuch*, p. 191.
145 *Cumhuriyet*, 19 November 1940.

7 Hostile encirclement: 1941

1 FO. 371/R890/236/44. Emphasis in original.
2 Howard, *Turkey, the Straits and US Policy*, p. 164.
3 Trumbull Higgins, *Winston Churchill and the Second Front 1940–1942*, pp. 71–3.
4 DGFP, D, vol. xii, No. 514, p. 816.
5 Trumbull Higgins, *Winston Churchill*, p. 50.
6 Churchill, *The Grand Alliance*, p. 17.
7 J. R. M. Butler, *Grand Strategy*, vol. 2, p. 383.
8 FO. 371/R481/236/44 (emphasis in original), tel. no. 124.
9 FO. 371/R646/113/67; *Grand Strategy*, vol. 2, p. 383.
10 Higgins, *Winston Churchill and the Second Front 1940–1942* pp. 50–1: The issue of infiltration of 'men in mufti' as the Foreign Office called them would become a particularly sensitive topic in the Cairo Conference in 1943.
11 Barutçu, *Siyasi Anılar*, p. 161.
12 Eden, *The Eden Memoirs: The Reckoning*, p. 205; Koliopoulos, *Greece and the British Connection*, pp. 228–30.
13 F. R. Atay, *Ulus*, 26 February 1941.
14 Koliopoulos, *Greece and the British Connection*, pp. 246–7; See also Barker, *British Policy*, p. 103: '[Eden] failed to budge the Turks an inch from their refusal to stir outside their frontiers'. The Turkish press was also directed during the visit not to print anything about the deficient nature of British help to Greece. See Alpay Kabacalı, 'Milli Şef Döneminin Örtülü Sansürü (Unofficial Censorship in the Period of the National Chief), *Tarih ve Toplum*, no. 38, January 1987, p. 20.
15 FO. 371/R2450/236/44. tel. no. 540.
16 Ibid.
17 Ibid.; Bulgaria joined the Axis on 1 March.
18 DGFP, D, vol. xii, no. 113, pp. 201–2; see also Van Creveld, *Hitler's*

Strategy, p. 64: 'On their way south (through Bulgaria) the German troops would have the Turkish army looking over their left shoulder . . .'

19 FO. 371/R2937/557/92; R2069/113/67: The Foreign Office felt that the Turks were guilty of 'wilful blindness' in their relations with Germany.

20 DGFP, D, vol. XII, no. 161, p. 286.

21 Barker, *British Policy*, p. 27.

22 A. Ş. Esmer, *Ulus*, 23 April 1941.

23 *Ulus*, 10, 11 April 1941.

24 Barutçu, *Siyasi Anılar*, p. 193.

25 F. R. Atay, *Ulus*, 23 May 1941.

26 Warren F. Kimball, *Churchill and Roosevelt. The Complete Correspondence*, vol. 1, *Alliance Emerging* (Princeton University Press, 1984), pp. 181–82, p. 184a; F. L. Loewenheim and H. D. Langley, *Roosevelt and Churchill. Their Secret Wartime Correspondence* (New York, 1975) p. 140.

27 G. Lenczowski, 'Turkey and World War II' in *The Middle East in World Affairs* (Cornell University Press, 1952).

28 DGFP, vol. XII, no. 529, p. 836; Barutçu, *Siyasi Anılar*, p. 185; Churchill, *The Grand Alliance*, p. 641; Koliopoulos, *Greece and the British Connection*, p. 250.

29 DGFP, D, vol. XII, no. 556, pp. 886–7.

30 FO. 371/R5366/1934/44.

31 DGFP, D, vol. XII, no. 607, pp. 985–6.

32 Ibid., No. 566, pp. 913–14. It is interesting that Papen, unlike Hugessen who imputed 'bazaar instincts' to the Turkish leaders should have a closer appreciation of the Turkish attitude.

33 Ibid., No. 161, pp. 230–1. The German High Command also appreciated the difficulties of taking on the Turkish army at that point in time. A Wilhelmstrasse memo dated 24 August stated: 'General Jodl explained that we did not have sufficient forces for a large campaign such as a war against Turkey would require . . .' See DGFP, D, vol. XII, No. 161, pp. 230–1. As early as 20 April Hitler had told Ciano that an attack on Egypt through Turkey would be 'dangerous' as Turkish resistance would be 'considerable'. See *Ciano's Diplomatic Papers*, Malcolm Muggeridge (ed.), Stuart Hood (trans.), p. 435.

34 FO. 371/R5495/1934/44. tel. no. 1256.

35 *Ulus*, 13 June 1941.

36 *Ulus*, 19 June 1941.

37 Yunus Nadi, *Cumhuriyet*, 20 June 1941.

38 Barutçu, *Siyasi Anılar*, p. 203.

39 CAB. 65/23. WM 73(41)2.

40 DGFP, D, vol. XIII, No. 367, p. 589.

41 *Undeclared War*, p. 512.

42 FO. 371/R6363/1934/44.

43 FO. 371/R7421/236/44.

44 FO. 371/R6399/1934/44.

45 DGFP, D, vol. XII, No. 637, p. 1080.

46 E. Erkilet, *Cumhuriyet*, 29 June 1941.

47 F. R. Atay, *Ulus*, 23 June 1941.

48 FO. 371/N3197/78/38.
49 Yunus Nadi, *Cumhuriyet*, 28 June 1941.
50 Ataöv, *Turkish Foreign Policy, 1939–1945*, p. 98; Barutçu, *Siyasi Anılar*, p. 222.
51 FO. 371/R6747/236/44.
52 FO. 371/R6535/1934/44.
53 FO. 371/R6772/236/44; R6823/236/44.
54 FO. 371/R7421/236/44.
55 Eden, *The Reckoning*, pp. 246–7.
56 DGFP, D, vol. xiii, No. 538, p. 849.
57 FO. 271/R6436/1934/44, tel no. 1551.
58 FO. 371/R5560/1934/44, tel. no. 1279.
59 Koçak, *Türkiye'de Milli Şef Dönemi*, p. 156.
60 E. Kedourie, 'Wavell and Iraq, April–May 1941', *Arabic Political Memoirs*, pp. 277, 279.
61 DGFP, D, vol. xii, No. 556, p. 914. German war material passed through Turkey addressed to Afghanistan and Iran. Vichy material went through addressed to Vichy's own frontier garrisons. See also Koçak, *Türkiye'de Milli Şef Dönemi*, p. 162.
62 Koçak, *Türkiye'de Milli Şef Dönemi*, pp. 162, 164. The Vichy forces were defeated at the end of July.
63 FO. 371/R6584/236/44. tel. no. 158.
64 DGFP, D, vol. xii, No. 586, p. 953.
65 FO. 371/R6658/236/44. tel. no. 1607.
66 FO. 371/R6703/236/44. tel. no. 1623.
67 Kimball, *Churchill and Roosevelt*, vol. 1, pp. 235, 236, C-113x; Loewenheim, Langley and Jonas, *Roosevelt and Churchill*, pp. 155–6.
68 *Undeclared War*, p. 803.
69 Churchill, *The Grand Alliance*, p. 477.
70 *Undeclared War*, p. 803.
71 Bruce Kuniholm, *The Origins of the Cold War in the Near East*, pp. 142–3.
72 CAB. 65. 23 (WM) 79(41)2; CAB. 65. 23 (WM) 84(41)1.
73 FO. 371/R7908/236/44, tel no. 2041.
74 Yunus Nadi, *Cumhuriyet*, 27 August 1941.
75 N. Sadak, *Akşam*, 26 August 1941.
76 *Cumhuriyet*, 27 August 1941.
77 N. Sadak, *Akşam*, 28 August 1941.
78 FO. 371/R8328/139/44, tel no. 2186.
79 FO. 371/R8358/R8363/139/44.
80 Kuniholm, *The Origins*, pp. 142, 143.
81 CAB 65/19. (WM) 98(41)5.
82 DGFP, D, vol. xiii, No. 294, p. 471.
83 Ibid., No. 358, p. 568.
84 Ibid., No. 402, p. 646. The Turco-German trade agreement was signed in Ankara on 9 October 1941.
85 Kuniholm, *The Origins*, p. 28. See also Fahir Armaoğlu: 'İkinci Dünya Harbinde Türkiye', p. 161.
86 FO. 371/R6927/R6923/40/44.

87 CAB. 65.19(WM) 101(41)4.
88 Shaw and Shaw, *History of the Ottoman Empire and Modern Turkey*, vol. 2, pp. 156, 157, 260–3.
89 Koçak, *Türkiye'de Milli Şef Dönemi*, p. 192. This recently published work gives a competent appraisal of the Pan-Turanian issue based on Turkish and German sources.
90 FO. 371/R6584/236/44.
91 Koçak, *Türkiye'de Milli Şef Dönemi*, p. 191.
92 P. W. Hostler, *Turkism and the Soviets*, pp. 172–5.
93 Koçak, *Türkiye'de Milli Şef Dönemi*, p. 191.
94 Ibid., p. 194.
95 Weisband, *Turkish Foreign Policy*, p. 193.
96 Koçak, *Türkiye'de Milli Şef Dönemi*, pp. 194, 195, 196.
97 DGFP, D, vol. XIII, no. 361, p. 371.
98 Ibid., p. 573.
99 Ibid., no. 194, p. 306.
100 Koçak, *Türkiye'de Milli Şef Dönemi*, pp. 201, 202, 203. Koçak's information comes from *Akten zur Deutschen Auswartiges Politik*. Serie E, Band III, 16 July to 30 September 1942, Nr. 238, 27 August 1942, Göttingen 1974.
101 Koçak, *Türkiye'de Milli Şef Dönemi*, p. 203.

8 'Active neutrality': 1942

1 F. R. Atay, *Ulus*, 3 January 1942.
2 Howard, *Turkey, the Straits and U.S. Policy*, p. 165.
3 Ibid., p. 166.
4 DGFP, D, vol. XIII, No. 295, p. 491.
5 Yunus Nadi, *Cumhuriyet*, 10 January 1942.
6 Ibid., 11 January 1942.
7 FO. 371/R148/24/44.
8 The *Ciano Diaries*, p. 456; A. Ş. Esmer in a private interview on 29 October 1977.
9 FO. 371/R2070/810/44.
10 FO. 371/R953/486/44. tel no. 290.
11 Von Papen, *Memoirs*, p. 488.
12 FO. 371/R953/486/44.
13 Ibid. This memo is marked 'most secret', and 'based on delicate sources'.
14 FO. 371/R5200/810/44, tel no. 1468.
15 FO. 371/R5215/810/44.
16 Howard, *Turkey*, p. 167.
17 *Ciano's Diplomatic Papers*, p. 483.
18 F. R. Atay, *Ulus*, 20 February 1942.
19 Ibid., 17 February 1942.
20 *Ulus*, 28 February 1942.
21 *Ulus*, 18 March 1942.
22 Howard, *Turkey*, p. 167.

23 FO. 371/R1533/24/44, tel. no. 451.
24 FO. 371/R1532/24/44. tel. no. 448.
25 FO. 371/2516/24/44.
26 Von Papen, *Memoirs*, p. 488.
27 FO. 371/R2380/486/44. tel. no. 679.
28 Ibid. Emphasis in original. Hugessen seems at least to have acquired one essential word for his Turkish vocabulary.
29 FO. 371/R3192/24/44.
30 FO. 371/R2993/24/44. tel. no. 923. The chances are that Menemencioğlu was sounding the Ambassador for information. Hugessen did in fact say: 'I was unable to make out how far he was exaggerating in order to alarm me and how far he was going on definite data . . .'
31 CAB. 65/26WM61(42)4.
32 F. R. Atay, *Ulus*, 13 June 1942.
33 Ibid., 18 June 1942.
34 FO. 371/R5690/488/44, tel no. 1589.
35 FO. 371/R4159/24/44, tel. no. 1333. Emphasis in original.
36 FO. 371/R4473/24/44, tel. no. 1257.
37 FO. 371/R4791/24/44.
38 FO. 371/R5690/486/44, tel. no. 1589.
39 FO. 371/R6369/481/44.
40 FO. 371/R2363/486/44.
41 Koçak, *Türkiye'de Milli Şef Dönemi*, p. 175.
42 Ibid., note 5.
43 See above p. 125.
44 FO. 371/R4087/24/44.
45 FO. 371/R5618/2713/44.
46 Ibid.
47 FO. 371/R7176/24/44. In July 1942 Numan Menemencioğlu had become Foreign Minister and Saraçoğlu Prime Minister after the death of Prime Minister Refik Saydam.
48 Ibid.
49 A. Ş. Esmer in a personal interview 29 October 1977.
50 Churchill, *Hinge of Fate*, p. 623.
51 R. Sherwood, *Roosevelt and Hopkins*, pp. 656–7.
52 Churchill, *Hinge of Fate*, p. 624.
53 FO. 371/R7897/24/44.
54 Churchill, *Hinge of Fate*, pp. 624–6.
55 FO. 371/R7978/24/44.
56 Ibid.
57 Ibid.
58 Howard, *Turkey*, p. 172; Weisband, *Turkish Foreign Policy*, pp. 146–8; Churchill, *Hinge of Fate*, pp. 624–6.
59 FO. 371/R8381/810/44 and Hugessen, *Diplomat in Peace and War*, pp. 185–6; Hugessen clearly stated in his memoirs: 'Unless they [Turkey] became a United Nation by abandoning their present attitude of neutrality, they could not expect to have a say in the peace settlement.'
60 FO. 371/R8732/24/44.

9 On the razor's edge: 1943

1 Higgins, *Winston Churchill*, p. 171.
2 Kimball, *Churchill and Roosevelt*, vol. 2, *Alliance Forged*, pp. 129–32; Loewenheim and Langley, *Roosevelt and Churchill*, p. 313.
3 Churchill, *Hinge of Fate*, pp. 632–5.
4 Sherwood, *Roosevelt and Hopkins*, p. 799.
5 USFR, *Conferences at Washington and Casablanca*, p. 634.
6 F. C. Erkin, *Les Relations Turco-Soviétiques*, pp. 220–1; FO. 371/R5378/55/44.
7 USFR, *Conferences at Washington and Casablanca*, p. 643.
8 Kuniholm, *The Origins*, p. 30.
9 Weisband, *Turkish Foreign Policy*, p. 134; Aydemir, *İkinci Adam*, vol. 2, p. 260.
10 Kuniholm, *The Origins*, p. 33.
11 Churchill, *Hinge of Fate*, p. 631.
12 The Menemencioğlu Text, p. 272. The Montreux Convention (signed 20 July 1936) determined that in wartime when Turkey was a non-belligerent the Straits would be closed to warships of all countries. The Convention specified further that Turkey could not offer air or naval facilities to an outside party.
13 Churchill, *Hinge of Fate*, p. 638.
14 FO. 371/R2281/R10304/1016/44; Erkin, *Les Relations Turco-Soviétiques*, p. 230.
15 FO. 371/R2425/55/44.
16 FO. 371/R10304/1016/44.
17 H. C. Yalçın, *Yeni Sabah*, 3 February 1943.
18 *Cumhuriyet*, 4 February 1943.
19 Yunus Nadi, *Cumhuriyet*, 14 February 1943.
20 Asım Us, *Vakit*, 3 February 1943.
21 Ahmet Emin Yalman, *Vatan*, 14 February 1944.
22 Hugessen, *Diplomat in Peace and War*, p. 190.
23 Weisband, *Turkish Foreign Policy*, p. 153, emphasis in original.
24 Sir Henry Maitland Wilson, *Eight Years Overseas*, p. 156.
25 Ehrman, *Grand Strategy*, vol. 5, p. 90.
26 Weisband, *Turkish Foreign Policy*, p. 153.
27 FO. 371/R2986/55/44.
28 Ibid.
29 Sir Henry Maitland Wilson, 'Operations in the Middle East', *London Gazette*, no. 37, 786. November 12 1946, and *Eight Years Overseas*, pp. 156–7.
30 Interview with Suat Hayri Ürgüplü, 1 November 1977.
31 *Eight Years Overseas*, p. 156–7.
32 Weisband, *Turkish Foreign Policy*, pp. 160–1; Foreign Ministry Berlin to Ambassador in Ankara, Berlin, 13 August 1943, *Captured Files* NA. T-120, Roll 2618, Frame E 364709.
33 FO. 371/R5310/55/44.
34 FO. 371/R5366/55/44.

35 FO. 371/R5444/7/44.
36 FO. 371/R5595/55/44.
37 Nadir Nadi, *Cumhuriyet*, 22 June 1943.
38 Yunus Nadi, *Cumhuriyet*, 28 June 1943.
39 FO. 371/R8244/55/44.
40 Churchill, *Closing the Ring*, p. 54.
41 FO. 371/R9066/55/44.
42 Churchill, *Closing the Ring*, p. 181.
43 Ibid., p. 182; Kuniholm, *The Origins*, p. 34.
44 Churchill, *Closing the Ring*, p. 184.
45 Ibid., p. 195.
46 FO. 371/R9672/55/44. The British lost Kos, Leros, and Samos in rapid succession.
47 FO. 371/R11160/6611/22. This writer has had numerous conversations with the inhabitants of Bodrum who took part in the evacuation of British forces from Kos. They all remembered the pellmell retreat and the awe inspired by German air power.
48 FO. 371/R10301/55/44.
49 Ahmet Emin Yalman, *Vatan*, 14 February 1944.
50 N. Sadak, *Akşam*, 20 November 1943.
51 Weisband, *Turkish Foreign Policy*, p. 165.
52 FO. 371/R10301/55/44.
53 Weisband, *Turkish Foreign Policy*, p. 166.
54 Ibid., p. 166.
55 Kuniholm, *The Origins*, p. 34.
56 Churchill, *Closing the Ring*, p. 255.
57 Kuniholm, *The Origins*, pp. 35, 36.
58 FO. 371/N6921/3666/38, pp. 20–1. Record of the Second Meeting of Tripartite Conference, 20 October 1943.
59 Ibid.
60 Churchill, *Closing the Ring*, pp. 256–7.
61 FO. 371/N6921/3666/38. Annex 21, p. 90.
62 Weisband, *Turkish Foreign Policy*, p. 173.
63 FO. 371/N6921/3666/38.
64 Kuniholm, *The Origins*, p. 36.
65 USFR, *Conferences at Cairo and Tehran*, Secretary of State to President, 1 November 1943, p. 144.
66 Ibid.
67 Ibid., Ambassador Harriman to President, 2 November 1943, p. 146; Kuniholm, *The Origins*, p. 36.
68 F. R. Atay, *Ulus*, 21 October 1943.
69 H. C. Yalçın, *Tanin*, 22 October 1943.
70 Ibid., 31 October 1943.
71 Weisband, *Turkish Foreign Policy*, pp. 177–8.
72 Menemencioğlu Text, p. 274.
73 Ibid., p. 280.
74 USFR, *Conferences at Cairo and Tehran*, p. 164.
75 Menemencioğlu Text, p. 275; Kuniholm, *The Origins*, pp. 36–7.

76 Menemencioğlu Text, p. 279.
77 USFR, *Conferences at Cairo and Tehran*, p. 166.
78 Ibid.
79 Eden, *The Reckoning*, p. 419. One finds repeated references to deafness on the part of leading Turks. Sir Henry Maitland Wilson in *Eight Years Overseas*, p. 151, commented that he noticed in Adana that İnönü, 'was handicapped by deafness as was his Foreign Secretary, Numan (after the Cairo Conference at the end of the year I began to doubt that deafness was a handicap in diplomacy . . .)' Similarly R. E. Sherwood in *Roosevelt and Hopkins* (p. 799) mentions, 'Some mad wag in Cairo circulated the report that all the Turks were wearing hearing devices so perfectly attuned to one another that they all went out of order at the same instant whenever mention was made of the possibility of Turkey's coming into the war.'
80 Menemencioğlu Text, p. 276.
81 Ibid., p. 280.
82 Eden, *The Reckoning*, p. 423.
83 USFR, *Conferences at Cairo and Tehran*, p. 187.
84 A. E. Yalman, *Vatan*, 6 November 1943.
85 Z. Sertel, *Tan*, 6 November 1943.
86 N. Nadi, *Cumhuriyet*, 6 November 1943.
87 Personal interview with A. Şükrü Esmer, 29 October 1977.
88 Sherwood, *Roosevelt and Hopkins*, p. 780.
89 Kuniholm, *The Origins*, p. 41; Erkin, *Les Relations Turco-Soviétiques*, p. 243; Aydemir, *İkinci Adam*, vol. 2, p. 266.
90 USFR, *Conferences at Cairo and Tehran*, pp. 492–7.
91 Ibid.
92 FO. 371/R1304/1016/44.
93 USFR, *Conferences at Cairo and Tehran*, p. 496.
94 Ibid., p. 536.
95 Ibid., p. 573.
96 Ibid., p. 588.
97 Ibid., p. 587.
98 Ibid., p. 589.
99 FO. 371/R1304/R2281/1016/44.
100 FO. 371/R11313/55/44.
101 FO. 371/R11108/55/44.
102 FO. 371/R12707/55/44.
103 Ibid.
104 Weisband, *Turkish Foreign Policy*, p. 202; USFR, *Conferences at Cairo and Tehran*, p. 664.
105 Menemencioğlu Text, p. 278.
106 Ibid.
107 Ibid., p. 279.
108 USFR, *Conferences at Cairo and Tehran*, p. 691.
109 Ibid., p. 695.
110 Ibid., p. 696.
111 Ibid., p. 714.

112 Menemencioğlu Text, p. 284.
113 USFR, *Conferences at Cairo and Tehran*, p. 730.
114 Ibid., p. 751.
115 Kuniholm, *The Origins*, p. 48, note 105; Kuniholm's source is D. Gordon and R. Dangerfield, *The Hidden Weapon: The Story of Economic Warfare* (New York 1947), p. 123.
116 USFR, *Conferences at Cairo and Tehran*, p. 744; also Sherwood, *Roosevelt and Hopkins*, p. 780.
117 USFR, *Conferences at Cairo and Tehran*, p. 817.
118 Interview with Suat Hayri Ürgüplü, 29 October 1977.
119 Kuniholm, *The Origins*, p. 46.
120 Eden, *The Reckoning*, p. 429.
121 Irving (ed.), *Breach of Security*, pp. 26–7.
122 L. C. Moyzisch, *Operation Cicero*.
123 Koçak, *Türkiye'de Milli Şef Dönemi*, pp. 291–2.
124 Interview with Suat Hayri Ürgüplü, 1 November 1977.
125 Koçak, *Türkiye'de Milli Şef Dönemi*, p. 287.
126 H. C. Yalçın, *Tanin*, 12 December 1943.
127 N. Nadi, *Cumhuriyet*, 12 December 1943.
128 Asım Us, *Vakit*, 12 December 1943.
129 FO. 371/R12987/55/44.
130 FO. 371/R13067/55/44; R13068/55/44.
131 FO. 371/R13069/55/44. See also the Menemencioğlu Text, p. 275 and Kuniholm, *The Origins*, pp. 36, 37.
132 FO. 371/R13069/55/44.
133 FO. 371/R13141/55/44.
134 FO. 371/R13159/55/44; Prem. 3, 447; R13459/55/44.

10 The Turkish gambit: 1944

1 FO. 371/R10541/789/44.
2 Menemencioğlu Text, p. 290.
3 FO. 371/R609/7/44.
4 FO. 371/R873/7/44.
5 Menemencioğlu Text, p. 287.
6 Ibid.
7 FO. 371/R1327/7/44; R874/7/44.
8 FO. 371/R587/7/44; Kuniholm, *The Origins*, p. 51.
9 FO. 371/R1345/7/44.
10 FO. 371/R3882/7/44.
11 FO. 371/R2501/7/44.
12 N. Sadak, *Akşam*, 13 February 1944.
13 P. Sefa, *Tasvir-i Efkâr*, 28 February 1944.
14 N. Nadi, *Cumhuriyet*, 29 February 1944.
15 N. Sadak, *Akşam*, 29 February 1944.
16 Yuluğ Tekin Kurat, 'İkinci Dünya Savaşında Türk Alman Ticareti', p. 102.
17 Kuniholm, *The Origins*, p. 52.

18 FO. 371/C4001/2/41.
19 USFR, 1944 (5), pp. 825–6.
20 *Tasvir-i Efkâr*, 25 April 1944.
21 Ibid.
22 N. Sadak, *Akşam*, 18 April 1944.
23 Ibid., 22 April 1944.
24 F. R. Atay, *Ulus*, 21 April 1944; N. Nadi, *Cumhuriyet*, 22 April 1944.
25 Erkin, *Les Relations Turco-Soviétiques*, p. 292.
26 Barker, *British Policy in South-East Europe*, p. 23.
27 Ibid., pp. 28, 35; FO. 371/R8662/55/44; R8078/68/44.
28 CAB. 66/49. WP(44)244.
29 FO. 371/R9286/3830/44.
30 Erkin, *Les Relations Turco-Soviétiques*, pp. 278, 279.
31 Keesing's Contemporary Archives, vol. 5, 1943–46, pp. 6, 526.
32 J. W. Roskill, *The War at Sea*, vol. 3, part 1, p. 317.
33 FO. 371/R9129/7/44.
34 Erkin, *Les Relations Turco-Sociétiques*, p. 277. The search revealed that the ship had 9 mm armour plate, depth charges, cranes of 31 tons capacity for transporting light armoured vehicles, 5 machine guns, 2 cannon, and submarine detection equipment.
35 Keesing's, vol. 5, 1943–46, pp. 6, 526.
36 FO. 371/R10541/789/44: This is a handwritten minute initialled 'W.M.', it probably belongs to A. W. Mohan of the Southern Dept.
37 Ibid.
38 FO. 371/R9637/3830/44. Mrs Nermin Streater, Menemencioğlu's niece, also concurs in the view that her uncle was made to resign to please the Allies. Her father, Mr Muvaffak Menemencioğlu, Numan Menemencioğlu's elder brother was dismissed at the same time from the *Anadolu Ajansı*, the official news agency of which he had been the director. Conversation with Mrs Nermin Streater, 9 June 1977.
39 *Yeni Sabah*, 17 June 1944.
40 H. C. Yalçın, *Tanin*, 17 June 1944.
41 Menemencioğlu Text, p. 294.
42 CAB. 66/49 WP(44) 242.
43 CAB. 66/49 WP(44) 244.
44 USFR, 1944(5), pp. 863–5.
45 USFR, 1944(5), pp. 862–3. Prime Minister Saraçoğlu had taken over the Foreign Ministry after Menemencioğlu's resignation and held both portfolios until Hasan Saka was appointed Foreign Minister in early 1945.
46 CAB. 65/47 WM88(44)3.
47 FO. 371/R10982/17/6.
48 FO. 371/R11508/7/44.
49 USFR, 1944(5), pp. 884–5.
50 H. C. Yalçın, *Tanin*, 1 June 1944.
51 Koçak, *Türkiye'de Milli Şef Dönemi*, p. 302.
52 Ibid., p. 298; F. R. Atay, *Ulus*, 9 May 1944.
53 Ibid., F. R. Atay, *Ulus*, 13 May 1944.

54 Koçak, *Türkiye'de Milli Şef Dönemi*, p. 299.
55 Ibid., p. 300 note 149, p. 301.
56 Ibid., p. 302.
57 CAB 66.48/WP(44)186.
58 CAB 66/51 WP(44)304.
59 See above pp. 152, 173.
60 FO. 371/R11873/7/44.
61 FO. 371/R15838/7/44.
62 FO. 371/R20344/7/44.
63 FO. 371/R16013/3830/44.
64 FO. 371/R18327/1723/44.
65 Ibid.
66 Ibid.
67 FO. 371/R10541/789/44.

11 The Soviet demands: 1945

1 F. R. Atay, *Ulus*, 24 February 1945.
2 Interview with Ahmet Şükrü Esmer, 29 October 1977.
3 USFR, 1945, Yalta Papers, *Conferences at Malta and Yalta*, p. 773.
4 Ibid., pp. 897–918.
5 Koçak, *Türkiye'de Milli Şef Dönemi*, p. 323.
6 H. C. Yalçın, *Tanin*, 24 February 1945.
7 *Yeni Sabah*, 24 February 1945.
8 Nadir Nadi, *Cumhuriyet*, 24 February 1945.
9 H. C. Yalçın, *Tanin*, 4 March 1945.
10 Necmettin Sadak, *Akşam*, 26 March 1945.
11 Haluk Ülman, *Türk-Amerikan Diplomatik Münasebetleri. 1939–1947* (Turkish–American Diplomatic Relations. 1939–1947), p. 52; Erkin, *Les Relations Turco-Soviétiques*, pp. 290, 293.
12 Weisband, *Turkish Foreign Policy*, p. 316; Erkin, *Les Relations Turco-Soviétiques*, p. 295. Although Weisband comments: 'Surprisingly, almost instantly, the wartime grievances of the British towards the Turks vanished . .' (p. 316), there was nothing 'surprising' or 'instant' about British support. We have already seen how as early as April 1944 the British were becoming aware that they could not afford to lose Turkey.
13 USFR, 1945(2), *Conferences of Berlin (Potsdam)*, pp. 256–8. The two treaties in question were the Ottoman–Russian Treaty of 22 December 1805 granting Russian warships facilities of passage through the Straits in the hope of securing the Czar's aid against Napoleonic France, and the Treaty of Hünkar İskelesi (8 July 1833) promising mutual assistance between the Ottoman and Russian Empires. This was a measure designed to procure Russian aid against Egypt during the Ottoman–Egyptian war of 1833. See Shaw and Shaw, *History of the Ottoman Empire and Modern Turkey*, vol. 1, p. 271, vol. 2, p. 34.
14 Erkin, *Les Relations Turco-Soviétiques*, p. 317–20.
15 FO. 371/R16339/4476/44.
16 FO. 371/R18776/4476/44.

17 FO. 371/R14529/R16406/R171521/R18187/477/7.
18 FO. 371/R18312/477/7.
19 H. C. Yalçın, *Tanin*, 29 June 1945.
20 Cavit Oral, *Bugün*, 28 June 1945.
21 FO. 371/R15837/177/44.
22 FO. 371/U10270/12/Reconstruction.
23 FO. 371/R16317/1272/44.
24 TCBMM, *Zabıt Ceridesi, Devre 7, 1945* (Minutes of the proceedings of the Grand National Assembly). See also *Ayın Tarihi*, no. 144, November 1945.
25 Ibid.

Conclusion

1 Conversation with retired Ambassador Ismail Soysal, 24 February 1987. Soysal notes that this story emanated from Menemencioğlu's private secretary at the time. Nasrettin Hoca (1208–37) is a quasi-legendary figure in Turkish folklore whose stories (usually bearing a light moral) are known in Anatolia, the Balkans, the Arab world, and in Central Asia.
2 A. B. Fox, *The Power of Small States*, p. 10.
3 D. Irving, *Hitler's War*, p. 590: 'Turkey had no desire to share Iran's fate – occupied, divided into spheres of interest and anaesthetized with a nice declaration of her independence.'
4 Fox, *Power of Small States*, p. 12.
5 F. A. Vali, *Bridge across the Bosphorous*, p. 354.
6 A. Ş. Esmer, *Ulus*, 20 May 1939.
7 Koçak, *Türkiye'de Milli Şef Dönemi*, pp. 394–5.
8 Kuniholm, *The Origins*, pp. 68–9.
9 Ibid., p. 70.
10 Van Creveld, *Hitler's Strategy*, p. 141.
11 See above p. 106, 107.
12 DGFP, D, vol. xiii, no. 393, p. 633.
13 H. C. Yalçın, *Tanin*, 4 March 1945.

BIBLIOGRAPHY

Unpublished documents

Great Britain: Public Records Office, Foreign Office Correspondence: FO 371: Turkey.

1934: vols. 17964, 17966, 17967.

1936: vols. 20093, 20094.

1938: vols. 21927, 21928, 21929, 21930, 21931, 21932, 21933, 21934, 21935.

1939: vols. 23007, 23062, 23063, 23211, 23283, 23284, 23288, 23290, 23291, 23292, 23293, 23294, 23296, 23297, 23739, 23741, 23742, 23743, 23744, 23746, 23747, 23748, 23749, 23750, 23753, 23756, 23787, 23821, 23846, 23862, 23867, 23868, 23869, 23870, 23871, 23873, 23952, 25004.

1940: vols. 24299, 24323, 24380, 24845, 24846, 24852, 24870, 24879, 24887, 24888, 24890, 24917, 24918, 24919, 24920, 24997, 25007, 25009, 25012, 25013, 25015, 25016, 25017, 25018, 25019, 25020.

1941: vols. 26518, 26907, 29484, 29500, 29730, 297131, 297132, 29740, 29777, 29779, 29780, 29782, 29830, 30031, 30059, 30060, 30067, 30068, 30076, 30089, 30090, 30091, 30092, 30093, 30094, 30095, 30103, 30124, 30125, 30126, 30127, 30128, 30153, 30205, 30231.

1942: vols. 31322, 33311, 33312, 33313, 33340, 33342, 33362, 33366, 33367, 33368, 33369, 33375, 33376, 33406.

1943: vols. 34158, 34163, 34173, 35175, 36917, 37030, 37031, 37064, 37080, 37226, 37281, 37321, 37400, 37401, 37064, 37080, 37226, 37281, 37321, 37400, 37401, 37402, 37403, 37404, 37406, 37465, 37466, 37468, 37469, 37470, 37471, 37472, 37473, 37474, 37475, 37476, 37477, 37478, 37479, 37480, 37482, 37491, 37509, 37510, 37516, 37517.

1944: vols. 39572, 39648, 42725, 44064, 44065, 44067, 44068, 44069, 44070, 44071, 44072, 44073, 44074, 44082, 44133, 44145, 44164, 44165, 44176, 44188, 44191, 44201, 44207, 42725.

1945: vols. 48149, 48220, 48697, 48709, 48710, 48750, 48751, 48765, 48775, 48795, 50678, 50938.

All the material used was found through the Foreign Office Catalogue, years 1934–45 under Turkey.

For reference purposes the Foreign Office classification is used. Hence in R10541/789/44, R indicates Southern Department. 10541 is the document number, 789 is the Foreign Office file number and 44 is the country code, in this case Turkey.

Cabinet Office Papers

War Cabinet Conclusions and Confidential Annexes; CAB/65. 'W.M.' series
1939–45. vols. 1, 2, 3, 4, 5, 6, 7, 8, 9, 10, 18, 19, 21, 22, 23, 26, 29, 31, 40,
42, 45, 47.
War Cabinet Memoranda: CAB/66. 'WP' series 1943–45. vols. 34, 41, 48, 49,
51.

Prime Minister's Office

Operational Papers, PREM. 3: vol. 447. 5A; Cairo Conversations and negotiations for Turkish entry into war.

Published documents
Great Britain

Documents on British Foreign Policy 1919–1939 (DBFP), E. L. Woodward and
Rohan Butler (eds.).
Series 1, vol. xiii. Turkey, February–December 1920; Arabia, Syria, and
Palestine, February 1920–January 1921; Persia, January 1920–March
1921.
Series 3, vol. v, April 4–June 8 1939; vol. viii, August 15–September 3 1939.

Germany

Documents on German Foreign Policy (DGFP) Series D.
Vol. vi The last months of peace. March–August 1939
Vol. vii The last days of peace. August 9–September 3, 1939.
Vol. ix The War Years. March 18–June 22, 1940.
Vol. x The War Years. June 23–August 31, 1940.
Vol. xii The War Years. February 1–June 22, 1941.
Vol. xiii The War Years. June 23, December 11, 1941.

United States

Department of State. Foreign Relations of the United States. (USFR).
The Conferences at Washington 1941–42 and Casablanca, 1943.
Foreign Relations of the United States: Conferences at Cairo and Tehran 1943.
Foreign Relations of the United States: Diplomatic Papers, 1944, vol. v.
Foreign Relations of the United States: The Conferences at Malta and Yalta, 1945.
*Foreign Relations of the United States: Diplomatic Papers, 1945, The Conference of
Berlin (The Potsdam Conference),* vols. i and ii.
Foreign Relations of the United States: Diplomatic Papers 1945, vol. viii.
Foreign Relations of the United States: Diplomatic Papers 1946, vol. vii.

Department of State, *Nazi–Soviet Relations 1939–1940: Documents from the Archives of the German Foreign Office,* Raymond J. Sontag and James Stuart
Beddie (eds.).

Soviet Union

Documents Secrets des Affaires Etrangères d'Allemagne. La Politique Allemande (1941–1943). Traduit de Russe par Madelaine et Michel Eristov.

Official publications

Great Britain

Foreign Office. *British and Foreign State Papers*. Treaty of Mutual Assistance between His Majesty in Respect of the United Kingdom, the President of the French Republic, and the President of the Turkish Republic, Ankara, October 19, 1939, Cmd. 6165, Treaty Series No. 4, House of Commons Sessional Papers, Vol. 12 (London. Her Majesty's Stationery Office 1940).

Royal Institute of International Affairs. Foreign Research and Press Service. *Review of the Foreign Press*. Series B, European Neutrals and the Near East. (Allied Governments, European Neutrals – Smaller European Enemies – and the Near East). 4 October 1939–27 June 1943. After 1943 Ser. N. compiled by Foreign Office Research Department: The Near and Middle East. 30 June 1943–27 June 1945.

House of Commons. *The Parliamentary Debates* (official reports) Fifth Series 1942–1945.

History of the Second World War. *Grand Strategy*. J. R. M. Butler, vol. 2, September 1939–June 1941, vol. 3, June 1941–August 1942. John Ehrman, vol. 5. August 1943–September 1944, vol. 6. October 1944–August 1945. HMSO, London 1956–7.

History of the Second World War. *Economic Blockade*, W. N. Medlicott, vols. 1 and 2, HMSO, London 1952–9.

History of the Second World War. *The War at Sea*, S. W. Roskill, vol. 3, part 1, HMSO, London 1960.

History of the Second World War. *British Foreign Policy in the Second World War*, Sir L. Woodward, vol. 4, HMSO, London 1975. Vol. 5. HMSO, London 1976.

Turkey

Türkiye Cumhuriyeti Başbakanlık Basın ve Yayın Umum Müdürlüğü. *Son Değişikliklere Göre Matbuat Kanunu*. (Office of the Prime Minister of the Turkish Republic. General Directorate of Press and Publications. The Press Law comprising recent Alterations), Ankara, Basın ve Yayın Umum Müdürlüğü Yayınları, no. 15, 1946.

Türkiye Cumhuriyeti *Maliye Tetkik Kurulu 1924–1948 Yılları Bütçe Giderleri* (Inspectorate of the Ministry of Finance. Budget expenditures between 1924–1948), Milli Eğitim Basımevi, Ankara 1948.

Türkiye Cumhuriyeti Başbakanlık İstatistik Umum Müdürlüğü (General

224   *Bibliography*

Directorate of Statistics), *İstatistik Yıllığı 1942–1945* (Statistical Yearbook 1942–1945), vol. 15, 1946.

Türkiye Cumhuriyeti Bayındırlık Bakanlığı: *Bayındırlık Dergisi* (Ministry of Public Works: Public Works Journal), December 1948.

Türkiye Büyük Millet Meclisi. (TBMM) *Zabıt Ceridesi.* (Tutanak Dergisi). (The Records of the Turkish Grand National Assembly). Devre vı ve vıı. (Sixth and Seventh Sessions) 1942–1946.

Türkiye Cumhuriyeti Başbakanlık Basın ve Matbuat Genel Müdürlüğü (General Directorate of Press and Publications), *Ayın Tarihi* (News of the month), 1939–1945.

Türk Devrim Tarihi Enstitüsü (The Institute of the History of the Turkish Revolution), *İnönü'nün Söylev ve Demeçleri* 1919–1938 (Speeches and statements of İsmet İnönü), Türk Devrim Tarihi Yayınları. no. 2, Ankara 1946.

Newspapers

Akşam
Cumhuriyet
İkdam
Son Posta
Son Telgraf
Tan
Tanin
Tasvir-i Efkâr
Ulus
Vakit
Vatan
Yeni Sabah
Yeni Asır

Interviews

Personal interview with Professor Ahmet Şükrü Esmer, İstanbul 29 October 1977. Ahmet Şükrü Esmer was a leading columnist in the Turkish press during the Second World War. He was regarded as the foremost authority on foreign affairs among the press corps. Esmer also had a distinguished career as an academic at the Political Sciences Faculty of Ankara University. He died in 1981.

Personal interviews with Suat Hayri Ürgüplü, İstanbul 29 October and 1 November 1977. Ürgüplü served as Minister of Customs and State Monopolies during the war. He later became a prominent politician in the 1970s. He died in 1981.

Personal interview with Mrs Nermin Streater, London 9 June 1977.

Other sources

Keesing's Contemporary Archives, vol. 5, 1943–6.

Tamkoç, Metin, *A Bibliography on the Foreign Relations of the Republic of Turkey 1919–1967. And Brief Biographies of Turkish Statesmen*, Middle East Technical University, Faculty of Administrative Sciences, Publication no. 11, Ankara 1968.

Memoirs

Aras, Tevfik Rüştü, *Görüşlerim* (My Views), Semih Lütfü Basımevi, İstanbul 1945. Aras was the Foreign Minister of the Turkish Republic from 1923 to 1938.

Atay, Falih Rıfkı, *Çankaya: Atatürk Devri Hatıraları* (Çankaya: Memoirs of the Atatürk era), vol. 2, Dünya Yayınları, İstanbul 1958. Atay was a leading journalist and the editor of the official *Ulus* during the war years. He is also well known for his numerous memoirs dealing with the Atatürk era.

Barutçu, Faik Ahmet, *Siyasi Anılar* (Political Memoirs.) *1939–1954*, Milliyet Yayınları, İstanbul 1977. Deputy from Trabzon during the war years. Deputy Prime Minister in the Hasan Saka government in 1947, and speaker of the CHP in opposition during the Democratic Party administration.

Cebesoy, Ali Fuad, *Milli Mücadele Hatıraları* (Memoirs of the National Struggle), Vatan Neşriyatı, İstanbul 1953. (Cebesoy was one of Mustafa Kemal's leading commanders, and a senior member of the Turkish General Staff during the Second World War.)

Cebesoy, Ali Fuad, *Ali Fuad Cebesoy'un Siyasi Hatıraları* (Ali Fuad Cebesoy's Political Memoirs), Vatan Neşriyatı, İstanbul 1957.

Eden, Anthony, *The Eden Memoirs: The Reckoning*, Cassel, London 1965.

Hugessen, Sir Hugh Knatchbull, *Diplomat in Peace and War*, Murray, London 1949.

Hull, Cordell, *The Memoirs of Cordell Hull*, vol. 2, The Macmillan Company, New York 1948.

İnönü, İsmet, *Hatıralar* (Memoirs), vol. 1, Bilgi Yayınları, Ankara 1985. (Series of taped interviews compiled by journalist Sabahaddin Selek and later published.)

Koyunoğlu, Arif Hikmet, 'Koyunoğlu'nun Anıları' (Koyunoğlu's Memoirs), *Tarih ve Toplum*, no. 36, December 1986, pp. 35–40. Koyunoğlu was an architect by training and was one of the first Turkish architects to take part in the construction of Ankara as the new Capital. His memoirs are interesting because they are one of the few written by a civilian and by someone who was not actually part of the Kemalist inner circle.

Massigli, René, *La Turquie devant la guerre: mission a Ankara 1939–40*, Librairie Plon, Paris 1964.

Menemencioğlu, Numan, Les Détroits vus de la Mediterranée: aperçus, études, souvenirs (unpublished memoirs), Menemencioğlu is one of the most important and one of the least known of Republican statesmen. His career in the Turkish Diplomatic Service spans both the Ottoman and the Republican periods. During the Second World War he served as General Secretary and Foreign Minister.

von Papen, Franz, *Memoirs*, Andrew Deutsch Ltd, London 1952.

Schacht, Hjalmar, *Account Settled*, Weidenfeld and Nicolson, London 1949.

Truman, Harry S., *Memoirs by Harry S Truman*. vol. 1, *Year of Decisions*, vol. 2, *Years of Trial and Hope*, Doubleday and Co., New York, 1956.

Us, Asım, *Gördüklerim, Duyduklarım, Duygularım: Meşrutiyet ve Cumhuriyet Devirlerine ait Hatıralar ve Tetkikler* (What I saw, heard and felt: Memoirs and Essays on the Constitutional and Republican Periods), Vakit Matbaası, İstanbul 1964. Us was a leading writer in the *Vakit* newspaper, a Deputy in the Assembly and a prominent member of the Turkish elite.

Wilson, Sir Henry Maitland, *Eight Years Overseas 1939–1947*, Hutchinson and Co., London 1949.

Books and periodicals

Adıvar, Halide Edip, 'Turkey and her Allies', *Foreign Affairs*, vol. 18, April 1940, p. 442.

Ahmad, Feroz, *The Turkish Experiment in Democracy, 1950–1975*, Hurst and Co., London 1977.

Akdağ, Mustafa, *Türkiye'nin İktisadî ve İçtimaî Tarihi* (The Economic and Social History of Turkey), 2 vols., Cem Yayınevi, İstanbul 1973.

Akşin, Aptülahat, *Atatürk'ün Dış Politika İlkeleri ve Diplomasisi* (Atatürk's Foreign Policy Principles and Diplomacy), part 2, İnkilâp ve Aka Kitabevi, İstanbul 1966.

Al-Qazzaz, Ayad, 'The Iraqi British War of 1941. A Review Article', *International Journal of Middle East Studies*, vol. 7, 1976, p. 591.

Allworth, Edward (ed.), *Central Asia. A Century of Russian Rule*, Columbia University Press, 1967.

Allworth, Edward (ed.), *The Nationality Question in Soviet Central Asia*, Praeger, New York 1973.

An Consantoir, 'Turkey, Rampart in the Middle East' (Anonymous article in Irish Journal of Military History), *An Cosantoir*, vol. 12, no. 7, 1952, p. 315.

Armaoğlu, Fahir H., 'İkinci Dünya Harbinde Türkiye' (Turkey in the Second World War), *Siyasal Bilgiler Fakültesi Dergisi* (Journal of the Faculty of Political Sciences Ankara University), vol. 13, no. 2, June 1958, p. 139.

Armaoğlu, Fahir H., *Siyasi Tarih, 1789–1960* (Political History 1789–1960), Sevinç Matbaası, Ankara 1964.

Ataöv, Türkkaya, *Turkish Foreign Policy 1939–1945*, Ankara Üniversitesi Siyasal Bilgiler Fakültesi Yayınları (Publication of the Political Sciences Faculty of Ankara University), no. 197–79, 1965.

Atatürk, Mustafa Kemal, *Nutuk*, Cilt 1–3 (Speech, vols. 1–3), Ankara Devlet Basımevi 1927. Translation: *A Speech delivered by the President of the Turkish Republic, Ghazi Mustafa Kemal*, Leipzig 1929.

Atay, Falih Rıfkı, *Kurtuluş* (The Liberation), Doğan Kardeş Matbaacılık, İstanbul 1966.

Avcıoğlu, Doğan, *Türkiye'nin Düzeni. Dün–Bugün-Yarın* (The Turkish Order. Yesterday. Today. Tomorrow), Tekin Yayınevi, İstanbul 1975.

Aydemir, Şevket Süreyya, *İkinci Adam* (The Second Man), 2 vols., Remzi Kitabevi, İstanbul 1976.

Badoglio, Pietro, *Italy in the Second World War*, Greenwood Press, Westport, Connecticut 1976.

Balta, Tahsin Bekir, *Türkiye'de Yürütme Kudreti* (Executive authority in Turkey), Ankara Üniversitesi Siyasal Bilgiler Fakültesi Yayınları. (Publication of the Political Sciences Faculty of Ankara University), no. 114–96, Ankara 1960.

Barker, Elizabeth, *British Policy in South-East Europe in the Second World War*, Macmillan, London 1976.

Bayur, Hikmet, *Türkiye Devletinin Dış Siyaseti* (The Foreign Policy of the Turkish State), A. Sait Matbaası, İstanbul 1942.

Bayur, Hikmet, *Atatürk: Hayatı ve Eserleri* (Atatürk: His Life and Achievements), Aydın Kitabevi, Ankara 1962.

Bilkur, Şefik, *Türkiye'nin Milli Geliri* (National Income of Turkey), Devlet İstatistik Enstitüsü (National Statistics Office), Ankara 1949.

Bilsel, Cemil, *Devletlerle Münasebetler: Bugün ve Yarın* (Relations with States: Today and Tomorrow), Kenan Kitabevi, İstanbul 1943.

Boveri, Margret, *Mediterranean Cross-Currents*, Oxford University Press, 1938.

Bryant, Arthur, *The Turn of the Tide 1939–1943. A Study based on the Diaries and Autobiographical Notes of Field Marshal the Viscount Alanbrooke*, Collins, London 1957.

Burçak, Rıfkı Salim, 'İngiliz-Fransız-Türk İttifakı. Ekim 19 1939'(Anglo-Franco-Turkish Pact of 19 October 1939), in *Siyasal Bilgiler Okulu Dergisi* (later became Siyasal Bilgiler Fakültesi Dergisi), vol. 4, 1949, nos. 1–2 and 3–4, pp. 347, 374.

Burçak, Rıfkı Salim, *Türk Rus İngiliz Münasebetleri, 1791–1941* (Turkish-Russian-British Relations 1791–1941), Aydınlık Matbaası, İstanbul 1946.

Cassels, Alan, *Mussolini's Early Diplomacy*, Princeton University Press, Princeton 1970.

Cem, İsmail, *Türkiye'de Geri Kalmışlığın Tarihi* (The History of Under-development in Turkey), Cem Yayınevi, İstanbul 1975.

Churchill, Winston S., *The Second World War*, vol. 3, *The Grand Alliance*. Vol. 4, *The Hinge of Fate*. Vol. 5, *Closing the Ring*. Vol. 6, *Triumph and Tragedy*. Cassel and Co., London 1950–54.

Ciano, Count Galeazzo, *The Ciano Diaries 1939–1943*, Malcolm Muggeridge (ed.), William Heinemann, London 1947.

Ciano, Count Galeazzo, *Ciano's Diplomatic Papers*, Malcolm Muggeridge (ed.), Stuart Hood (trans.), Odhams Press, London 1948.

Collier's, 'Turkish Toss Up' (Anonymous), *Collier's*, 23 August, 1941.

Davison, Roderic H., 'Lausanne Thirty Years After', *Middle East Journal*, vol. 7, Summer 1953.

Davidson, Roderic H., 'Turkish Diplomacy from Mudros to Lausanne', in *The Diplomats*, Felix Gilbert and Gordon Craig (eds.), Princeton University Press, Princeton 1953.

Davison, Roderic H., *Turkey*, Prentice Hall, New Jersey 1968.

Davos, R., *Faşist Almanya'nın Türkiye'ye Yayılışı* (The expansion of Fascist Germany into Turkey), T. K. P. Yayınları 1977.

Deutsch, Karl, W., *The Analysis of International Relations*, Prentice Hall, New Jersey 1968.

Dodd, C. H., *Politics and Government in Turkey*, Manchester University Press, Manchester 1969.

East, Gordon, *Mediterranean Problems*, Thomas Nelson and Sons Ltd., London 1940.

Erkilet, Emir H., *İkinci Dünya Harbi ve Türkiye* (Turkey and the Second World War), İnkilap Kitabevi, İstanbul 1945.

Erkin, Feridun Cemal, *Les Relations Turco-Soviétiques et la question des Détroits*, Başnur Matbaası, Ankara 1968.

Esmer, Ahmet Şükrü, 'Türk İngiliz Dostluğunun Temelleri' (The Foundations of the Turco-British Friendship), *Siyasi İlimler Mecmuası* (Journal of Political Sciences), Ankara, no. 94, January 1939, pp. 1–5.

Esmer, Ahmet Şükrü, *Siyasi Tarih 1789–1939* (Political History 1789–1939), Maarif Matbaası, İstanbul 1944.

Esmer, Ahmet Şükrü, *Siyasi Tarih 1919–1939* (Political History 1919–1939), Ankara Üniversitesi Siyasal Bilgiler Fakültesi Yayınları. (Publication of the Political Sciences Faculty, Ankara University), nos. 30–32, Ankara 1953.

Esmer, Ahmet Şükrü, 'The Straits: Crux of World Politics', *Foreign Affairs*, vol. 25, 1946–47, p. 290.

Esmer, Ahmet Şükrü, 'İkinci Dünya Savaşında Türk Dış Politikası' (Turkish Foreign Policy in the Second World War) in *Olaylarla Türk Dış Politikası 1919–1973* (Turkish Foreign Policy by Events 1919–1973), Ankara Üniversitesi Siyasal Bilgiler Fakültesi Yayınları (Publications of the Political Sciences Faculty of Ankara University), no. 279, Sevinç Matbaası, Ankara 1974.

Feis, Herbert, *Churchill, Roosevelt, Stalin. The War They Waged and the Peace They Sought*, Princeton University Press, Princeton 1957.

Fisher, Roger, *Basic Negotiating Strategy*, Harper and Row, New York 1969. Allen Lane, The Penguin Press, London 1971.

Forrestal, James Vincent, *The Forrestal Diaries. The Inner History of the Cold War*, W. Millis and E. S. Duffield (eds.), Cassel, London 1952.

Fox, Annette Baker, *The Power of Small States: Diplomacy in World War II*. University of Chicago Press, Chicago 1959.

Frey, Frederick W., *The Turkish Political Elite*, The MIT Press, Cambridge, Massachusetts 1965.

Gafencu, Grigore, *The Last Days of Europe. A Diplomatic Journey in 1939*, Frederick Muller Ltd., London 1947.

Gönlübol, Mehmet, 'Lausanne'dan sonra Türk Dış Politikası' (Turkish Foreign Policy after Lausanne), in *Olaylarla Türk Dış Politikası 1919–1973* (Turkish Foreign Policy by Events). Ankara Üniversitesi Siyasal Bilgiler Fakültesi Yayınları. (Publication of the Political Sciences Faculty of Ankara University, no. 279). Sevinç Matbaası, Ankara 1974.

Gönlübol, Mehmet, and Sar, Cem, *Olaylarla Türk Dış Politikası 1919–1973*

Gövsa, I. A., *Türk Meşhurları Ansiklopedisi* (Encyclopedia of Famous Turks), Yedigün Neşriyatı, İstanbul 1946.

Graves, P. P., *Briton and Turk*, Hutchinson, London 1941.

Halder, Generaloberst, *Kriegstagebuch* (War Diary), 3 vols. W. Kohlhammer Verlag, Stuttgart 1964.

Hershlag, Z. Y., *Introduction to the Modern Economic History of the Middle East*, E. J. Brill, Leiden 1964.

Higgins, Trumbull, *Winston Churchill and the Second Front 1940–1942*, Oxford University Press, New York 1957.

Hirzowicz, Lukasz, *The Third Reich and the Arab East*, Routledge and Kegan Paul, London 1966.

Hodge Vere, Edward, *Turkish Foreign Policy 1918–1948*, Ambilly Annemasse 1950.

Hostler, Charles Warren, *Turkism and the Soviets: The Turks of the World and Their Political Objectives*, George Allen and Unwin, Ltd., London 1957.

Howard, H., 'The Straits after the Montreux Conference', *Foreign Affairs*, vol. 15, 1936–7, p. 199.

Howard, H., *The Partition of Turkey. A Diplomatic History 1913–1923*, University of Oklahoma Press, 1931.

Howard, H., *Turkey, the Straits and US Policy*, The Johns Hopkins University Press, 1974.

Hughes, H. S., 'The Early Diplomacy of Italian Fascism, 1922–1932', in *The Diplomats, 1919–1939*, Martin Gilbert and Gordon Craig (eds.), Princeton University Press, Princeton 1953.

Irving, David, *Hitler's War*, Hodder and Stoughton, London 1977.

Irving, D. and Watt, D. C. (eds.), *Breach of Security*, William Kimber, London 1968.

Kabacalı, Alpay, 'Milli Şef Döneminin Örtülü Sansürü' (Unofficial censorship in the Period of the National Chief), *Tarih ve Toplum*, no. 38, January 1987, pp. 19–22.

Kahn, David, *The Codebreakers*, London 1963.

Kara, Nihal, 'Türkiye'de Çok Partili Sisteme Geçiş Kararının Nedenleri' (The Reasons for the Transition to Multi-Party Politics in Turkey), *Yapıt*, no. 8, December–January 1984–5, pp. 64–76.

Karal, Enver Z., *Türkiye Cumhuriyeti Tarihi 1923–1950* (History of the Turkish Republic), Maarif Basımevi, İstanbul 1954.

Karpat, Kemal H., *Turkey's Foreign Policy in Transition 1950–1974*, E. J. Brill, Leiden 1975.

Kedourie, Elie, *The Chatham House Version and Other Middle-Eastern Studies*, Frank Cass, London 1970.

Kedourie, Elie, 'Wavell and Iraq, April–May 1941', in *Arabic Political Memoirs and Other Studies*, Frank Cass, London 1975.

Keyder, Ç. and Pamuk, Ş., '1945 Çiftçiyi Topraklandırma Kanunu Üzerine Tezler' (Some views on the 1945 Land Reform Act), *Yapıt*, December–January 1984–5.

Khadduri, Majid, *Independent Iraq: A Study of Iraq Politics since 1932*, Oxford University Press, London 1958.

Kimball, Warren, F., *Churchill and Roosevelt. The Complete Correspondence*, Vol. 1, *Alliance Emerging*, Vol. 2, *Alliance Forged*, Princeton University Press 1984.

Kinross, Lord, *Atatürk. The Rebirth of a Nation*. Weidenfeld and Nicolson, London 1964.

Kirk, George, 'The USSR and the Middle East in 1939–1945: Turkey' in *Survey of International Relations. The Middle East in the War, 1939–1946*, Oxford University Press, London 1952.

Kıyak, Sadi, *Dışişleri Bakanlığı Mevzuatı ve Basın Yayınla İlgili Hükümler* (Laws and Regulations concerning the Ministry of Foreign Affairs and Rulings on Press and Broadcasting), Başbakanlık Devlet Matbaası, Ankara 1947.

Klinghoffer, A. J., *The Soviet Union and International Oil Politics*, Columbia University Press, New York 1977.

Koçak, Cemil, 'İkinci Dünya Savaşı ve Türk Basını' (The Turkish Press and the Second World War), *Tarih ve Toplum*, no. 35, November 1986, pp. 29–34.

Koçak, Cemil, *Türkiye'de Milli Şef Dönemi (1938–1945)* (The Period of the National Chief in Turkey), Yurt Yayınevi, Ankara 1986.

Koliopoulos, John S., *Greece and the British Connection. 1935–1941*, Oxford University Press, Oxford 1977.

Kuniholm, Bruce R., *The Origins of the Cold War in the Near East. Great Power Conflict and Diplomacy in Iran, Turkey, and Greece*, Princeton University Press, Princeton 1980.

Kurat, Yuluğ Tekin, 'İkinci Dünya Savaşında Türk-Alman Ticareti' (Turkish–German Trade during the Second World War), *Belleten*, vol. 25, nos. 97–100. Türk Tarih Kurumu Basımevi (Journal of the Turkish Historical Society), Ankara 1961.

Kurat, Yuluğ Tekin, 'Elli Yıllık Cumhuriyetin Dış Politikası' (Fifty Years in the Republic's Foreign Policy), *Belleten*, vol. 39, nos. 153–6. Türk Tarih Kurumu Basımevi, Ankara 1975.

Langer, William L. and Gleason, Everett S., *The Undeclared War*, Peter Smith, Gloucester, Massachusetts 1968.

Lenczowski, George, *The Middle East in World Affairs*, Cornell University Press, New York 1952.

Lewis, B., *The Emergence of Modern Turkey*, Oxford University Press, 1968.

Lewis, Geoffrey, *Turkey*, Ernest Benn Ltd., London 1965.

Loewenheim, Francis L., Langley, Harold D. and Jonas, Manfred (eds.), *Roosevelt and Churchill. Their Secret Wartime Correspondence*, Saturday Review Press, E. P. Dutton and Co. Inc., New York 1975.

Melek, Abdurrahman, *Hatay Nasıl Kurtuldu* (How Hatay was liberated), Türk Tarih Kurumu Basımevi (Publication of the Turkish Historical Society), Ankara 1966.

Miller, William, *The Ottoman Empire and its Successors, 1801–1922*, Cambridge University Press, 1923.

Monroe, Elizabeth, *The Mediterranean in Politics*, Oxford University Press, 1938.

Morgenthau, Hans J., *Politics Among Nations. The Struggle for Power and Peace*. Alfred A. Knopf, fifth edn., New York, 1973.

Mowat, R. B., *A History of European Diplomacy 1914–1925*, Edward Arnold and Co., London 1928.

Moyzisch, L. C., *Operation Cicero*, Constantine Fitzgibbon and Henrich Fraenkel (trans.), Wintage, London 1950.

Nadi, Nadir, *Perde Aralığından* (Through a Crack in the Curtain), Cumhuriyet Matbaacılık ve Gazetecilik TAŞ, İstanbul 1964.

Okday, Şefik, *Büyükbabam Son Sadrazam Ahmet Tevfik Paşa* (My Grandfather the Last Grand Vezir, Ahmet Tevfik Paşa), Bateş Bayilik, İstanbul 1986.

Olaylarla Türk Dış Politikası (1919–1973) (Turkish Foreign Policy by Events), Parts 1–3; Part 1, 1919–1939 by Prof. Dr Mehmet Gönlübol and Dr Cem Sar. Part 2 1939–1945 by Prof. Dr Ahmet Şükrü Esmer and Dr Oral Sander. Part 3 1945–1965 by Prof. Dr Mehmet Gönlübol, Prof. Dr Haluk Ülman, Prof. Dr A. Suat Bilge, Dr Duygu Sezer. Ankara Siyasal Bilgiler Fakültesi Yayınları (Publication of the Political Sciences Faculty of Ankara University), no 279, Sevinç Matbaası, Ankara 1974.

Petrov, Vladimir, *'June 22, 1941', Soviet Historians and the German Invasion*, University of South Carolina Press, Columbia, SC 1968.

Phillips, Ernest, *Hitler's Last Hope: A Factual Survey of the Middle-East War Zone and Turkey's Vital Strategic Position with a Special Chapter on Turkey's Military Strength by Noel Barber*, W. H. Allen and Co., London 1942.

Robertson, Esmonde M., *Mussolini as Empire Builder. Europe and Africa 1932–1936*, Macmillan Press, London 1977.

Robinson, R. D., *The First Turkish Republic*, Harvard University Press, Cambridge, Massachusetts 1963.

Roosevelt, Elliot, *As He Saw It*, Duell, Sloan and Pearce, New York 1946.

Rund, S. R., 'The Army of the Crescent and Star', *Infantry Journal*, vol. 60, no. 2.

Sadak, Necmettin, 'Turkey Faces the Soviets', *Foreign Affairs*, vol. 27, 1948–9, p. 449.

Salvemini, Gaetano, *The Origins of Fascism in Italy*, Harper and Row, New York 1973.

Sander, Oral and Sar, Cem, *Olaylarla Türk Dış Politikası* (1919–1973) (Turkish Foreign Policy by Events). Part 2 1939–1945. Ankara Üniversitesi Siyasal Bilgiler Fakültesi Yayınları (Publication of the Political Sciences Faculty of Ankara University), no. 279, Sevinç Matbaası, Ankara 1974.

Savcı, Bahri, 'Modernleşmede Devlet Başkanımızın rolü' (The Role of our Head of State in the Modernisation process), in *Prof. Dr Yavuz Abadan's Armağan*, Siyasal Bilgiler Fakültesi Yayınları (Publication of the Political Sciences Faculty of Ankara University), no. 280, Ankara 1969.

Sevengil, Kadri Kemal, *Milli Şef'in Söylev, Demeç ve Mesajları* (Speeches, Statements and Messages by the National Chief), Akay Kitabevi, İstanbul 1945.

Shaw, Stanford J. and Shaw, Ezel Kural, *The History of the Ottoman Empire and Modern Turkey*. 2 vols., Cambridge University Press, 1976.

Sherwood, Robert E., *Roosevelt and Hopkins: An Intimate History*, Harper and Bros., New York, 1950.

Sonyel, S. R., *Turkish Diplomacy 1918–1923*, Sage Publications, London 1975.

Tamkoç, Metin, *The Warrior Diplomats*, University of Utah Press, Salt Lake City 1976.

Tarakçıoğlu, Reşit M., *Ruslarla Olan Komşuluklarımız (Our Neighbourly Relations with the Russians)*, Ayyıldız Matbaası, Ankara 1966.

Taylor, A. J. P., *The Origins of the Second World War*, Hamish Hamilton, London 1961.

Toker, Feyyaz, 'Ali Riza Türel'in Cevapları', *Cumhuriyet*, 7 December 1959.

Toynbee, Arnold, 'The Franco-Turkish Dispute over the Sanjak of Alexandretta', *Survey of International Affairs*, vol. 14, 1936, p. 767.

Toynbee, Arnold, *The Western Question in Greece and Turkey*, Howard Fertig, New York 1970.

Trumpener, Ulrich, *Germany and the Ottoman Empire 1914–1918*, Princeton University Press, Princeton 1968.

Tunçay, Mete, 'İkinci Dünya Savaşı'nın Başlarında (1939–1941) Türk Ordusu' (The Turkish Army in the first years of the Second World War 1939–1941), *Tarih ve Toplum*, no. 35, November 1986, pp. 34–42.

Tunçay, Mete, *Türkiye Cumhuriyeti'nde Tek Parti Yönetimi'nin Kurulması (1923–1931)* (The Institution of the Single Party Regime in the Turkish Republic, 1923–1931), Yurt Yayınları, Ankara 1981.

Ülman, Haluk, *Türk Amerikan Diplomatik Münasebetleri 1939–1947* (Turkish–American Diplomatic Relations 1939–1947), Ankara Üniversitesi Siyasal Bilgiler Fakültesi Yayınları (Publication of the Political Sciences Faculty of Ankara University), no. 128, Sevinç Matbaası, Ankara 1961.

Vali, Ferenc A., *Bridge Across the Bosphorous: The Foreign Policy of Turkey*, The Johns Hopkins University Press, Baltimore 1971.

Van Creveld, Martin L., *Hitler's Strategy 1940–1941: The Balkan Clue*, Cambridge University Press, 1973.

Villari, Luigi, *The Expansion of Italy*, Faber and Faber, London 1930.

Wallach, Jehuda, *Bir Askeri Yardımın Anatomisi* (The anatomy of one case of military aid), Genelkurmay Basımevi (Publication of the Turkish General Staff), Ankara 1985.

Walder, David, *The Chanak Affair*, Hutchinson, London 1969.

Ward, Barbara, *Turkey*, Oxford University Press, London 1942.

Ward, R. E. and Rustow, D. A. (eds.), *Political Modernisation in Japan and Turkey*, Princeton University Press, Princeton 1964.

Weisband, Edward, *Turkish Foreign Policy 1943–1945. Small State Diplomacy and Great Power Politics*, Princeton University Press, Princeton 1973.

Wilson, Henry Maitland, 'Operations in the Middle East', *London Gazette*, no. 37, 12 November 1946.

Wiskemann, Elizabeth, *Undeclared War*, Constable and Co., London 1939.

Woodhouse, C. M., 'The Intermittent King', *The Times Literary Supplement*, 28 July 1978, pp. 860–1.

Wright, Edwin M., 'Iran as a gateway to Russia,' *Foreign Affairs*, vol. 20, 1941–2, p. 367.

Xydis, Stephen G., 'New Light on the Big Three Crisis over Turkey', *Middle East Journal*, vol. 14, 1960, p. 420.

Zhivkova, Ludmila, *Anglo-Turkish Relations 1933–1939*, Secker and Warburg, London 1976.

INDEX

234 *Index*

Cairo, Eden–Menemencioğlu meeting at, 154, 155
Çakmak Fevzi Marshall, 38, 46, 63, 124, 131, 148, 163
Çakmak Line, 39
Çanakkale, 67, *see also* Dardanelles
Capitulations, 14, 69, 70
Casablanca Conference, 134, 145
Caucasus, 93, 130, 131, 179, 180, 182
Cebesoy Ali Faut, 44, 63
Chamberlain, Neville, 94, 99
CHP, *see* Republican Peoples' Party
chrome: exports to Germany, 26, 128, 129; exports to Britain, 27, 28; end of exports to Germany, 168–69
Churchill, Sir Winston; views on help to Greece, 113; view of Turkey as source of manpower, 117; obsession with second front in the Balkans, 118, 142, 155; anxiety caused in Turkey by attitude towards Soviets, 123–24; role in Casablanca Conference, 145; personal involvement in Aegean campaign, 150–51 views on forcing Turkey into war, 152, 156, 157, 165
Ciano, Count Galeazzo, 112, 136, 208 note 121
Cicero, 163
Clodius, Karl, 26, 128
Committee of Union and Progress (CUP), 58, 59
COMPASS (operation), 113
compromise peace, 53, 98, 133–35, 137–40
Constitution (Turkish), *see* Law of Fundamental Organization
Cos, *see* Kos
Council of Ministers (Bakanlar Kurulu), Turkish Cabinet, 42
credit agreements: with Britain and France, 26, 35; with Germany, 26, 28
Crete, effect of British defeat in, 120
Cripps, Sir Stafford, 96
Cumhuriyet newspaper, 8, 9, 10
Cumhuriyet Halk Partisi (CHP), *see* Republican People's Party
Curzon, Lord, 14, 68
Cyprus, Eden–Saraçoğlu meeting in, 119
Czechoslovakia, 33, 36

Daladier, Eduard, 93
Dardanelles, *see also* Straits, 76, 152,

178, 206 note 20, 204 note 56
Darlan, Admiral, 93
defense, *see* army, re-armament, armaments credit
Dill, Sir John, 118, 119
Dodecanese islands, 76, 121, 141, 149–51

economic policy (Turkish), 12–17; Liberalism, 18; Etatism, 17–21
economic warfare: the "chrome war", 128; pre-emptive buying, 168; question of strategic exports, 168–69, 170
Eden, Sir Anthony, 68, 118, 119, 124, 127, 138, 152, 154
Edirne, 121, 125
Egypt, 113, 114, 115, 139, 219 note 13
electoral system, 42, 43
Enver Pasa, 42, 67, 118, 130, 131, 201 note 42
Erden, Ali Fuat, General, 131
Erkilet, Hüseyin Hüsnü, General, 131
Erkin Feridun Cemal, 44
Erzurum Congress, 65
Esendal, Memduh Şevket, 130
Esmer Ahmet Şükrü, 8, 10, 63
etatism, 17–21
expansionism (rejection of), 2
export trade, 23–30

Finland, 90, 91, 93
Five Year Plans, 18, 19, 20
foreign loans, 20, 30
Forschungsamt, German codebreaking service, 61, 203 note 18
France: as factor in Anglo-Turkish Negotiations, 75–76; Maginot Line, 97; involvement in projected bombing of Baku oil, 93; effects of collapse on Turkey, 97–100; British destruction of French fleet, 100–2; Turkish disappointment with, 117

Gafencu, Grigore, 74
General Directorate of the Press (Matbuat Umum Müdürlüğü), 8
Gerede, Hüsrev, 63, 97, 201 note 23
Germany: economic preponderance in Turkey, 23–28; German advisers for Ottoman Army, 59; increase of influence on Turkey, 60; effects of victories over Allies, 97–98; efforts to